THE GOLDEN D

As both an order and a magical tradition in the 19th century, the Hermetic Order of the Golden Dawn is responsible for planting the seeds of magic that today have sown magical organizations throughout the world. The Golden Dawn and its reverberating facets are now meticulously depicted in the ongoing series *The Golden Dawn Journal*.

Book One: Divination explores the underlying mechanism and methods of divination, including those most favored by the Golden Dawn. As "divination is the process of establishing communication with the Gods of the collective unconscious" (Steven Marshall), *Book One* reveals how, when, and why the divinatory process works and examines whether or not it can always be trusted. Included in this fascinating foray are explorations into psychological considerations in divination, particular forms of divination and particular methods within those forms. *Book One* delves into all aspects of ceremonial magic and the Hermetic Tradition, including Tarot readings from meetings of the original Golden Dawn members!

The Golden Dawn Journal, Book One presents the world's best known occult and magical organization in a clear and practical way, providing a vehicle for communication, exploration and discussion for anyone interested in understanding the universe and his or her role in it.

About the Editors

Both Chic and Tabatha are Senior Adepts of the *Hermetic Order of the Golden Dawn,* the only such group operating in the United States and Canada that has a Vault which was consecrated by Israel Regardie and into which Regardie performed initiations for the purpose of establishing a Second Order with valid initiatory succession from the original Mother temple in London. They are the authors of *The New Golden Dawn Ritual Tarot* (deck and book) and *Secrets of a Golden Dawn Temple*.

To Write to the Editors

If you wish to contact the editors or would like more information about this book, please write to the editors in care of Llewellyn Worldwide and we will forward your request. Both the editors and publisher appreciate hearing from you and learning of your enjoyment of this book and how it has helped you. Llewellyn Worldwide cannot guarantee that every letter written to the editors can be answered, but all will be forwarded. Please write to:

Chic Cicero and Sandra Tabatha Cicero
c/o Llewellyn Worldwide
P.O. Box 64383-850, St. Paul, MN 55164-0383, U.S.A.

Please enclose a self-addressed, stamped envelope for reply, or $1.00 to cover costs.
If outside U.S.A., enclose international postal repy coupon.

Free Catalog from Llewellyn

For more than 90 years Llewellyn has brought its readers knowledge in the fields of metaphysics and human potential. Learn about the newest books in spiritual guidance, natural healing, astrology, occult philosophy and more. Enjoy book reviews, new age articles, a calendar of events, plus current advertised products and services. To get your free copy of *Llewellyn's New Worlds of Mind and Spirit*, send your name and address to:

Llewellyn's New Worlds of Mind and Spirit
P.O. Box 64383-850, St. Paul MN 55164-0383, U.S.A.

THE GOLDEN DAWN JOURNAL

Book 1
Divination

Edited by

Chic Cicero
Sandra Tabatha Cicero

1994
Llewellyn Publications
St. Paul, Minnesota 55164-0383

FIRST EDITION
1st Printing, 1994

Cover design by Chic and Sandra Tabatha Cicero
Color for cover design by Christopher Wells

ISBN 1–56718–850–8

Permissions:
Cross and Triangle artwork copyright © Sandra Tabatha Cicero
Archangel drawings copyright © Sandra Tabatha Cicero
Hieroglyphic chart copyright © M. Isidora Forrest
Illustration for article entitled "What to do for an Oracle
       Addiction" copyright © Lloyd Nygaard
Sections from the letters from Miss Annie E.F. Horniman to W.B.
       Yeats containing her Tarot readings as found in MS 18,312 are
       reproduced thanks to the Council of Trustees of the National
       Library of Ireland
Illustrations of the Tarocco Italiano fabrica del Dotti Milano, 1845,
       copyright © 1985 are reproduced by permissions of Osvaldo
       Menegazzi
Article copyright © Gareth Knight
Article copyright © Dolores Ashcroft-Nowicki
Article and diagrams copyright © Adam Forrest

Llewellyn Publications
A Division of Llewellyn Worldwide, Ltd.
P.O. Box 64383, St. Paul, MN 55164–0383

Printed in the United States of America

*This book is dedicated
to those Initiates who were present
at a very special event:
The consecration
of the Vault of the Adepti
by Israel Regardie
(Isis-Urania Temple, Georgia—1982).
L.V.X.*

**Forthcoming Books in
The Golden Dawn Journal Series**

*Qabalah: Theory and Magic
The Art of Hermes
The Magical Pantheons
Egyptian Magic
The Invisible Temple
The Hermetic Goddess
Cross and Triangle
Of Planets and Angels
Enochiana
Alchemy*

CONTENTS

Preface

The Golden Dawn Journal is an ongoing series of books designed to reflect the magical teachings and philosophy of the Hermetic Tradition. Each issue of *The Journal* will focus on articles written by various authors who have had experience in Western ceremonial magic; particularly the type of magic espoused by the Hermetic Order of the Golden Dawn and its off-shoots.

As an Order and a magical tradition, the Golden Dawn is responsible for planting many of the seeds of knowledge that have spouted today in the form of numerous magical organizations throughout the world. Few could argue against the fact that the teachings of the Golden Dawn were fundamental to much of what now constitutes 20th Century magic. One of the tasks of *The Golden Dawn Journal* will be to provide a survey of historical and contemporary Golden Dawn magic, with some articles comparing Golden Dawn techniques with those of other magical traditions. *The Journal* will concentrate on serious exploration of the techniques used in the Hermetic Tradition, as well as an investigation into the archaic roots of ceremonial magic. Practical advice for the working magician will be featured.

Another reason for presenting *The Journal* series is to provide readers with articles on subjects which may not be exclusively concerned with the Golden Dawn, but which are nonetheless of interest to Hermetic students. The focus of such articles as these will not be so much with Golden Dawn content as with Golden Dawn perspective. *The Journal* will express the views of many of today's practicing Golden Dawn magicians, as well as respected occultists from outside of the Order. Many of today's magical groups have their roots in the

Hermetic Tradition, and *The Journal* will explore the parallel ideas and views common to all. By showcasing these shared ideas, as well as new Golden Dawn rituals and information from respected sources, *The Golden Dawn Journal* will confirm that the Golden Dawn system of magic, far from becoming obsolete and stagnant, is in fact alive and well and providing new vitality for modern students of the Western Esoteric Tradition. It is our belief that the willingness to share ideas is important for the spiritual growth of magical groups and individuals alike. For we are all neophytes of the Hermetic Arts, and what we seek is the One Truth, the Quintessence, the Summum Bonum, the Stone of the Wise.

— *Chic Cicero*

Introduction

hy should a highly respected organization like the Golden Dawn, credited as a leading authority in spiritual development, teach its students the art of divination, which some see as a low occult practice? The answer is clear enough to anyone who has ever contemplated the images of Divine Beings in the starry night sky or heard the whisperings of Nature Spirits from a river, cool breeze or wooded hillside. There is no part of us that is not of the Gods, for as Hermes taught, "As above, so below." That statement is one of the Truths that we, as magicians, live by. The Universe that we live in is *Divine*. Every blade of grass, every least bacterium, and even the lowly gravel in your driveway exists through the Creative Will of the Divine. No event that occurs in a Divine Universe comes about by chance or mere coincidence, even if its reasons and results are beyond our ability to comprehend it. Nothing in a Divine Universe is without meaning or significance.

The word *divination* is based upon the Latin word *divinatio* which means, "the faculty of foreseeing." The root word is itself based upon the Latin word for "divine power" or "of the Gods," and thus exposes the meaning of the word *divination* which is "to make divine." This sheds an entirely different light on the subject of divination; instead of an anti-logical parody of science wrapped in folklore and superstition, we begin to see the emergence of a spiritual science that deals with discovering the Divine significance of "chance" events. And like other methods included in the magical arts, divination has existed as a tool for psychic well-being and spiritual health long before the development of modern psychology (which has often borrowed heavily from the techniques of ceremonial magic—putting new names on old magical ideas).

To many people in the non-magical world (as well as few in the magical world) divination is seen as a low form of occult application. Divination has received this unjustified reputation from those practitioners who have abused it for the usual non-Divine reasons: to gain money, power and influence over others. Given the opportunity, some unscrupulous individuals will find a way to corrupt *any* noble human endeavor in order to enrich themselves at the expense of others. This should not for one moment deter the sincere student from full exploration of the divinatory arts in order to gain a better understanding of the Divine Universe and his/her role in it. Performed correctly and for the right reasons, divination can open up the mind of the *diviner* to the wonders of the spiritual realms and an appreciation of the subtle framework behind the visible Universe. In addition to this, the various methods of divination are among the best-known exercises for stimulating and enhancing the faculties of intuition, clairvoyance and imagination.

The history of divination is as old as humanity's first awareness of the Divine. Since mankind was first able to discern a Higher Power that lay beyond the physical world, humanity has strived to touch upon and communicate with that Eternal Force that empowers the Universe. Prayers and invocations to Deities developed out of the human desire to *talk to* the Divine—to worship the Gods and petition them for favorable conditions. Ritual trance and meditation developed out of the human desire to receive communications from the Divine; to let the Gods *talk to* humans and enrich humankind with a Higher Wisdom. Divination, too, developed as a means of interaction with the Gods; a method by which one could interpret and comprehend the Will of the Divine.

The forms of divination that developed were as varied as the inventive minds from which they sprang. The earliest type of divination was probably as simple as gazing into a fire, or listening to the wind. It often did not seem to matter what form the divination took; it was more important that the diviner be able to quiet the mind enough to attune with the Higher Forces and then perceive certain signs or symbols by means of an *inner perception* or *symbolic vision* that could interpret the Divine implications of the symbols.

In the ancient world, atmospheric signs such as rain, wind, and lightning were considering the precursors of major events—all of which had Divine implications. In societies where warfare against other tribes or nations was a way of life, divination was often employed strategically, to petition the Gods' advice on the best course of action to take against one's enemies. One of the earliest recorded forms of such a divination used militarily was *The Mingling of Arrows* mentioned in the Book of Ezekiel: "For the king of Babylon stood still at the crossways, at the head of the two ways, in order to resort to divination. He has shaken the arrows. He consulted with images and looked into the liver." The king put the names of his enemies on the arrows, placed them back into the quiver, and shook them up. Whichever arrow he then drew from the quiver, bore the name of the enemy he would attack. (The second type of divination mentioned in the above quote was *extispicy* or the inspection of entrails, a rather messy form of divination that dated back to a primitive time when nomadic tribes would move into a new region; but not before inspecting the viscera of animals to determine if the surrounding area was conducive to good health.)

Divining Arrows were at one time employed in the great mosque at Mecca. One arrow was inscribed with the words, "My Lord hath commanded me." On a second arrow was written, "My Lord hath forbidden me." A third arrow was blank. If the first arrow was drawn, the diviner concluded that the enterprise in question had Divine sanction. If the second arrow was drawn, the opposite conclusion was reached. If the blank arrow was drawn, the divination was started again until a decisive answer was reached.

The *Casting of Lots* or *Sortilege* was an early eastern form of divination frequently employed to determine a person's guilt or innocence in a criminal matter. The early Christians and Muslims often divined by opening a holy book (the Bible or Koran) and reading whatever portion of the text first appeared.

One rather inventive form of divination practiced in ancient times was known as *Alectromancy*. A circle was drawn on the ground and divided into as many parts as there were letters in the alphabet. A grain of wheat was then placed on every letter. After several incantations were repeated, a white rooster was placed within the circle. Wherever the bird pecked at the grain indicated the letters revealing the name of a person in question.

Crystallomancy, or divination by means of scrying into a crystal ball, precious stone, or mirror was practiced in very early times, and is still a very popular method today. The operator would gaze into the object for a considerable period of time, to compose his/her mind for whatever revelation was forthcoming.

Hydromancy was similar to the technique just mentioned, but instead of a crystal ball, the diviner would gaze into a still pool or bowl of water. A related technique known in Egypt at a very early period was *Scyphomancy*, or divination by the cup. A cup was filled with wine or some other appropriate beverage and scryed into. Whenever a Divine name was spoken, some of the wine was poured on the ground as an offering to the Deity.

Geomancy was a form of divination that had connections with both the Earth and with astrology. The earliest form of this method was the practice of casting pebbles on the ground or poking holes in the dirt from which were determined certain characters or figures. These figures were assigned specific astrological principles which had a direct influence on the outcome of the divination. Today the figures of Geomancy are usually generated by using pen and paper. Somewhat similar to Geomancy was the practice of *Lithomancy*, or divination by reading the veins and markings on particular stones.

Dactylomancy was a method of divining by rings. A circular ring was suspended by a thread within a glass container. Involuntary movements of the diviner's hand would cause the ring to strike the glass; one strike for an affirmative answer, or two strikes for a negative reply. Modern forms of Dactylomancy include the use of a *pendulum* or the *Ring and Disk* (a method practiced by Adepts of the Second Order of the Golden Dawn).

Pyromancy was the art of divining by Fire. When a divining Fire burned quickly and vigorously, it was considered a good omen. If it was difficult to light or slow to burn, it was considered a bad sign. Sometimes the shape of the flame or the number of separate flaming points had a direct bearing on the prediction.

Cheiromancy, the reading of lines or ceases on the palm of a hand, dates back to antiquity and is still popular today. The same is true of *Oneiromancy*, the interpretation of dreams.

Many methods of divination preferred today also have their roots in ancient times. The *I Ching* or Chinese Book of Changes employs dried yarrow sticks or coins to randomly generate one of 64 figures known as "hexagrams," These hexagrams contain certain combinations of cosmic principles that are symbolic of various physical and psychic situations. The casting of *Runes*, a Norse magical alphabet carved on wood blocks or stones and "thrown" as a divining tool is also quite popular with today's practitioners. However, the most prevalent form of divination in modern times, especially among students of the Western esoteric teachings is undoubtedly *Cartomancy* or divination through cards. Most Cartomancers employ the *Tarot*, a pictorial book of occult knowledge that encompasses not only the divinatory arts but also a progressive system for spiritual attainment and initiation.

Most scholars agree that Tarot was invented in the 14th Century. However it was not until the 19th Century that the modern Hermetic Tarot fully blossomed under the teachings of the Hermetic Order of the Golden Dawn. The various correspondences between the systems of Tarot and the mystical *Qabalah*, first surmised by Eliphas Levi, became a greatly expanded system of esoteric knowledge under the guidance of S.L. MacGregor Mathers. In fact, virtually *all* of the various occult sciences taught in the Outer Order of Golden Dawn (Astrology, Qabalah, Geomancy, Tarot, etc.) were incorporated into a *comprehensive and unified* body of knowledge comprising the Golden Dawn's Inner Order curriculum, which included Enochian, Assumption of Godforms, Rising in the Planes, and various forms of practical ritual work. In order for an Adept to be able to perform Enochian magic safely and correctly, for example, s/he had to be quite skilled in the knowledge of Tarot, Geomancy, Astrology and Qabalah. In the higher ritual workings of the Order, a thorough understanding of all of these "separate" techniques was and still is essential. The correspondences between each of these methods must become second-nature to the magician, who is then able to focus the mind on the astral manipulations necessary for ceremonial work.

The divinatory methods embraced by the Golden Dawn, have become fundamental to the understanding of the *Divine Universe* by today's hermetic students. These techniques are now used by magicians of many different traditions to *communicate* with the Creator of the Divine Universe by seeking out knowledge from within. This, too, is a fulfillment of the Hermetic Axiom mentioned at the beginning of this introduction, for by learning how to interpret the subtle cosmic influences *within* us

(Man—the Microcosm) we then can learn to interpret those subtle unseen influences that exist *outside of ourselves* (the Macrocosm) through a universal law of *correspondences*.

Aside from the employment of certain aspects of divinatory systems within the initiation rites and higher ritual workings of the Golden Dawn, the *science of divination* itself is taught primarily through the techniques of Tarot and Geomancy. A basic knowledge of Astrology is also required on the part of the student. (By comparison, divination by *Enochian Chess* and by the *Ring and Disk* of a Theoricus Adeptus Minor plays a lesser role.) Originally, the Golden Dawn's method of Tarot divination known as the *Opening of the Key*, (fully explained in the article by Cris Monnastre) was not taught below the Grade of Adept; Outer Order students learned the Celtic Cross method instead. Popularized by A.E. Waite, the simple Celtic Cross Spread is proof that many of the basic teachings expounded by the Golden Dawn have become fundamental to virtually all areas of 20th Century occultism.

The ability to perform an accurate divination comes easily to a few, but for most of us it takes a lot of study, practice, intuition, and a working knowledge of correspondences. It requires a balanced approach on the part of the diviner; an approach that actively involves all parts of the psyche: intellect and emotion, ego and Spirit. The type of divinatory system chosen is not important. The most essential requirement is that the diviner should have some basic set of symbols that s/he is thoroughly familiar with, and which express a distinct meaning. These meanings should be precise and clear, but nonetheless *elastic* enough to permit the psychic powers of perception to come into play. The question asked in a divination should be precise and to the point, and the selection of symbols should always be random in order to engage the subconscious mind in the interpretive process.

In this first issue of *The Golden Dawn Journal*, we present several articles by various authors on the subject of divin-ation. The topics covered range from: explanations on how and why the process of divination works, traditional techniques of Tarot and Geomancy (along with new information on both), new Tarot spreads, historical information derived from the actual Tarot readings of an original member of the Golden Dawn, explorations of both Roman and Græco-Egyptian divin-atory techniques, Gypsy Runes, and new systems of divination developed by accomplished magicians in the field. We also present a section that will become a permanent fixture of *The Journal* series known as the Editor's Forum, where all of our authors are asked to respond to a specific question that relates to the theme of the current issue. It is our hope that the Forum can supply the reader with a wide range of opinions and practical advice from both working magicians and well-known authorities.

It is also our hope that after reading this book, students and Initiates alike are better able to interpret the subtle nuances of the Divine Universe in which we live, work, and do magic. Like any practice that can be either sublimated or abused by its practitioners, divination should be respected as a powerful tool for personal growth and change. Through better understanding of the mechanics and philosophy of the art, we trust that the sincere student will never abase the *Divine* in *divination*.

— Chic Cicero
Sandra Tabatha Cicero

The Psychology of Divination

Steven Marshall

In treading the magical path on the road to wholeness, the goal becomes the process. The Goal of the Quintessence, the Stone of the Philosophers, reveals itself as an interior alchemy of transforming the human psyche into the spiritual gold of the enlightened human being. This is the divine art of Hermes, the alchemy of the Self. The process of spiritual growth is not an unconscious one that we can rely on nature alone to effect, but one that must be accomplished through a combination of human artifice and spiritual insight. The development of certain skills, the learning of particular knowledge and an understanding of the mysteries of our own psychology constitute necessary resources in journeying the conscious path of spiritual development. One of the areas of skill and knowledge prescribed on the magical path is the art of divination.

The psychological alchemy facilitated by the practice of divination provides a key to magical development that can serve the devout seeker throughout the spiritual quest. The word *divination* has its root in a Latin word meaning "of the Gods." Divination is the process of establishing communication with the Gods of the collective unconscious. One of the patron Gods of divination is Hermes, the psychopomp of the soul and the Messenger of the Gods. In myth, Hermes traverses the Underworld, the Heaven-world and the middle realm of humanity. He is the Lord of the Crossroads where these three realms meet. Thus the art of divination involves a psychological process where the underworld, heavenly and human areas of the psyche come together in a meaningful way.

The three levels of the human psyche that are involved in the practice of divination are called the Nephesh, the

Neschama and the Ruach in the teachings of the Qabbalah. The Nephesh relates to the animal soul, the subconscious and the realm of the personal unconscious. The Ruach corresponds to the conscious ego, and the Neschama includes the higher divine genius, the superconscious and the realm of the collective unconscious. The Neschama and the Nephesh both communicate through the language of symbols and images. The ego consciousness communicates primarily through the language of the written or spoken word, the "logos." The Ruach cannot communicate directly with the Neschama, as it must rely on the Nephesh to convert "the word" into the symbol language that the Neschama can perceive. The Ruach communicates with the Nephesh by means of words that have emotional or image-stimulating meaning to the Nephesh, much in the same way a dog may learn to associate certain words with certain behaviors or consequences. The Nephesh is also responsible for sensory perception.

In a divination, the Nephesh first sends the image of the visual pattern of the symbols to the Ruach. The Ruach must then ask the Nephesh to request insight from the Neschama for interpreting the symbols presented. The Nephesh presents the pattern of divinatory symbols to the Neschama and the Neschama returns a mythic symbol, a dream motif or other archetypal symbol of its meaning to the Nephesh. The Nephesh returns to the Ruach the archetypal symbol clothed in the internal images and elementary words that might have conscious meaning to the Ruach. These internal images may be kinesthetic, visual or auditory. They may often arise as imaginative stories, such as a child may relate. Many of these steps in communication can often go awry. One of the primary functions of divination on the magical path is to clear out these channels of communication and improve the relationships between these three areas of the psyche.

The role of divination in our spiritual growth involves the development of a symbol system whereby one can address and communicate with the Gods, the archetypes of the collective unconscious. The purpose in practicing divination is to discover an interior guidance through building a bridge between a synchronistic pattern of symbols in physical time and space and the timeless world of the archetypal psyche. When one has awakened one's sense of the working out of interior archetypes in external events, divination has served one of its primary purposes in psychological transformation.

The symbols of any divination system represent archetypes within the psyche that can be perceived in differing images personal to a particular individual's experience. However, because of the collective nature of these archetypes, the images and symbols of the various divination systems exhibit surprising similarities. Most of the popular methods of divination can be understood in terms of the symbolism of numbers, letters, Astrology and the Elements.

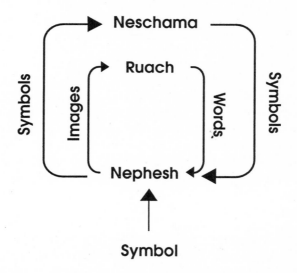

The value of the psychological paradigm, as compared to others, is that psychology is the fundamental basis of any symbol system. Because the symbols of many divination systems are the projections of the collective symbols of number, Astrology and the Elements, learning the interpretations of these symbols in one divinatory system opens one to the interpretation of many others. Through an understanding of the psychology of divination, practicing one system of divination with that psychological process in mind can prepare one to accurately divine through many others with a minimum of retraining. A limitation of this approach comes when traversing wide cultural boundaries. When the collective symbols of number, Astrology and Element differ considerably, the interpretation appropriate to that culture must be learned and, to a considerable extent, internalized before this paradigm can be applied.

Many might assume that divination is concerned with the development of intuition, but the mystic and psychologist, Carl G. Jung, describes four gateways of experience through which one may approach the symbolic patterns of a divination. These gateways are the four psychological functions: intuition, thinking, feeling and sensation. The practice of divination requires attention to all four. One may begin the practice of divination with a fully developed intuitive function but, if the thinking function is undeveloped, one may experience blocks in the analysis of the visual pattern or verbalizing those intuitive insights. If the feeling function is undeveloped, one may be unconscious of the feeling dimension that the divination is addressing or the synthesis of the various images becomes blocked. If the sensation function is neglected one may have difficulty focusing the attention on the visual pattern and get lost in intellectual or intuitive abstractions having nothing to do with the divination. The long form of I Ching divination with yarrow stalks or the generation of figures in geomancy is highly recommended for those with undeveloped sensation functions.

According to the schools of depth psychology, the most neglected function of the psyche is primarily unconscious, while the primary function is the one that the conscious ego most relies upon to interpret life experiences. When we approach the practice of divination one must call upon that mysterious and neglected fourth function that is most closely associated with the archetypal realm of the collective unconscious. The frustration and confusion experienced by those beginning the practice of divination testify to this difficulty in accurately interpreting the symbolic patterns of a divinatory system and translating them into definite images from the indefinite realm of the archetypes themselves. When the undeveloped function is forced to express itself it works against the primary function, which is mutually excluded by it. This temporary suspension of the familiar means of cognition allows insights and imaginations from the unconscious psyche to break through.

Every system of divination begins with attention to the sensation function. The manipulation of cards, rune staves, coins or computer interfaces, and the perception of the pattern of visual symbols generated require the use of the sensation function. If the sensation function is undeveloped, then, it is during this period of calling upon the sensation function that the insights from the unconscious often arrive. During the sensate experience of casting a chart, casting a hexagram, or simply taking in the visual content of the symbols, the interior images or spontaneous thoughts required to interpret the divination arise. After the pattern of symbols has been generated and visually perceived, then the revelations of the archetypal psyche can be interpreted and verbalized through the psychological triangle of manifestation: the functions of thinking, feeling and intuition.

If the thinking function is undeveloped, insights arrive when one begins to analyze the pattern of symbols according to learned information. In attempting to access the neglected function, the insights come from the unconscious. If thinking is the primary function, too much analysis can keep one locked in intellectual searches for something that fits which can block the interpretation.

If the feeling function is undeveloped, beginning to synthesize the various pieces of information or develop the human connections brings forth the necessary insights. If feeling is the primary function, too much emphasis on the human connection can get one caught up in making everything feel good and limit the accuracy of the interpretation.

If the intuitive function is undeveloped, all attempts to transcend the strictly visual content to find the imaginative content and meaning triggers the influx of illumination regarding the divination. If intuition is the primary function, one can ignore the visual content or literal meaning of a symbol and get carried away in false imaginings and personal projections.

When calling upon the undeveloped function and suspending the activity of the primary function, divination becomes an exercise in the conjunction of the opposites of one's inner and outer reality. Outside, the pattern of symbols can be seen as pictures with definite content and form, while, inward, lies the indefinite and unstructured material of the magical imagination that provides them with meaning.

"Active imagination" is the term that Jung used to describe the integration of the unconscious process into consciousness. The unconscious process is circular rather than linear. When the unconscious is presented with a symbol, a circle of thoughts or images begin to cluster around the central sym-

bol; thoughts that may not relate to each other in any linear
fashion but are extensions of the seed symbol. This cluster of
thoughts or images then reveals a connecting thread of meaning between them that connects the symbol with a key word or
key image that can be applied to whatever situation comprises
the subject of the divination.

To begin the practice of divination, one must first learn the
basic correspondences and divinatory meanings of the symbols
included in the divinatory system to be used. This provides the
appropriate "grist for the mill" of the unconscious and a Rosetta
Stone for interpreting the thoughts and images that may arise
during a divination. It also provides the Interface for the Ruach,
the ego consciousness to communicate with the Nephesh, the
personal unconscious through the symbolic language it under-
stands. Without this preliminary study one will be blocked by
difficulties in verbalizing the impressions evoked by the pattern
of symbols in the divination, or may simply free associate in a
manner that no longer relates to the symbol at all.

In applying these divinatory meanings, a definite
sequence is required. First attend to the visual image of the
symbol and its literal meaning to impress the Nephesh; next
recall the associated key words and key images given by the
learned correspondences and divinatory meanings, so as to
include the mediating Ruach; then, finally, activate the magical imagination to receive from the Neschama the specific
meaning that associates the symbol with the human situation
that is the subject of the divination. These three areas of the
psyche also correspond to the four psychological functions. The
sensate function relates to the Nephesh, the thinking and feeling functions relate to the Ruach, and the intuitive function
relates to the Neschama.

The application of the four psychological functions to
interpreting a divination occurs in a definite sequence as well.
First, one must note the visual image of the symbol and its literal meaning by use of the sensate function. Next, one must
explore whether the symbol feels good or bad and whether it
has favorable or unfavorable portents in the human dimension
of life by use of the feeling function, then one must correlate
the information provided by the sensate and feeling function
with its basic correspondences and divinatory meanings by use
of the thinking function. Finally, one makes an intuitive projection relating the symbol to a particular situation in life.

Often the sensate and feeling functions are not given their proper due when interpreting a divinatory symbol. When interpreting a symbol note whether it faces right or left, whether it is upside down or right side up, or whether it is truly the symbol that one, at first glance, assumes it to be. Also, if one has no feelings at all about a symbol, it cannot be very meaningful. Without the feeling function, one may be able to express an interpretation precisely and rationally according to learned information, but relevance to the human situation may be lacking.

The practice of divination in the work of the magician is to demonstrate the Macrocosmic activity of the powerful and unconscious archetypes in the Microcosm of human life. A divinatory system is not a collection of individual symbols but a complex, living organism. The manner in which the symbols in a divination relate to each other reflects the patterns in one's life, much as the sequencing in a DNA strand determines the physical characteristics of an organism. All the symbols of the divinatory system are alive and well, or not so well, within us. The function of divination is to project selected archetypal symbols that are of special significance to the individual at a particular time. Carl Jung described the connection of meaning between two events associated in time as "synchronicity."

Synchronicity is an acausal connecting principle whereby chance events, such as the casting of the I Ching or the lighting of a cricket on the hearth, may bear a relationship of meaning to a psychological or external event occurring simultaneously in an individual's life. A hypothetical example might be a woman who notices a crow pecking at her window and later finds out that her life partner died at about the same time. Obviously, there is no causal connection between the two events, but when the symbolic life intrudes upon our consciousness one discovers a connection of meaning. If she happened not to notice the crow or the crow had no meaning for her, there would be no synchronicity. In the works of Carlos Castaneda, the Yaqui sorcerer, Don Juan, constantly points out the significance of particular omens to the psychological events taking place in the author. In much the same fashion our unconscious psyche produces a spontaneous relationship of meaning between a random pattern of symbols and events in human life.

Most often, the symbols appearing in a divination represent areas of life that have been consciously neglected. One reason that a divination may give indications of external events is that unconscious contents striving to get our attention can often be projected into the human events of life. Performing a divination may give us an opportunity to look at these neglected areas of life before they come out and beat us over the head to get our conscious attention.

The symbols appearing in a divination may be interpreted in much the same way as a dream. Dreams often portray aspects of ourselves that we have neglected in our waking lives, and likewise with a divination. More than anything else, each symbol in a divination is a question and an invitation for the individual to explore one's sensations, feelings, thoughts and intuitions about a particular area of life that one has neglected.

Though a deeper understanding of a present life situation may throw light on the future, one must be particularly cautious in making predictions. A divination is much like the mirror of Galadriel, it shows not what will be but what might be, if the present course is unaltered. Although divination greatly expands one's perception of the particular implications of a situation, it can not provide the whole picture. For someone to make important decisions or plans solely on the basis of a divination would be foolhardy. Divination is not a tool for shirking our responsibility for directing our own life but a means of bringing our unconscious life to light, so that we might live it more consciously. A wider view of a problem and an increased understanding of our own hidden motives may help us formulate solutions or receive some counsel that can help us through a particular trial in our lives.

Interpreting a divination for oneself or others with whom we are emotionally enmeshed is usually ill-advised, at first. The reason for this is because if one cannot interpret the meaning of one's projections in one' s own life or in those with whom one is relating, how can one look at a pattern of symbols without the same prejudices and one-sided attitudes. During a successful divination, the diviner feels a certain playful, almost tricksterish, detachment from the situation, which is perhaps the mercurial archetype that governs divination coming through. If the diviner is too invested in the outcome of the divination, s/he may give good, empathetic support for the Querent's psyche, but the accuracy of the divination can easily be lacking. A divination may be a useful projective tool in a counseling session, but counseling and divination require two entirely different interactions.

On the other hand, divination can foster self-discovery. One practice for using divination as a method of self-exploration is to pick a symbol for the day, keep a careful diary, and witness where the meaning of the symbol correlates with the day's events. Another practice is to perform a divination just before going to bed, record the results, and reflect on any dreams of that night or the next that might pertain to the divination.

Divination is an attempt to consciously utilize the powers of the unconscious, but the unconscious does not grant its powers easily. In divination, we attempt to bridge the gap between an ego-consciousness, bound by the limitations of time and space, and the realm of the unconscious where time and space have no meaning. The process of entering into the "dream time" where a symbol system comes alive with numinosity and speaks to us in an oracular fashion does not happen by simply performing a divination and applying cookbook interpretations or the associations of one's personal unconscious. In beginning the art of divinatory interpretation, the symbols often seem dead and mute, rather than possessing the numinosity necessary for an effective interpretation. In such instances, one is forced to rely on the intellectual exercise of attempting to pick a meaning from those learned and memorized or spontaneously coming up with one of one's private associations, either of which is seldom satisfactory. Intellectual study of the symbolism and meaning of the divinatory symbols is an important preparation to be able to translate the language of the Gods into an intelligible message but, if one is not in touch with the realm of the archetypal psyche, the Neschama, one's intellectual knowledge of the symbols is not very useful. One can become caught in a closed loop of communication between the Ruach and the Nephesh that does not include the divine insight of the Neschama. It is for this reason that some form of invocation becomes a necessary preliminary to any divination.

With continual practice, one can begin to consciously and willfully enter the twilight state of consciousness where one has access to the powers of the unconscious. An oracular reading of a divination gives one a powerful communication with the Gods of the collective unconscious—it interconnects the heavenly, human and underworld areas of the human psyche, giving a message that is uniquely personal and powerful to the individual, a message to which clings a numinosity that strikes us on a deep and fundamental chord of the psyche.

Divination describes a process whereby we can obtain knowledge about our lives from the abode of the Gods, the realm of the archetypes. The word "divination" comes from a time when people believed in denizens of another world who had a more omniscient view than those of this world, a time of oracles and soothsayers whose speech was as much an occasion for dread as for hope. Such is the archetypal world of the psyche that we address in the practice of divination, divining an oracular message that can give meaning to the perplexities and vagaries of life. Such is the world where Gods walk and legends speak, where the mythic truths of our being give a meaning that both transcends human limitations and heals the division between the divine and human dimensions of life. Such is the step on the path to wholeness.

ABOUT THE AUTHOR

Steven Marshall is currently an ordained priest of the Ecclesia Gnostica and pastor of the Queen of Heaven Gnostic Church. He has studied and practiced various forms of divination for the past 28 years, including Astrology, dowsing, runes, Tarot, and the I Ching. He has studied with the BOTA for the past thirteen years. He attended courses in alchemy, Qabbalah and Astrology with the Paracelsus Research Society in 1975 and 1976. A Baccalaureate degree in Psychology and a background in Jungian studies has given him a distinctly psychological approach to the occult sciences. In 1984, after twelve years of study and writing, he collaborated with an artist in the design, production and publication of a deck of the Major Arcana, *The Tarot of Initiation*.

Divination & The Magical Tarot

Gareth Knight

f I have learned anything from forty years' acquaintance with the Tarot it is that it is a *living* magical system. That is to say, that it is no mere assemblage of symbolic images. It is this too, of course, but its sequence of images on seventy-eight pieces of card forms the physical body for an inner intelligence.

Some practitioners in the Golden Dawn tradition have recognized this, at least in part, by visualizing an overseeing angelic presence whenever they work with the Tarot. In keeping with favored correspondences this angelic presence is sometimes invoked under the name of HRU. However, I have found that the Spirit of the Tarot can be very effectively approached and contacted more directly, by invocation of one of its images.

And of all the images that are open to choice I have found the best to be the Fool. This image of combined innocence and wisdom comes across as a free spirit who is readily contactable by anyone who cares to make the effort. It has proved to be a very friendly and approachable archetype as testified in reports from various students, many of them complete beginners, that I have published in my book on practical divination, *The Magical World of the Tarot* (Aquarian/Harper-Collins 1991).

Once this introductory contact has been made, which is very flexible and adaptable to the needs and assumptions of the individual concerned, then the more technical aspects of working with the Tarot can be developed by working with the image of the Magician. Under this persona the Spirit of the Tarot controls upon his altar the rest of the archetypal images and elemental powers.

This applies whether the purpose of the student is divinatory, meditational or magical. To many aspirants to initiation and spiritual self-knowledge, divination is something of a poor relation. And any Tarot teacher will be aware that there are two specific audiences. One is oriented toward the Tarot as a source of inner wisdom; the other toward the Tarot as a source of outer guidance.

To cater to an audience that contains individuals who choose to polarize vociferously from either end of the spectrum can be quite demanding. Yet there should be no conflict between the two approaches. They are to be found upon a common spectrum. And each approaches the same body of truth, if from a different direction.

The difference of direction is initially one of motivation. Yet whether a student is seeking personal inner wisdom, or practical advice upon events in the outer world, the common denominator is one of approaching and inner sage, or guru, or source of superior intelligence. If we keep this firmly in mind most problems will evaporate.

The Tarot is quite capable of looking after itself and will respond to any approach, and in a way that is most appropriate to the individual concerned. The teacher's task is best seen in terms of being a facilitator. Not to lecture, but simply to make the necessary connections and then keep out of the way. The Tarot will then prove its own ability as teacher. It will teach the magical aspirant ways to inner wisdom. It will teach the seeker of divinatory powers the best way to develop them. And like any wise teacher, it will respond in the way best suited to each individual student.

The ability to work with the Tarot requires no special gifts. Psychic or intuitive abilities are of course a help, but these abilities are where you find them. These inner senses of perception are the natural heritage of most of the human race, and like the outer senses of perception, simply need to be used to be developed. And in pursuit of this self development, the Tarot is a superb means of self instruction.

This is because the Tarot contains both the theory and the practice of the Hermetic Tradition. It is a complete pictorial primer of Mystery teaching. Anyone who buys a Tarot deck, or receives one as a gift from some well meaning relative or friend, becomes the custodian, did they but know it, of a powerful tool of self-initiation.

All of this should give us a profound respect for the unknown adepti who originally gave the Tarot to the world. There are various claims and disputes as to how, where and when the system originated. This does not really matter. Many of the images are perennial, and could be traced back to remote antiquity, but the device as it stands today seems to have been bequeathed to us by the Hermetic schools of the Italian Renaissance. These contemporaries of Marsilio Ficino, Pico della Mirandella and other illuminati learned in turn from the documents released into the West by the fall of Byzantium in 1453, when ancient manuscripts from monastic libraries and archives were scattered by the Islamic conquest, to be collected and translated by the princes of the Italian city states.

These archetypal concepts, in the form of the Tarot, they structured into what amounts to no less than a magical time bomb. And it has been waiting to go off ever since!

At first the Tarot seems to have been produced in the form of a set of beautiful meditational *objets d`arts*, encrusted with gold leaf, circulated amongst the same aristocracy who commissioned artists of the caliber of Botticelli to paint symbolic pictures such as the *Prima Vera*, the Birth of Venus, Venus overcoming Mars, or such closely related images as Fortitude, (one of the traditional Cardinal Virtues, as well as a Tarot image now usually called Strength).

Then the spread of the recently invented printing press enabled copies of the images to be widely circulated, and along with playing cards, they became part of a popular game. As such, the images percolated through European society for three hundred years.

Rosicrucian adepts of the early seventeenth century knew of their esoteric significance. This is plain from images like the Lightning Struck Tower, which are described, for example, in that strange magical document *The Chymical Marriage of Christian Rosencreutz*. Yet it was not until the end of the eighteenth century, some two hundred years further on, that the esoteric significance of the Tarot was openly proclaimed, in Court de Gebelin's *Le Monde Primitif*.

From then on nineteenth and twentieth century occultists have made it a part of their own magical systems, at first taught privately and then more widely published, in the works of Eliphas Levi, "Papus" and others in France, and of A.E.

Waite and other adepti of the Golden Dawn in England, and later (via Paul Foster Case and Manley P. Hall) in America.

In 1910, A.E. Waite published *The Pictorial Key to the Tarot*, complete with original pictorial designs for the suit cards. These have been very influential ever since, as comparison of Waite's designs with many later versions will show. In this, he broke away from the tradition of heavy handed secrecy that invested the occultism of his time. As such, he deserves more credit as a pioneer than he often receives, for he has not been such a "dead weight" on the esoteric tradition as some of his critics would have us believe.

He also translated and published Tarot works from the French, which speaks for a considerable broadness of mind in view of the differing systems of Qabalistic attribution on either side of the English Channel. This should also serve to demonstrate that there is no "one and only true" method of allocating Tarot, and other forms of symbolism, to the Qabalistic Tree of Life, for French and English speaking students have been happily and successfully pursuing their own systems now for well over a century.

Yet all of this activity was only preparing the ground for that which was yet to come. In the late 1960's, the Tarot time-bomb finally went off. Since then, Tarot cards have not only become readily available but have proliferated widely. It is difficult to believe that when I was writing *A Practical Guide to Qabalistic Symbolism* in 1960 I found it impossible to find a Tarot deck on sale in the whole of London, whereas now there must be well over a hundred different versions to choose from, some on sale even in novelty sections of department stores. This is a real, and unprecedented, democratization of the "secret" and "esoteric" wisdom. No longer so secret, no longer just for the few.

If there is one thing to be learned from this diversification of images of the Tarot it is that at root it is an essentially *magical* system. That is to say that it works in terms of images in the visual imagination. And although there is an overall structure to the corpus of Tarot images as a whole, and also a sustainable coherence in the essential inner integrity of each individual image, nonetheless all of them are capable of a considerable degree of transformation.

Now in terms of practical magic, *transformation* is a very important principle. There is the somewhat bizarre tradition of the medieval magician standing in his circle of art and commanding some frightful entity before him to "Transform! Transform!" into a shape or form more acceptable to his taste.

Behind this somewhat superstitious and fearsome imagery lies an important technique. This is, that we can interface with, and learn from, inner communicators via a system of mental or astral imagery, but for meaningful communication to take place this imagery has to be capable of flexibility.

Of course this flexibility must not become so flexible that it becomes formless. If so, we find ourselves wandering in a labyrinth of the fantastic or the phantasmagorical. There are indeed instances in published work where this fault is evident. Not least, in the early nineteenth century fortune telling devices spawned from the fancy of society clairvoyants such as Etteila or Madame LeNormand, in which the underlying discipline of Tarot form no longer "in-forms" the imagery. In more modern terms this is akin to trying to seek wisdom from juvenile fantasy games, or from the jungle of the personal subconscious. What we are trying to achieve is a means of rational communication between the planes, and this is not to be obtained through the false avenues of surrealist imagery, dream or nightmare phantasms, or the obsessive visions of psychosis, hallucinogens or narcotics.

Yet if we stick to a rigid system of images, seventy-eight in number in the case of the Tarot, we are confining ourselves to a somewhat restricted language. As a practical example of this, we can try putting ourselves in the position of the Spirit of the Tarot. Suppose for a minute or two that you are the Spirit of the Tarot and that Cinderella is consulting you just prior to her ugly sisters going off to the ball. Try to tell her in ten cards, using the well-known Celtic spread, what she can expect. It's not too easy is it? Yet that is what we expect of the Tarot whenever we consult it.

It is for this reason that naturally gifted cartomancers that I have observed tend to read cards not singly but in pairs of three—for this obviously gives a wider and more subtle language of communication. Reading in pairs increases the symbolic word count from 78 to (78 x 78) or 6084; reading in sets of three increases it another 78-fold, to 474,552. Whilst using reversed images would increase these figures yet again to 156 single images, 24,336 paired images, or 3,796,416 composite three-fold images. Obviously this vastly increases the flexibility of interpretation, and gets one away from the pedestrian approach of most Tarot "how to" books, ploughing through "stock meanings" for each card. It would be beyond any book, or even the average computer program, to lay down some four million different "meanings."

However, we can also achieve the flexibility of a meaningful and subtly expressive language by approaching the Tarot in a magical way. That is, by allowing the images to transform, to move, to speak to us. It then becomes rather more than a statistical experiment equivalent to tossing a coin umpteen times, as a quasi-scientific approach to divination would imply. Rather are we using the basic images and their position within a spread as a means of *tuning* our consciousness to the intelligent source that lies behind the oracle.

In practical terms what we need to do first of all is to "make friends" with our images. This will automatically tune our consciousness in the right way, just as making friends with people in the outer world brings about a greater rapport with them.

When we look at how the Golden Dawn adepti approached the Tarot, it is plain that they did so in a very magical way. In plain terms, they allowed the images to transform and adapt themselves within their own minds.

In the original Golden Dawn Tarot, insofar as there was an original one, we find ourselves with a series of images that, although plainly Tarot, owes a lot to coming through the vision of S.L. MacGregor Mathers. As far as can be ascertained, originally, members of the Order had to copy their own from a single master set. Israel Regardie's version as rendered by Robert Wang would seem to be a fair representation of the kind of thing that members would end up with. In undertaking this exercise they no doubt unconsciously picked up a great deal of first hand contact with the Intelligence behind the images. Plain simple working with the images in this way can be a powerful stimulus even for those who think they have no psychic abilities. Drawing the images, (however inadequately in aesthetic terms) has a talismanic effect by the very act of physical expression. Inner-plane archetypal ideas are being made manifest in the world of outer activity. Even the simple act of coloring in a set of ready-made line drawings can prove beneficial—a useful halfway house for those who feel themselves completely lacking in graphical skills. Ideally, however, students would render their own images from first principles, and this is a method that I have found excellent for the basic training of seriously committed magical students.

However, whilst producing one's own set can be an excellent training and discipline it is not the necessary means for on-going work with the Tarot. This is because the physical production of the images is a "fixing" of them. We may illustrate the process in alchemical terms. For practical working we need the images to be in a state of "solution," that is, relatively changeable whilst still retaining their essential quality or "quintessence." And then to pass to a state of "volatility" as the intuitive faculty engages with the meaning behind them, to be "distilled" into a specific realization of what is meant in relation to a specific reading.

It is therefore quite in order to use any form of cards that may come to hand. Obviously those most congenial to the personal temperament of Querent and Consultant will be preferable, but for my own part I am more than happy to use the ordinary exoteric Marseilles Tarot rather than any esoteric version. This is because the very crudeness of the old images allows the imagination freer flow, and other people's esoteric theories are not thrust upon one. One of the problems for example with Aleister Crowley's often beautiful and intelligent designs is their over-complexity, and the agenda of philosophical and personal idiosyncrasies that is thrown in as well. Although this may be welcome and helpful to dedicated Thelemites, for me it simply gets in the way, and the same might well be said of any "esoteric" set.

And if one has made a point of contacting the various cards individually, starting with the Fool and the Magician, and proceeding through the remaining Trumps and on into the Elemental Lesser Arcana (as I have demonstrated in *The Magical World of the Tarot* and in *Tarot and Magic*) then each card, however crudely designed a piece of pasteboard, will be effective as a tuning device in consciousness. It will trigger the imaginative faculty to enable the relevant images to move, speak, transform, and generally communicate in a subtle and intimate fashion.

Sometimes a crystal ball can be useful as an adjunct to this process, but only if the individual feels comfortable with it. Like all magical devices, including the appurtenances of ritual, or the Tarot cards themselves, they are means to an end, not ends in themselves—and the real action takes places in the creative imagination.

So much for the individual cards, let us turn to the actual process of divination itself, for here again we shall see that we are undertaking a very magical operation.

Whether or not the participants are dressed for the part, the act of divination on behalf of another is a form of ritual magic. It is a polar working conducted by two officers. In terms of function the Querent is acting as an Officer of the Western Portal and the Consultant as Officer of the East, or Magus.

Figure 1 illustrates the dynamics of the situation, with the Querent and Consultant seated at either side of the spread, whilst hovering over the table as it were, is the Spirit of the Tarot. This unseen Presence will have affected the fall of the cards via the subconscious shuffling and cutting process under-taken by the two physical officers. It will continue by contribut-ing to the interplay of impressions, interpretations, intuitions between Querent and Consultant as they converse with each other and consult over the spread.

The process of divination will be the more successful the more the three lines of communication in the diagram are effectively operating. If one or more are to some extent blocked, (either by a Querent insensitive to the Spirit of the Tarot, or through a lack of rapport between Querent and Consultant) then the chances of a successful reading become more remote. Should the Consultant be a dabbling tyro, with no real link to the Spirit of the Tarot, then the chances of success are likely to be zero. However, such is the power and ingenuity of the Spirit of the Tarot that it has been known to work even through the unlikeliest of outer plane collaborators.

If we become involved in group work we find the kind of inner dynamics shown in Figure 2. In this instance we have the kind of situation that I have found useful in workshops for beginners. The group sits round in a circle and anyone present is free to comment upon the spread that is laid in the center—one member of the company playing the role of Querent and the leader of the workshop taking the part of chief Consultant or Magus of what is, in effect, close to the dynamics of a ritual lodge. Here we see that all present are able in potential to speak and interpret on behalf of the Spirit of the Tarot, and the group element facilitates this very strongly. It is an excellent

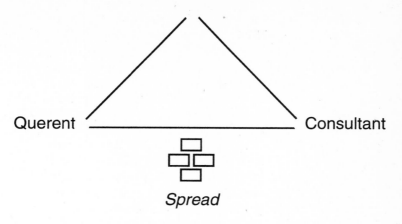

Spirit of the Tarot

Querent   Consultant

Spread

Figure 1

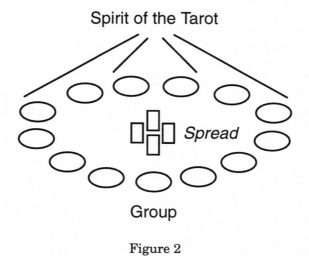

Spirit of the Tarot

Spread

Group

Figure 2

way to build up a group mind for the occasion and to bring out the latent abilities of individuals present.

As I have said, the Tarot is an excellent teacher in its own right. So much so that once a rapport has been built with it then one no longer really needs to read books upon the subject. Eliphas Levi claimed that a prisoner in solitary confinement could learn the mysteries of the universe if he were able to consult the Tarot in his cell. This is something of a high claim but there is much truth in it. I have certainly learned more about the Tarot through sitting alone in a contemplative state and allowing the cards to drift through my hands and fall into various patterns, than ever I have learned from printed sources. This role of Spirit of the Tarot as direct teacher is represented in Figure 3.

Note that once again we have lines of communication or psychic force in the form of a triangle. As students of the Qabalah will know, three is the basic number of form, as represented by the third Sephirah, Binah. And the Paths upon the Tree of Life are also a complex structure of triangles, whilst the Sephiroth themselves naturally fall into a threefold series of triads. It may therefore be worth following up this concept to see how far it leads us.

For example, we could have made Figure 1 a little more complex by drawing in lines of force to and from the actual spread of cards upon the table. This would give us the diagram shown in Figure 4, where besides drawing in these lines we have drawn circles to represent the Spirit of the Tarot, the Querent and the Consultant. Students of the Qabalah will recognize a familiar type of figure beginning to build up. It is as if we are looking at one segment of the Tree of Life.

This similarity becomes more marked if we now elaborate this simple diagram to include the Higher Self of the Querent, the Higher Self of the Consultant, and what corresponds to these in the oracle itself, the Higher Fount of Wisdom in the Spirit of the Tarot. This is represented in Figure 5 which shows what should prove to be a very effective divination indeed, wherein the Higher Selves of all concerned are in colloquy. This may be recognized in Qabalistic terms as the Daath/Yesod magical circuit.

And we can go on to complete a full Tree of life if we so wish, as in Figure 6. Here, the actual physical laying out of the cards by shuffling and cutting by Querent and Consultant are

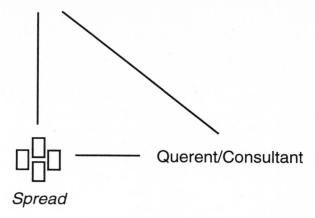

Figure 3

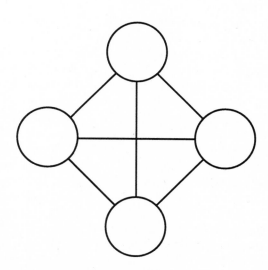

Figure 4

represented by Malkuth and the heavier lines between Malkuth and Hod (for Querent) and Netzach (for Consultant).

In the full Tree spread we also have spiritual dynamics entering in. In practical terms this is a divination becoming a revelation from the source of all being. This is perhaps the formula for an "infallible divination"—which is at least conceptually possible, if not often achieved. We enter here upon a divide that might be drawn between inspired prophecy, and divination as more generally experienced and understood.

The Tree of Life pattern is sometimes used more overtly, as a pattern for making a spread in general divinatory work. Indeed this forms part of the method described in the Golden Dawn knowledge papers. For my own part I have to say that I find that method rather too elaborate and intellectually contrived.

I prefer to go back to basics, and to regard the space whereon the cards are to be spread as a field that is apparently black but filled with potential. This potential is of space and time and not realized until the actual cards fall in their particular places upon it. I generally lay out 21 cards in the form of a spiral, starting in the center and swirling outwards in a threefold ring. The first card laid represents the center of the question, the concern in the heart of the Querent in the here and now. The remaining cards take much of their significance from the part of the table where they are laid.

The nature of this potential is represented in Figure 7. The cards toward the top of the table represent more spiritual factors; those toward the bottom of the table more material considerations. At the same time cards towards the left hand side represent past considerations and those towards the right hand represent future possibilities. It follows that the first card laid is quite a significant one, being the central point between spirit and matter and between past and future. It represents the heart of the matter and of the Querent. There is not space here to go into the detail of this particular spread but those so interested can find it all in *The Magical World of the Tarot.*

However, these principles of the dynamics of the table of art extend to various other forms of spread, and in keeping with what I have said about the self instructional nature of the Tarot, it quite possible for anyone to develop their own particular spread by meditations based upon these very broad basic principles.

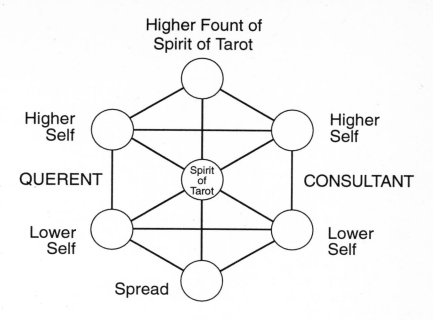

Figure 5

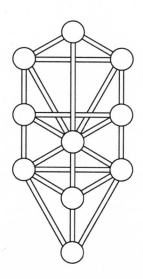

Figure 6

It is interesting to note, for example, that the principles form a general background to A.E. Waite's so-called Celtic Spread, which is arguably the most popular spread in use today. Without getting into the minutiae of analysis, it may be seen from Figure 8 that an arrow can be drawn across the spread, representing a progress from past to future and from subliminal to spiritual as it goes from left to right and bottom to top.

An appreciation of these basic principles can serve to clarify the mind when considering the merits of any particular spread. In particular might this be said of the Waite spread. Despite its simplicity, different instructional manuals give as many different ways of laying out the cards, particularly in the order and significance of those that form the equal-armed cross. Any studious student seeking enlightenment through reading all the literature is likely to get more confused the more they read. Waite himself sat on the fence somewhat in this respect and past or future depended upon which way the Significator faced.

From reading all the literature one is left with the impression that, although most esoteric commentators seem to thrive by taking in each other's washing, in the process of so doing they put it into a fine old muddle. It is really not good enough to trot out that hoary old excuse for slip-shod scholarship or plain ignorance, that these are "deliberate blinds" to protect the sacred wisdom from the unworthy and uninitiated.

The point we would make is that the way through the labyrinth is relatively easy to find. It is not through the academically respected method of comparing texts. One might as well study a dozen defective maps. The Ariadne's thread is provided by realizing and acting upon the fact that the Tarot is a magical system, and that it will open up like a flower to any who approach it in the right way.

This approach is two-fold. First a purging of the mind of all intellectual lumber save the most basic of first principles. Secondly the faith and sensitivity to build the images in the mind, relate to them personally, and let them transform. The Spirit of the Tarot will do the rest.

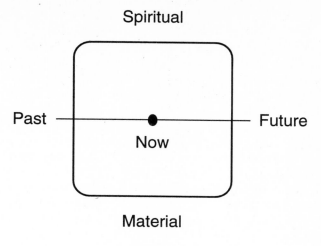

Figure 7

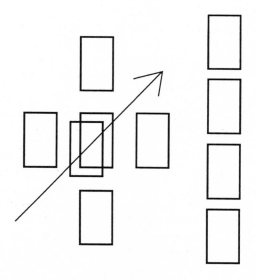

Figure 8

33

ABOUT THE AUTHOR

Gareth Knight was magically trained in the Society of the Inner Light, the fraternity founded by Dion Fortune, herself a former initiate of the Golden Dawn under the tuition of Moina MacGregor Mathers and Brodie-Innes. Early in life he wrote *A Practical Guide to Qabalistic Symbolism* which includes Tarot symbolism as applied to the Tree of Life, using the Golden Dawn system. Latterly he has written two books devoted exclusively to Tarot, *The Magical World of the Tarot* (Aquarian/Harper Collins) and *Tarot and Magic* (Destiny Book) —the first applied to divination, the latter to ritual and astral working. His latest publications are *Evoking the Goddess in the Western Mystery Tradition* (Destiny Books) and *Magic and the Western Mind* (Llewellyn).

The Golden Dawn Method
of Tarot Divination

Cris Monnastre

an reaches toward his future. Like Michelangelo's Adam of the Sistine Chapel, he reaches for the very finger of God itself and hopes that by contact with that which is beyond himself he will somehow become more than he is. Even while directing his consciousness to awareness of the present moment; while embracing all experience of the "now" with absorption and intensity; he still programs and affects his internal and external experience of what he calls his "future." But as inevitably as day follows night, he continually sets his vision beyond himself, beyond what he alone can do or see, hear or touch, and commands his universe with increasing precision and impelling audacity. He liberally illumines the Earth with what was once only an Edison's dream. He communicates over incaluable distances, even beyond his own planet. He walks upon the Moon!

Yet through all the evolving cycles of unending time, he has only begun to contest his most formidable challenge, the control of his own consciousness. Only by plumbing that depth, by digging the wells of his own mind dry, will he gain an unimagined status within his own universe. There have always been those who ran ahead of humanity in invention, art, industry or government. But even beyond these there were fewer still who ran so far ahead that they appreciated a humanity evolved beyond the possibilities of its most remarkable achievements, and this vision surfaced exempt from rational explanation and argument. So they retired inward with the device of symbol, a universal exchange medium linking macrocosm and microcosm. These few had their ingenious systems and calligraphies, laid like unperceived foundations upon which reason and logic could never balance.

Perhaps they called themselves the fire philosophers or Essenes, Gnostics or alchemists, Qabalists or Rosicrucians, but in some way they all symbolized an enlarged existence and lateral reality. Living in seclusion or overtly defying established tradition, struggling through persecution or ingratiating death, they always assured us there were answers to unlock man's questions about himself, to announce somehow to his own ego an unthinkable destiny. And exoteric science limped along apologetically behind, slowly catching up as it verified what needed no verification. The vision alone would fulfill all prophecies!

The Tarot

Of all the approaches to this reality, one of the most outstanding is the Tarot. And of all the techniques for introducing us to the Tarot, divination excels; in particular the Golden Dawn method of Tarot Divination. The prediction of events in themselves is but a secondary part of divination. Emphasis must really be placed upon the development and demonstration of those intuitive and psychic faculties which divination nurtures in gentle growth.

There are those esotericists who look upon approaching the Tarot by way of divination as coming through the back door; and indeed, corrupting any divinatory technique to the level of fortune telling or pointless curiosity delays if not greatly threatens the progress of integration and spiritual development. But approached with considerable preparation by correlating the Tarot with basic Astrological and Qabalistic material and in the spirit of genuine inquiry, the student can be exposed to the rich mosaic of his life mirrored in universal symbol. The majority of students are initially attracted to the Tarot as a divinatory tool. They should be supplied with a practical study plan for approaching this technique. After a general survey of the Tarot, the divination process and the Golden Dawn Tarot manuscripts, such a study plan will be outlined here.

The Golden Dawn method of divination is in a class of its own. Although somewhat more lengthy and complex than other methods, it outdistances them in thoroughness and the detail it yields and is an excellent means of helping the student coordinate these diverse correspondences. Of course, it is to the Golden Dawn itself, a semipublic occult order of prominence founded at the turn of the last century, to which we are still in debt for the dissemination of so much regarding occult techniques and formulae. Its system of initiation is unrivaled. As far as can be ascertained, the earliest record of this particular technique is from the Golden Dawn material. Although it has mistakenly been attributed to Aleister Crowley by some authors, it was more than likely either the creation of MacGregor Mathers or received from those who preferred that their identities remain secret. This technique is found in the "Book T" manuscripts, Volume IV of *The Golden Dawn* by Israel Regardie.

The Tarot deck is divided into two sections, a Major and Minor Arcana (arcane means "secret or hidden knowledge reserved for those duly initiated"). The Major Arcana consists of 22 cards called *Keys, Trumps or Atu*. The Minor Arcana consists of 56 cards divided into four suits: Wands (Clubs), Cups (Hearts), Swords (Spades) and Pentacles (Diamonds). It is this section of the Tarot which is the forerunner of our modern-day playing cards.

The History of the Tarot

The Tarot is more than a deck of cards with a controversial history. It is the Rota Mundi of the Rosicrucians, and in David Conway's *Magic – An Occult Primer*, the author remarks, "Behind these quaint little figures in their medieval settings are said to be the most profound secrets of Hermetic Philosophy." Tarot symbolism is also found in the ciphers of Sir Francis Bacon, and the Seal of the United States; and it is no small coincidence that Levi's *Transcendental Magic*, the *Apocalypse* and Mabel Colin's *Light on the Path* correspond to the Tarot numerically by their subdivisions.

The history of the Tarot is replete with contradiction. Crowley's observation from *The Book of Thoth*, "The origin of the Tarot is quite irrelevant, even if it were certain. It must stand or fall as a system on its own merits," is some solace to one trying to unravel the skeins of fact from fiction. The Tarot can only be documented from the late fourteenth century during the reign of Charles VI of France; however, the overall conjecture is that the Tarot extends further back into history over many thousands of the years. There are many diverse theories, even legends; that the Tarot is of Egyptian origin (even though this theory was presented a quarter of a century before the deciphering of the Rosetta Stone); that it was created by a group of adepts in Fez to insure the preservation of an esoteric mystery wisdom during the projected evolving changes in culture and language; that it was invented by (or left in the custody of) the gypsies (Bohemians) to safeguard this mystery tradition during times of religious and political persecution under the guise of gambling and fortune telling.

Among the Tarot's advocates were Gringonneur, Alliette, Papus, Knight-Littel, Gebelin, Levi and many others; but in this past century its champions stood out as especially influential in the Western occult fabric: Mathers, A.E. Waite, Crowley and Case. And these four grew in some way from the fertile soil of the Golden Dawn.

Levi referred to the Tarot as "...a hieroglyphic monument which alone explains all the mysterious writings of high initiation." And so, in the tradition of a wisdom reserved for those initiated, perhaps the Tarot to this day continues to withhold its select mysteries from those who consider it with only casual interest.

The Archetypes

The Tarot has often been linked with Jungian archetypes, those inherited ideas or modes of thought derived from the experience of the human race and present in the unconscious of each individual. By working with these unique designs one connects with immense sources of power, knowledge and inspiration. Crowley refers to the Tarot as a universal pantacle, a symbolic representation of the macrocosm. Appreciating that we are the universe-in-little or microcosm, we are seeing *ourselves* mirrored in the Tarot when we work with it! Each of the cards represents a mode of consciousness identical with our own growth and development potential and reflects some aspect of the magnificent universe around and within us! To realize this and hold in our hands the very "keys" which can unlock the mysteries is ineffable indeed!

Since the Tarot is a means of exploring our unconscious mind, and the content of that unconscious affects our lives dramatically, the Tarot is useful in guiding us through our expectations of the future. We must discipline ourselves against negative suggestion, however, so we do not bring about the very thing that we fear through our anxious emotional attitudes.

Jung defined the *coincidence* of events, one partaking in the quality of the other even though they are not causally related, as synchronicity. Therefore the birth moment mapped in an Astrological chart has that quality of, is symbolic of, or "explains", the individual it represents. The pattern of the fall of *I Ching* coins takes on the quality of the question asked at the same moment. The shuffling of a deck of Tarot cards does the same. In the introduction to the Wilhelm/Baynes edition of the *I Ching* it is stated, "The axioms of causality are being shaken to their foundations: we know now that what we term natural laws are merely statistical truths and thus must necessarily allow for exceptions."

"Time," as Claude Bragdon explains in *A Primer of Higher Space*, is very probably a dimension of a four-dimensional *solid*; what we observe as birth, the span of life (or "future") and then death, exist as a unity, a *spatial* unit that we can only perceive from a radically altered state of consciousness. Simply, if you stood high upon a mountain summit and observed two automobiles approaching each other from a great distance but on the same course, you could easily "predict" a head-on collision although the cars were not as yet aware of each other from their own points of view. We have already overcome time and space with telegraph, telephone, television and satellites, but man's destiny is to reach beyond these mechanical devices with the instrument of his own consciousness!

The Golden Dawn manuscripts on the Tarot are an abundant source of important and suggestive correspondences and description; they can be explored and cultivated with infinite possibility, as can all the Golden Dawn material. "By names and images are all powers awakened and reawakened." In his introduction to the second edition of *The Golden Dawn* Israel Regardie suggests we remember this singular idea when we are confronted with a deluge of complex symbolism and technique. This is equally valid regarding the Tarot manuscripts.

That man's five senses give lie to reality is no new idea. In *Maps of Consciousness*, Ralph Metzner remarks, "The filtering mechanisms by which the incoming (sense) data are screened are genetically and culturally transmitted programs (patterns); we see what we are programmed to see." There are those symbols (as contained within the Tarot) which reverberate to restructuring forces which "...initiate streams of associations leading to enlarged and healing perspectives," We are programmed (reprogrammed!) to our own images and patterns! The images we hold within our consciousness *inevitably* determine all our experience and environment. From this we learn that by fixing our consciousness upon the Tarot symbols we are doing much more than investigating our unconscious process through divination; we are also redesigning this inner world of ours! Approaching Tarot divination is a multifaceted business in that learning how to develop our intuitive response to life, we are really only seeing an infinitesimal segment of this overwhelming process whose hidden significance is not only challenging but regenerative.

The Divinatory Faculty

At this juncture the student must realize that even to begin to gain any real benefit from working with the Tarot it must be assimilated into his consciousness in a practical and vital way. All of its symbolism must be absorbed and actually become a part of the student's warp and weft. This cannot be accomplished to great advantage only by memorizing the card meanings or, worse, not memorizing the meanings at all and attempting divination with the aid of a book. By coordinating the Tarot with the appropriate Astrological and Qabalistic correspondences, all facets of the student's personal occult inventory are heightened. This kind of preparation will bring about a divinatory faculty, facilitating an intuitive and psychic response to the Tarot symbols. The more one studies the Tarot, the more one reflects with amazement at the mind or minds which conceived of this incredible and inexhaustible tool for exploring one's existence! Those who approach this technique of Tarot divination without adequate preparation either fail to learn sufficiently or use this technique and delay their progress in this direction significantly. Crowley reminds us, "It is for the student to build these living stones into his living temple." How is this accomplished? In his books on magical technique, William Gray continually emphasizes that for a symbol to become a dynamic part of our being, there must be a *mutual absorption.* "We must enter into it and it must enter into us." Paul Foster Case suggests as one approach that the student *look* at least one card of the Major Arcana daily; it is even more advantageous and evocative to "tune" into the card's symbolism (as one tunes in a radio station) by also mediating upon its corresponding color at the same time. For most of us seeing is the first and best step toward understanding. In *The Symphony of Life*, Donald Hatch Andrew says: "There is every reason to believe that matter in this vast space is linked to every other bit of matter by gravity. There is every reason to believe that the de Broglie music of every portion of this space penetrates every other portion of it. Then nearness or farness is not a question of *space separation* but a question of *tuning*." The power/knowledge source symbolized by Tarot is not separated from us by space or time. We need only adjust to its wavelength, so to speak. As we are penetrated by radio and television waves we are also living and moving *now* within a sea of ultra dimensional learning potential. With "sight through symbol" we link with a power/knowledge source extending beyond our limited three-dimensional awareness. We will only make this connection if we become the symbols and systematically discipline our consciousness toward their absorption.

To begin we will follow a practical study plan outlined below and create a notebook just for the Tarot. Nearly every occult authority agrees with the necessity of keeping some kind of personal written record. As Crowley has observed, to attempt occult work without it is like setting out to sea without charts for navigation. This notebook will aid in accomplishing that "mutual absorption" so necessary. It becomes an extension of one's consciousness and reflects a gradual inner growth.

First of all, select a Tarot deck. For the purposes of this article and the accompanying divinatory technique, it is advantageous to select one of the Tarot decks adhering to the traditional designs of the Golden Dawn system: Waite, Crowley, Case, Wang, or the recently published *New Golden Dawn Ritual Tarot* by Sandra Tabatha Cicero.

As a prerequisite, the student *must* memorize the Astrological symbols of the Planets and signs of the Zodiac. No other Astrological knowledge is necessary. This should only take a minimal amount of time, but these symbols and ideas must become as familiar as the alphabet if progress is expected. An abbreviated list is provided here. Additional correspondences can easily be obtained from any book on basic Astrology, and the student is encouraged to increase his familiarity with as many correspondences as time and interest will permit. These symbols are the foundation upon which the Tarot will be built. Card by card, stone by stone, this inner temple is erected with care and precision.

Astrological Correspondences

Planets		**Signs**		**Houses**
☉	Vitality	♈	Impulse	1. The self, the first 24 months of life
☽	Reflection	♉	Practicality	2. Finances, self-worth
☿	Intellect	♊	Diversity	3. Communications, local travel, kindred
♀	Love	♋	Emotion	4. Home, close of life
♂	Energy	♌	Drama	5. Children, sports, romance, speculation
♃	Expansion	♍	Labor	6. Health, employment, service
♄	Restriction	♎	Sociality	7. Partnerships, the public, marriage
♅	Invention	♏	Regeneration	8. Joint finances, sex, legacies
♆	Inspiration	♐	Idealism	9. Higher education, religion, law
♇	Transformation	♑	Executiveness	10. Prominence, career, honors
		♒	Humanitarian	11. Hopes and fears, love received
		♓	Poetry	12. Self-undoing, institutions

Preliminary Instructions

Having selected a Tarot deck, purchase a loose-leaf notebook. With tab dividers allow one section per card (78 in all). Having assimilated the above Astrological material, we are ready to begin our study program preparatory to learning the Golden Dawn divinatory technique. This preparation will consist of absorbing the Tarot symbols a few minutes each day as well as memorizing the key ideas relating to each card. Do not think this is in any way unnecessary. When Tarot divination is approached without adequate preparation, it is a waste of time if not even deleterious. The material presented is organized over six weeks, a brief period of time, considering the amount material reviewed. Even if the card meanings have been memorized already, this additional study program will still be of the utmost benefit.

The Tree of Life

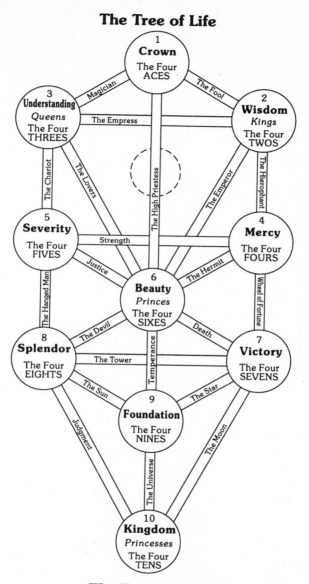

The Four Worlds

YOD	HEH	VAV	HEH (Final)
Fire	Water	Air	Earth
Wands	Cups	Swords	Pentacles
Originative	Creative	Formative	Physical
Initiating	Pleasures	Difficulties	Business (Material)

As one part of our daily exercise we will follow Case's suggestion in *The Tarot – A Key to the Wisdom of the Ages* and spend five minutes looking at each card. Since we want to explore 78 cards in only six weeks we will work with several cards each day as outlined below. Case remarks that by looking at the Tarot carefully and regularly, "...you transfer their designs from the printed cards to your own brain cells. Your brain is an instrument analogous to a radio set. When you thus modify its mechanism you attune it to the states of consciousness symbolized by the Tarot designs." He adds that the Tarot's evocative effect is increased by looking at the corresponding color with each card.

The six-week study plan is outlined below. Week 1 concentrates on the Major Arcana; Weeks 2 through 5, the four suits of the Minor Arcana: Wands, Cups, Swords and Pentacles. Week 6 reclassifies all 78 cards under the seven ancient Planets. These correspondences are collected from a variety of sources, while the Golden Dawn Tarot manuscripts, containing some of the most comprehensive material on the Tarot, are the parent source. The manuscripts also contain excellent descriptions of many of the cards and the student is urged to read and to absorb these as well.

The Study Plan

Before beginning the week's work, find sheets of colored construction paper corresponding to the color column. Enter these sheets in your notebook for the appropriate card.

Week 1, Major Arcana. Instructions: try to work in the early morning when you are refreshed, relaxed and not likely to be disturbed. Work with three cards per day, four cards on the seventh day. Place the card on top of the appropriate color sheet in your notebook. look at it for five minutes and note down any impressions or ideas. Take note of the corresponding Hebrew letter and Astrological correspondence. What additional ideas do they convey? Memorize the abbreviated card meanings. (The abbreviated meanings are a composite of several authoritative sources on the Tarot.) The student will want to refer to the appropriate diagram for an added perspective in which the Major Arcana is illustrated on the Zodiac.

Once again find the corresponding color sheets for each of the cards being worked with in the following study plans.

Major Arcana on the Zodiac

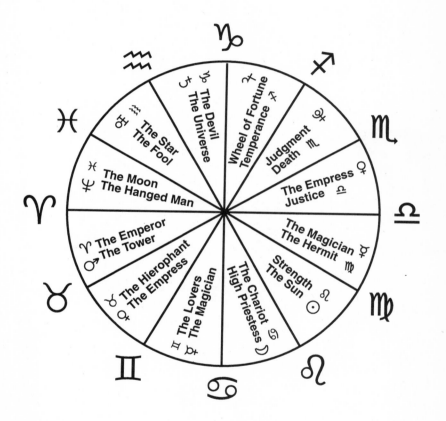

Tarot Decans

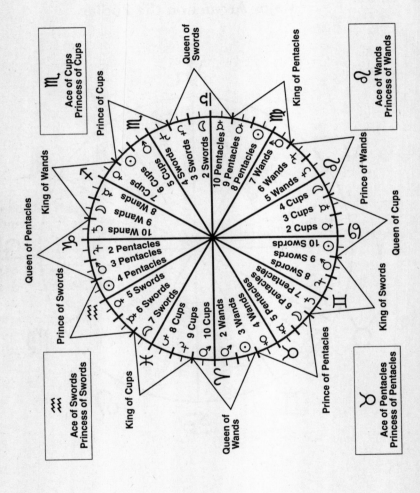

Week 2, Minor Arcana (Suit of Wands). Instructions: this week we begin with the suit of Wands. Work with two cards per day in the above outlined manner. Note the decan (division of 10 degrees of the Zodiac, see diagram of Tarot decans) and the Astrological correspondences. (Note: the rulers of the Tarot decans are not the same as the rulers of the Astrological decans.) Memorize the card meanings. The four Court cards of each suit—King, Queen, Prince and Princess—usually refer to actual people in divinations. Over the next four weeks study the diagram of the Qabalistic Tree of Life with the Minor Arcana placed upon it. Note below this glyph on the diagram how the four suits of the Minor Arcana correspond to the letters of the Tetragrammaton, *Yod-Heh-Vav-Heh* and the four Worlds of the Qabalists.

Weeks 3 - 5, Minor Arcana (Suit of Cups, Swords, and Pentacles). Instructions: see Week 2 Instructions.

Week 6, Ancient Planets. Instructions: this final week we will reclassify the Major and Minor Arcana according to the seven ancient Planets. Observe how these Planets correspond to the Tree of Life as portrayed in the accompanying diagram. (Note: all 78 cards do not correspond to the glyph itself in this same way. There are connecting "Paths" to which the Major Arcana correspond.) The classification of the Week 6 Study Plan is to create Planetary families to aid in the absorption of key ideas associated with each Planet. After five minutes of looking at each group of cards, note down any impressions or ideas under the appropriate section in your notebook. *Important:* review the memorized meaning of each card within its family.

Each day's session should take no more than 20 minutes, a small investment of time toward a technique which will be of inestimable value for your entire lifetime!

STUDY PLAN FOR WEEK 1 – (Major Arcana)

Day	Astro. Corresp.	No.	Card Name	Hebrew Letter	Color	Interpretation
Day 1	Uranus	0	The Fool	Aleph (ox)	Yellow	Originality, folly
	Mercury	1	The Magician	Beth (house)	Yellow	Occult power, skill, mind
	Moon	2	High Priestess	Gimel (camel)	Blue	Duality, unconsciousness, fluctuation
Day 2	Venus	3	The Empress	Daleth (door)	Green	Beauty, pleasure, dissipation
	Aries	4	The Emperor	Heh (window)	Red	Reason, control, dominion
	Taurus	5	The Hierophant	Vav (nail, hook)	Red-orange	Inspiration, alliance, (marriage)
Day 3	Gemini	6	The Lovers	Zayin (sword)	Orange	Love, attraction, harmony
	Cancer	7	The Chariot	Cheth (fence)	Yel-orange	Victory
	Leo	8	Strength	Teth (serpent)	Yellow	Courage, power
Day 4	Virgo	9	The Hermit	Yod (open hand)	Yel-green	Guidance, protection
	Jupiter	10	Wheel of Fortune	Kaph (fist)	Violet	Good fortune, success
	Libra	11	Justice	Lamed (ox-goad)	Green	Legality, material matters, justice
Day 5	Neptune	12	The Hanged Man	Mem (water)	Blue	Spiritual union, reversal
	Scorpio	13	Death	Nun (fish)	Blue-green	Transformation -spiritual & material
	Sagittarius	14	Temperance	Samekh (prop)	Blue	Adaptation
Day 6	Capricorn	15	The Devil	Ayin (eye)	Blue-violet	Materiality
	Mars	16	The Tower	Peh (mouth)	Red	Conflict, danger, awakening
	Aquarius	17	The Star	Tzaddi (fish-hook)	Violet	Hope, influence
Day 7	Pisces	18	The Moon	Qoph (back of head)	Red-violet	Voluntary change, deception
	Sun	19	The Sun	Resh (head)	Orange	Wealth, riches, success
	Pluto	20	Judgment	Shin (tooth)	Red	Decision, renewal
	Saturn	21	The World	Tau (cross)	Blue-violet	Synthesis, success

STUDY PLAN FOR WEEK 2 – (Suit of Wands—FIRE)

Day	Card Name	Decan /or Sub-Element	Astro. Cor.	Color*	Interpretation
Day 1	Ace of Wands	Root of Fire	—	White	Beginning
	2 of Wands	1st d. of Aries	Mars in Aries	Grey	Dominion
Day 2	3 of Wands	2nd d. of Aries	Sun in Aries	Black	Established Strength
	4 of Wands	3rd d. of Aries	Venus in Aries	Blue	Perfected Work
Day 3	5 of Wands	1st d. of Leo	Saturn in Leo	Red	Strife
	6 of Wands	2nd d. of Leo	Jupiter in Leo	Yellow	Victory
Day 4	7 of Wands	3rd d. of Leo	Mars in Leo	Green	Valor
	8 of Wands	1st d. of Sagitt.	Mercury in Sagitt.	Orange	Swiftness
Day 5	9 of Wands	2nd d. of Sagitt.	Moon in Sagitt.	Violet	Strength in reserve
	10 of Wands	3rd d. of Sagitt.	Saturn in Sagitt.	Black, olive russet, citrine	Oppression
Day 6	King of Wands	Fire of Fire	Sagittarius	Grey, red	Honest
	Queen of Wands	Water of Fire	Aries	Black, red	Friendly
Day 7	Prince of Wands	Air of Fire	Leo	Yellow, red	Friendly, departure
	Princess of Wands	Earth of Fire	Leo	Black, red	Messenger, brilliance

* The colors given here for the Minor Arcana reflect the colors of the ten Sephiroth of the Tree of Life as given in the Queen (Briah) Scale. This is to emphasize the important relationship that exists between the Minor Arcana cards and the Spheres on the Tree. The colors given for the Court cards reflect two pigments: that of the Elemental color of the Tarot suit, and the Briah color of the specific Sephirah which is assigned to the Court card in question. For example: The Kings relate to Chokmah (grey) while the Queens relate to Binah (black).

STUDY PLAN FOR WEEK 3 – (Suit of Cups—Water)

Day	Card Name	Decan /or Sub-Element	Astro. Cor.	Color	Interpretation
Day 1	Ace of Cups	Root of Water	——	White	Fertility
	2 of Cups	1st d. of Cancer	Venus in Cancer	Grey	Reciprocity
Day 2	3 of Cups	2nd d. of Cancer	Mercury in Cancer	Black	Abundance
	4 of Cups	3rd d. of Cancer	Moon in Cancer	Blue	Contemplation, blended pleasure
Day 3	5 of Cups	1st d. of Scorpio	Mars in Scorpio	Red	Pleasure's loss
	6 of Cups	2nd d. of Scorpio	Sun in Scorpio	Yellow	Beginning of success
Day 4	7 of Cups	3rd d. of Scorpio	Venus in Scorpio	Green	Illusory success
	8 of Cups	1st d. of Pisces	Saturn in Pisces	Orange	Abandoned success
Day 5	9 of Cups	2nd d. of Pisces	Jupiter in Pisces	Violet	Material success
	10 of Cups	3rd d. of Pisces	Mars in Pisces	Black, olive russet, citrine	Lasting success
Day 6	King of Cups	Fire of Water	Pisces	Grey, blue	Subtle, violent, artistic
	Queen of Cups	Water of Water	Cancer	Black, blue	Poetic
Day 7	Prince of Cups	Air of Water	Scorpio	Yellow, blue	Indolent, approach
	Princess of Cups	Earth of Water	Scorpio	Black, blue	Studious youth, news

STUDY PLAN FOR WEEK 4 – (Suit of Swords—AIR)

Day	Card Name	Decan /or Sub-Element	Astro. Cor.	Color	Interpretation
Day 1	Ace of Swords	Root of Air	—	White	Conquest
	2 of Swords	1st d. of Libra	Moon in Libra	Grey	Peace restored
Day 2	3 of Swords	2nd d. of Libra	Saturn in Libra	Black	Sorrow
	4 of Swords	3rd d. of Libra	Jupiter in Libra	Blue	Rest from strife
Day 3	5 of Swords	1st d. of Aquarius	Venus in Aquarius	Red	Defeat
	6 of Swords	2nd d. of Aquar.	Mercury in Aquar.	Yellow	Earned success
Day 4	7 of Swords	3rd d. of Aquar.	Moon in Aquarius	Green	Unstable effort
	8 of Swords	1st d. of Gemini	Jupiter in Gemini	Orange	Waste of energy
Day 5	9 of Swords	2nd d. of Gemini	Mars in Gemini	Violet	Despair & cruelty
	10 of Swords	3rd d. of Gemini	Sun in Gemini	Black, olive russet, citrine	Ruin, end of delusion
Day 6	King of Swords	Fire of Air	Gemini	Grey, yellow	Suspicious
	Queen of Swords	Water of Air	Libra	Black, yellow	Perceptive, widowhood
Day 7	Prince of Swords	Air of Air	Aquarius	Yellow	Domineering
	Princess of Swords	Earth of Air	Aquarius	Black, yellow	Active youth

STUDY PLAN FOR WEEK 5 – (Suit of Pentacles—EARTH)

Day	Card Name	Decan /or Sub-Element	Astro. Cor.	Color	Interpretation
Day 1	Ace of Pentacles	Root of Earth	——	White	Wealth
	2 of Pentacles	1st d. of Capri.	Jupiter in Capri.	Grey	Harmonious change
Day 2	3 of Pentacles	2nd d. of Capri.	Mars in Capricorn	Black	Growth
	4 of Pentacles	3rd d. of Capri.	Sun in Capricorn	Blue	Earthly power
Day 3	5 of Pentacles	1st. d. of Taurus	Mercury in Taurus	Red	Adaptation, material trouble
	6 of Pentacles	2nd d. of Taurus	Moon in Taurus	Yellow	Material success
Day 4	7 of Pentacles	3rd d. of Taurus	Saturn in Taurus	Green	Success unfulfilled
	8 of Pentacles	1st d. of Virgo	Sun in Virgo	Orange	Skill in affairs
Day 5	9 of Pentacles	2nd d. of Virgo	Venus in Virgo	Violet	Material gain
	10 of Pentacles	3rd d. of Virgo	Mercury in Virgo	Black, olive russet, citrine	Wealth
Day 6	King of Pentacles	Fire of Earth	Virgo	Grey, black	Reliable
	Queen of Pentacles	Water of Earth	Capricorn	Black	Generous
Day 7	Prince of Pentacles	Air of Earth	Taurus	Yellow, black	Laborious
	Princess of Pent.	Earth of Earth	Taurus	Black	Deliberate youth

STUDY PLAN FOR WEEK 6 – (Planetary Families)

(Cards ruled by a specific Planet)

Day	Family of:	Key words	Major Arcana (Sign)	Major Arcana (Planet)	Minor Arcana
Day 1	Saturn	- Restriction + Discipline	♑ The Devil ♒ The Star	♄ The Universe	5w,Qp,3s,As, 10w,Ps,8c,PSs,7p
Day 2	Jupiter	- Waste + Expansion	♓ The Moon ♐ Temperance	♃ Wheel of Fortune	6w,Kw,4s,Kc, 2p,9c,8s
Day 3	Mars	- Violence + Energy	♈The Emperor ♏ Death	♂ The Tower	7w,Qw,5c,Ac,3p,
				♅ Judgment	Pc,10c,PSc,2w,9s
Day 4	Sun	+ Vitality	♌ Strength	☉ The Sun	8p,Aw,6c,Pw,4p, PSw,3w,10s
Day 5	Venus	- Dissipation + Love	♉ The Hierophant ♎ Justice	♀ The Empress ♆ Hanged Man	9p,Qs,7c,Ap,5s Pp,4w,PSp,2c
Day 6	Mercury	- Scatteredness + Intellect	♊ The Lovers ♍ The Hermit	☿ The Magician ♅ The Fool	10p,Ks,8w,Kp 6s,5p,3c
Day 7	Moon	- Weakness + Reflection	♋The Chariot	☽ High Priestess	2s,Qc,9w, 7s,6p,4c

Abbreviations: w = Wands, c = Cups, s = Swords, p = Pentacles, A = Ace, K = King, Q = Queen, P = Prince, PS = Princess

The Art of Tarot Divination

As man reaches toward knowledge of his future, he realizes that he can grasp it, experience and examine it with the fresh wonderment of a small child holding and exploring some fascinating new discovery. With an evolving and altered consciousness, man observes, makes *contact* with that four-dimensional solid or reality which appears as the flow of his very life! He does not do this sporadically, but with gentle care and systematic investigation revealing those carefully patterned angles, planes and curves of his own life-solid, exposing that unity, the beauty of which knows no ungraceful or dissonant content, no error of the Grand Architect's hand. With time and dedicated experiment, divination can promote an enlivening perspective regarding the awareness of this life-reality.

From those first dark, interior stirrings of imagination, from the first man who embraced the mystery of a Full Moon sky and ached to explore the hidden secrets of a startling universe, with each patterned repetition of stars in their journey toward unimaginable destinations, and with the readings of omens or coins, shells or yarrow sticks, man has always labored to *know*. At times, to know what future events portend on this physical plane; at other times, to dive inward, daring the raging and colossal confines of inner life; but always to cajole, to seduce, to demand nature relinquish one more secret of her hidden existence. Whether man descended into the caverns of Delphi (as he again "descends" into the depths of the unconscious) or gave perfunctory attention to raving Cassandras, instinctively he knew he would fly with wings at the speed of light and outwit his self-made illusion of "time!"

There are other techniques of divination besides Tarot: *I Ching*, Geomancy, horary Astrology and many others, all valid and useful, depending upon the thought, practice and care with which they are approached. All divination has historically been the art and fancy of kings; but *Tarot* is what Stephan Hoeller calls "The Royal Path of Life."

We have already traced the lineage of the Tarot divination technique under consideration, but before outlining its outstanding features, we will canvas and outline its parent schema, the "Book T" manuscripts of the Golden Dawn.

1. The Titles of the Tarot Symbols

20 Cards

    a) The 16 Court cards and four Aces symbolically described in terms of the four elements.

36 Cards

    b) The 36 "small" cards, those numbered two through ten of the Minor Arcana with abbreviated divinatory interpretations listed by decanates.

22 Cards

    c) The 22 major Trumps with descriptions depicting their Astrological correlations.

78 Cards Total

These abbreviated titles should be read through many times, allowing their images and poetic language to sink deeply into one's consciousness.

2. The Descriptions of the 78 Tarot Symbols.

What comprises this section are descriptions of the design and symbolism of all 78 Tarot cards *except* the Major Arcana. The divinatory interpretations of this Arcana are given but not a description of these 22 cards themselves. If it were not for this omission, the student would be able to design his own complete deck from the original Golden Dawn descriptions! Also included within this section are interesting, evocative and detailed descriptions of the 16 Court cards as well as other miscellaneous material.

3. Explanation of the Divinatory Technique

After memorizing the abbreviated meanings of the 78 Tarot cards, it is especially recommended that the student read the material outlined above, adding additional ideas, symbolism and correspondences to one's consciousness regarding these 78 cards. The brief divinatory correspondences provided here offer only the *barest* framework upon which an infinitely elaborate edifice of the Tarot can be built. It is advisable to have the deck in hand while working through "Book T," correlating each card to whatever information is pertinent.

The real value of Tarot divination flowers within the consciousness only with regular practice. An isolated experiment or haphazard approach to this technique scatters energy and suggests to the unconscious a casual, even careless, opinion of it. The unconscious only responds in kind with inaccurate and disappointing results. Divination should only be attempted when one is fresh and not rushed. Since the entire procedure takes approximately one hour, it is unlikely one will have the stamina to experiment with more than two or three questions at a sitting.

A Tarot deck should be used only by its owner and kept in a safe and personal place among one's choice belongings. The more one works with a deck, keeps it within one's aura, the more the "mutual absorption" occurs and the Tarot becomes a vital part of one's consciousness.

The Opening of the Key

This method of divination is referred to as "The Opening of the Key." It consists of five separate procedures or "Operations," developing any question in unusually great detail. As explained in the "Book T" manuscripts, each Operation is symbolically linked with some grouping of Tarot cards and this schema relates to the Tree of Life as projected in a sphere.

Operation 1 (8 cards) One (Kether; 4 Aces) - ten (Malkuth; 4 Princesses). Initiating energy resolved into final manifestation on the physical plane.

Operation 2 (12 cards) The Court cards - four Kings, Queens, Princes - of the four suits, correlated with the 12 Astrological houses or areas of life-experience.

Operation 3 (12 cards) The 12 Keys (Trumps) of the Major Arcana, related to 12 signs of the Zodiac.

Operation 4 (36 cards) The small cards (numbering 2-10 of the Minor Arcana), related to the 36 decanates of the Zodiac.

Operation 5 (10 cards) The 10 Sephiroth of the Tree of Life, related to seven ancient Planets and the three "Mother Letters."

The divination takes approximately one hour to complete and record in the Divination Journal; such a length of time prevents the operator (reader) or Querent (person asking the question) from asking frivolous questions. In any method of divination (*I Ching*, Geomancy, etc.) it is ordinarily suggested that only one question be developed at a time, and that particular question only once in any given 24-hour period. The question should be an important one of singular emotional concern to the Querent. It should not be an "if" or "either/or" structure, but one clear question regarding the problem. Often the process of coming to grips with the essence of the existing problem in creating once concise statement and by singling out the relevant issues will alone be conducive to a clearer perspective.

Ask yourself the questions: What is really wrong? What alternatives do I have? What is my part in the matter? What is within me to attract such circumstances, decisions or tensions? Tensions are a part of life, a necessary and growth-producing part. Existence manifests itself in opposites and our three-dimensional awareness must experience it as such to prod us on to greater achievement, a more mature handling of life, a more liberated experience of our divine potential in a four-dimensional unity experience.

Elsewhere in *The Golden Dawn* it is suggested, preferred in fact, that the person performing the divination have no emotional involvement with the question; that aside from nothing to "gain or lose" from the information received during the divination, the diviner feel no animosity, attraction or any emotional attachment toward the Querent or matter under consideration. This is an *excellent* practice for developing real skill in divination and a neutrality which accelerates one's progress in this art as no other exercise can.

The Golden Dawn Method

Read these explanations over many times while experimenting with a deck of Tarot cards at the same time to grasp the movement of the different Operations. Do not perform an actual divination until you are very familiar with the flow within each Operation, the order in which they occur, and all additional details. Certain guidelines must be memorized (as eventually, the entire divination procedure itself) to yield credible results. There is no point in hurrying through the fundamentals of a technique which will be used to such advantage for an entire lifetime!

The Five Operations of the Opening of the Key

Select a Significator. This is the one card from the pack of 78 used to represent the Querent. The Golden Dawn material suggests this card be selected from the 16 Court cards according to physical description and age:

> *Wands & Cups:* Generally fair-haired and fair-complexioned.
> *Swords & Pentacles:* Generally dark-haired and dark-complexioned.
> *Kings:* Men. *Queens:* Women. *Princes:* Young Men.
> *Princesses:* Young Women.

Note: "Book T" is liberally confusing in its usage of the terms *King, Lord, Queen, Knight, Knave, Prince* and *Princess*, as they refer to the 16 Court or "picture" cards. (These are the four picture cards at the end of each suit, as opposed to the Major Arcana (Trumps) which depict scenes and figures as well.) The four Court cards of each suit represent Yod (Fire), Heh (Water), Vav (Air), Heh (Earth), the four letters of Tetragrammaton. All possible "Book T" designations are listed here.

	Golden Dawn	*Also Called*
Yod (Fire)	King	Lord, Knight
Heh (Water)	Queen	
Vav (Air)	Prince	King, Knight
Heh (Earth)	Princess	Prince, Knave

Before the Querent takes the deck, it is advisable that he attune with the intelligences of the Tarot through some kind of invocation. The following invocation is recommended in Israel Regardie's *The Golden Dawn:*

"In the Divine name IAO, I invoke thee, thou Great Angel HRU, who art set over the operations of this Secret Wisdom. Lay thine hand invisibly on these consecrated cards of art, that thereby I may obtain true knowledge of hidden things, to the glory of the ineffable Name. Amen."

(Read right to left.)

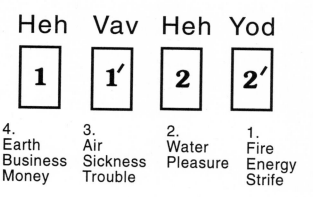

Heh	Vav	Heh	Yod
1	1′	2	2′

4.	3.	2.	1.
Earth	Air	Water	Fire
Business	Sickness	Pleasure	Energy
Money	Trouble		Strife

Example 1

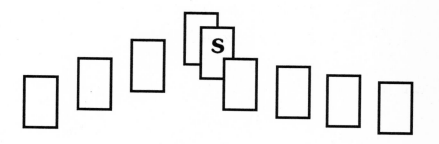

Example 2

59

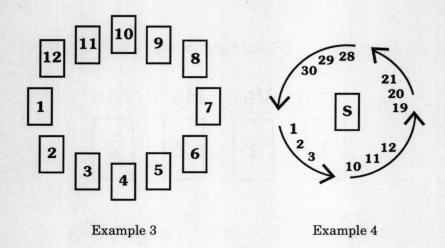

Example 3   Example 4

1. Crown - Primal Will

2. Wisdom - Archetypal father

3. Understanding - Archetypal mother

4. Mercy - Beneficence

5. Severity - Karmic law

6. Beauty - Redeemer

7. Victory - Emotion

8. Splendor - Intellect

9. Foundation - Astral Light

10. Kingdom - physical, material world

Example 5

60

Each of the five Operations is divided into two parts: a "counting" in some type of design and a "pairing" of cards. The "counting" is labeled "A", the "pairing" is labeled "B".

1A, First Operation; The Opening of the Question

1. The Querent shuffles the deck and stops when he "feels" like stopping.

2. Placing the deck face down, he cuts it in half to his *right* and then cuts *each* of these decks in half again to the right. The result is four stacks of cards representing the four letters of Tetragrammaton.

3. Each stack is carefully turned over to reveal the bottom cards and an interpretation of these four cards gives a general indication of the matter. Note: for now observe the basic interpretations of these four cards.

4. The person performing the divination looks for the Significator in each of the four decks *without disturbing* their order. Upon finding it, he discards the other three decks and notes the general meaning of the stack with the Significator in it. (See example 1.) He carefully spreads out the remaining deck in the shape of a horseshoe—i.e., cards above the Significator going to the right, cards below the Significator going to the left. (See Example 2.)

5. The diviner is ready to perform the first operation, which refers to the beginning of the matter, possibly the immediate past, depending upon what the cards indicate in this part of the divination.

6. The divination proceeds by a counting method. The student will have to memorize the following rules. (According to the "Book T" manuscripts, these are not arbitrarily chosen numbers, but represent some aspect of occult/Tarot symbolism.)

   Count 5 for an Ace.
   Count 7 for a Princess *(Page or Knave as designated)*.
   Count 4 for a King, Queen of Knight.
   Count their own number for the small cards:

6 of Cups, *10* of Swords, *3* of Wands, etc....
Count 3 for Trumps:
0 (The Fool) 12 (The Hanged Man) 20 (Judgment)
(The 3 Mother Letters of the Hebrew Alphabet)
Count 12 for cards of the Major Arcana
corresponding to the 12 signs of the zodiac.
Count 9 for each card of the Major Arcana
corresponding to one of the ancient Planets.

7. Start counting with the Significator in the direction
   it is looking. (If the Significator is looking straight
   ahead, the count proceeds to the left.) Count the
   Significator as No. 1 of the first count and proceed
   around the horseshoe as if it were a circle. Any card
   one lands upon is always No. 1 of the next count.
   This continues until a card is landed upon which
   has already been read and a "loop" results if any
   further count is continued.

8. Interpret these cards in terms of their meaning, the
   matter being questioned, and the suits of the card
   on each side of the card being interpreted. Weave a
   story around the question.

1B, First Operation

The second part of this first operation is pairing.
Cards are paired from *opposite ends* of the horseshoe until no more pairs can be made. The
Operator interprets each pair together, while
further elaborating the story.

2A, The Second Operation; The 12 Houses, The Development of the Matter

1. The Querent shuffles the entire deck again,
   thinking of the matter in question.

2. He *does not* cut the deck, only sets it face down
   upon the table.

3. The Operator deals out 12 stacks of cards, face
   down, representing the 12 houses of a horoscope.
   (See example 3)

4. The Operator goes through each pack to find the Significator. That pack is set aside; the rest are discarded. Special note is taken of which of the 12 house stacks the Significator is in and the following divination is interpreted accordingly.

5. As in 1A (4), the other stacks are discarded and this small pack is arranged in a horseshoe; be careful not to destroy the order. It is then "counted" and interpreted.

2B, The Second Operation

As in 1B (1), the cards are paired from opposite ends of the horseshoe and interpreted.

3A, The Third Operation; the 12 Signs, Continuing the Development

1. The same as 2A, except the 12 stacks represent the 12 signs of the Zodiac (attributed to the appropriate Trumps from the Major Arcana).

2. Take special note of which sign the Significator falls in. The Operation proceeds as 2A (5).

3B, The Third Operation

As in 1B (1), the cards are paired from the opposite ends of the horseshoe and interpreted.

4A, The Fourth Operation; The 36 Decanates, Further Development

1. The Querent shuffles the full deck, does not cut it, and places it on the table, face down.

2. The Operator takes the deck face up and, without destroying the order of the cards, finds the Significator.

3. The Significator and all the cards *below* it are placed on top of the cards above it. The Significator is now the top card.

4. The cards are placed face down on the table.

5. Dealing from the bottom of the pack, the Operator places the Significator (first card) upon the middle of the table. Thirty-six cards are then dealt counterclockwise (still from the bottom of the deck), in order, in the 36 decanates. (See Example 4)

6. The reading is counted from the Number 1 card (not the Significator), in counterclockwise motion, as explained in 1A.

4B, The Fourth Operation

The cards are paired: 1-36, 2-35, 3-34, 4-33, etc., and interpreted as previously explained.

5A, The Fifth Operation; The 10 Sephiroth, The Conclusion

1. The entire deck is shuffled by the Querent, not cut, and set face down on the table.

2. The Operator deals the entire deck into 10 stacks according to the glyph of the Tree of Life. (See Example 5)

3. The Operator then finds the packet in which the Significator falls.

4. This packet is arranged in the horseshoe pattern as explained in 1A (4) and interpreted accordingly.

5B, The Fifth Operation

The horseshoe arrangement is paired as in 1B (1) and interpreted accordingly. This concludes the fifth and final operation of the Opening of the Key.

The Concept of Time

The interpretation of "time" in a Tarot divination is always a perplexing matter. Case offers the only opinion: "Experience alone will enable you to judge time with any degree of accuracy, and no rules can be given. If you are possessed of the psychic qualifications necessary to a diviner, you will 'feel' time." This is good advice, but we might elaborate further with a few general considerations from the Tarot's symbolic framework. The four elements correspond with the four divisions of the day and with other divisions of "four" which we find within our time structure:

Elements	4 Seasons	Lunar Cycle
Air	Spring	New Moon & first phase
Fire	Summer	2nd phase
Water	Autumn	Full Moon & 3rd phase
Earth	Winter	4th phase

Divisions of the Day	Minor Arcana
Dawn to noon	Swords—Ace through Court cards
Noon to sunset	Wands—Ace through Court cards
Sunset to midnight	Cups—Ace through Court cards
Midnight to dawn	Pentacles—Ace through Court cards.

It is also significant to observe that the 12 Trumps corresponding to the 12 signs of the zodiac are also appropriately divided into the 12 Astrological segments of the solar year, as Aries: Trump 4, The Emperor—March 21—April 19, etc.

The remaining 10 Trumps of the Major Arcana (corresponding to the Planets and the luminaries of our solar system) relate with regard to "time" by their orbits:

Sun	Key 19	
Moon	Key 2	28 days
Mercury	Key 1	88 days
Venus	Key 3	224 days
Mars	Key 16	687 days
Jupiter	Key 10	12 years
Saturn	Key 21	29.5 years
Uranus	Key 0	84 years
Neptune	Key 12	165 years
Pluto	Key 20	248 years

An additional classification is Crowley's illustration of the central Astrological correspondences of each of the decan sets per sign. Beginning with Aries, these relate to the days of the week:

Sunday	3 of Wands
Monday	6 of Pentacles

Tuesday	9 of Swords
Wednesday	3 of Cups
Thursday	6 of Wands
Friday	9 of Pentacles
Saturday	3 of Swords

With these correspondences thoroughly assimilated, the idea of "time" interpretation should be no real obstacle.

Additional Guidelines

Both Israel Regardie's *The Golden Dawn* and Paul Foster Case's *Tarot—A Key to the Wisdom of the Ages* are virtually identical in the following guidelines:

Kings and Queens—actual men and women.

Princes—coming or going of a matter. (*The Golden Dawn* elaborates that if the Prince faces in the direction opposite of the count, this represents "...the coming of a person or event, or phase of an event..." If it is looking in the same direction of the count, this represents "...the departure of a person or the going off or wane of some event."

Princesses—young people; opinions, thoughts. Thoughts and opinions are in harmony with the subject of the reading if the Princess is looking in the same direction as the count; they are not in harmony with the subject if the Princess is looking in the opposite direction.

Both Regardie and Case list the following additional points:

Wands—Energy, opposition, quarrel
Cups—Pleasure, merriment
Swords—Trouble, sadness, sickness, death
Pentacles—Business, money, possessions.
Major Trumps—Strong forces beyond the
Querent's control
Court Cards—Society, meetings of many persons
Aces—Strength generally. Aces are always strong cards

If a spread contains:

4 Aces—Great power and force
3 Aces—Riches, success
4 Kings—Swiftness, rapidity
3 Kings—Unexpected meetings, (Kings as a rule show news)

4 Queens—Authority and influence
3 Queens—Powerful friends
4 Princes—Meetings with the great
3 Princes—Rank and honor
4 Princesses—New ideas or plans
3 Princesses—Society of the young
4 Tens—Anxiety, responsibility
3 Tens—Buying, selling, commerce
4 Nines—Added responsibilities
3 Nines—Correspondence
4 Eights—Much news
3 Eights—Much journeying
4 Sevens—Disappointments
3 Sevens—Compacts, contracts
4 Sixes—Pleasure
3 Sixes—Gain, success
4 Fives—Order, regularity
3 Fives—Quarrels, fights
4 Fours—Rest, peace
3 Fours—Industry
4 Threes—Resolution, determination
3 Threes—Deceit
4 Twos—Conferences, conversations
3 Twos—Reorganization, recommendation

Reversed Cards: In the Golden Dawn system, cards which appear upside down must remain so, but it the basic meaning of the card is unchanged.

Dropped cards: If the cards are dropped in shuffling or any other accidental way, abandon the divination and start again. If it is an important matter, wait 12 to 24 hours.

Suit Influence: While "stopping" on any card, always read and interpret the two cards on either side of it. (Air and Earth are contraries, as are Fire and Water. Air is sympathetic with Water and Fire, and Fire is sympathetic with Air and Earth.) Three cards of the *same* suit intensify the interpretation according to the card meanings. Two cards negative in suit to the center card weaken the center card's interpretation. One card positive and one card negative to the center card cancel each other out and do not affect the center card's meaning.

Divining for Money: This is a decision each person must arrive at for himself: he must keep in mind, however, that a highly developed facility with any of the occult arts and sciences is *never* a commodity to be bought or sold. Through progressive development, the aspiration and personal ideals should embody the life-giving element of the Sun, whose rays shine upon all unconditionally, demanding no payment, but exacting a high respect for its phenomenal force and power.

It is far better to learn the Tarot well enough to divine for oneself rather than to pay someone else for this technique, since a large part of its value is in the preparatory work. Remember, all answers are within.

The Importance of Keeping a Written Record

A divination performed in the spirit of genuine inquiry into the cycles of manifestation is like freezing a moment of time, immobilizing one infinitesimally small particle of life's movement—caught and trapped for our repeated observation and interpretation through the symbols of whichever divinatory technique we have selected. We have crystallized a rare jewel in a divination—a jewel to admire and delight in, to examine in all facets of its unique structure. For our own purposes of self-discovery we have stopped time, but we must still preserve this captured moment so that we may return again and again and further examine it for our own self-growth.

A written record is an ideal method of "collecting" our divinations, and for two reasons: (1) we preserve a record of the symbols and our interpretation of them, and (2) with repeated study of previous divinations as compared with how events actually transpired, our intuitive faculties are greatly heightened. We begin to appreciate fully our own responses under various influences and pressures, and that ability which is loosely termed "psychic" very gradually and gracefully unfolds into what we recognize only as a heightened awareness, an intense sensitivity to all stimuli.

Aleister Crowley was adamant about keeping a record of all magical work and progress. It is our yardstick by which to measure our inner growth. The benefits of a Divination Journal far exceed the little effort required for its keeping. A blank Divination-Journal form is provided with this article.

A form should be completed for each divination so that a permanent record is kept for all divinatory work. The top section is filled in first: the Sun and Moon signs, the phase of the

Moon, any outstanding Astrological transiting aspects, the Planetary ruler of the day, the ruler of the hour, the Significator, and the question. The above data can be very revealing regarding "cycles" after one has completed a thousand or more divinations.

The rest of the form is self-explanatory, with each of the five operations having an "A" and a "B" section. The "Card Lists" are a record of only the cards counted in the first part of each Operation and "pairs" are for the second part of the operations.

In using the Divination-Journal form, once the top section has been completed, interpret the cards of each operation freely and do not allow "writing" information on the form to interfere with a spontaneous response to the card symbols. Record the cards and summary interpretation *after* each "A" and "B" section before the cards are picked up and shuffled again.

Remember that most cards or groups of cards have alternative interpretations. Try to react as spontaneously as possible, using the symbols of the cards to evoke an inner feeling/sense about the matter under consideration. When another person is involved, the divination should be a dialogue, a sharing of ideas and observations where both profit from the experience.

The Tarot Trump No. 13 very rarely, if at all, signifies actual physical death, and a preferred interpretation is change or transformation. All apparently negative cards should be interpreted as meaningful and important tension, the necessary impetus to propel one on to greater good and fulfillment.

Some Final Suggestions

The Tarot is as versatile as it is complex. Its combinations are limitless, its value for problem-solving as open-ended as the use made of it. One can never exhaust its possibilities. Work with the Tarot creatively...and doggedly. Always attempt to apply it in some way to the problems of daily living, for these are the "keys" to our inner resources of knowledge, power and inspiration. From few other sources could we hope to garner as much as from the Tarot. It has the symbolic "maps" we need to lead us to the answers on *all* issues, answers which are within us already, but which we need to uncover.

Meditation and divination are two important techniques for using the Tarot and should be explored to their utmost.

Divination No. _____ For: _____ Date: _____

☉ -____ ☽-____ Phase: _____ Aspects: _____ Time: _____

Day of: _____ Hour of: _____ Significator: _____

Question: _____

First Operation (A. Horseshoe, B. Pairing)   Interpretation: _____

          Heh *Vav* *Heh* *Yod*   _____

4 cards   ___ ___ ___ ___   _____

Significator ___ ___ ___ ___   Interpretation: _____

                                     Card List:

A. Interpretation: _____

1 ____	6 ____	11 ____	16 ____
2 ____	7 ____	12 ____	17 ____
3 ____	8 ____	13 ____	18 ____
4 ____	9 ____	14 ____	19 ____
5 ____	10 ____	15 ____	20 ____

B. Interpretation: _____

1 ____ & ____	6 ____	& ____
2 ____ & ____	7 ____	& ____
3 ____ & ____	8 ____	& ____
4 ____ & ____	9 ____	& ____
5 ____ & ____	10 ____	& ____

Second Operation (A. Houses, B. Pairing)   **Card List:**   House: _____

A. Interpretation: _____

1 ____	6 ____	11 ____	16 ____
2 ____	7 ____	12 ____	17 ____
3 ____	8 ____	13 ____	18 ____
4 ____	9 ____	14 ____	19 ____
5 ____	10 ____	15 ____	20 ____

B. Interpretation: _____

1 ____ & ____	6 ____	& ____
2 ____ & ____	7 ____	& ____
3 ____ & ____	8 ____	& ____
4 ____ & ____	9 ____	& ____
5 ____ & ____	10 ____	& ____

Third Operation (A. Signs, B. Pairing)   **Card List:**   Sign: _____

A. Interpretation: _____

1 ____	6 ____	11 ____	16 ____
2 ____	7 ____	12 ____	17 ____
3 ____	8 ____	13 ____	18 ____
4 ____	9 ____	14 ____	19 ____
5 ____	10 ____	15 ____	20 ____

B. Interpretation: _____

1 ____ & ____	6 ____	& ____
2 ____ & ____	7 ____	& ____
3 ____ & ____	8 ____	& ____

_____

_____

Fourth Operation (A. Decanates, B. Pairing)

A. Interpretation: _____

_____

_____

_____

_____

_____

_____

_____

_____

B. Interpretation: _____

_____

_____

_____

_____

_____

_____

_____

_____

_____

Fifth Operation (A. Tree of Life, B. Pairing)

A. Interpretation: _____

_____

_____

_____

_____

B. Interpretation: _____

_____

_____

_____

_____

Actual Outcome: (Date: _____) _____

_____

_____

Status of Divination: _____

_____

_____

_____

4 _____ & _____ 9 _____ & _____
5 _____ & _____ 10 _____ & _____

Card List:

1 _____ 10 _____ 19 _____ 28 _____
2 _____ 11 _____ 20 _____ 29 _____
3 _____ 12 _____ 21 _____ 30 _____
4 _____ 13 _____ 22 _____ 31 _____
5 _____ 14 _____ 23 _____ 32 _____
6 _____ 15 _____ 24 _____ 33 _____
7 _____ 16 _____ 25 _____ 34 _____
8 _____ 17 _____ 26 _____ 35 _____
9 _____ 18 _____ 27 _____ 36 _____

1 _____ & _____ 10 _____ & _____
2 _____ & _____ 11 _____ & _____
3 _____ & _____ 12 _____ & _____
4 _____ & _____ 13 _____ & _____
5 _____ & _____ 14 _____ & _____
6 _____ & _____ 15 _____ & _____
7 _____ & _____ 16 _____ & _____
8 _____ & _____ 17 _____ & _____
9 _____ & _____ 18 _____ & _____

Card List:

1 _____ 6 _____ 11 _____ 16 _____
2 _____ 7 _____ 12 _____ 17 _____
3 _____ 8 _____ 13 _____ 18 _____
4 _____ 9 _____ 14 _____ 19 _____
5 _____ 10 _____ 15 _____ 20 _____

1 _____ & _____ 6 _____ & _____
2 _____ & _____ 7 _____ & _____
3 _____ & _____ 8 _____ & _____
4 _____ & _____ 9 _____ & _____
5 _____ & _____ 10 _____ & _____

Below is a list of additional recommendations in making the Tarot a part of one's daily life experience. All of these exercises have one purpose and that is to saturate your consciousness with the Tarot symbols.

1. Meditate upon one card of the Major Arcana each day. At the end of 22 days, return to card number 0 and repeat the entire cycle indefinitely.

2. Numerous inspirational books have been written on the Tarot with meditations on individual cards or combinations. (Such as Case's *The Book of Tokens*.) It is an occult tradition to read these various meditations aloud, thereby endeavoring to sympa thetically vibrate with the consciousness of the author.

3. The seven days of the week are ruled or "lorded over" by the seven Planets: Monday—Moon, Tuesday—Mars, Wednesday—Mercury, Thursday— Jupiter, Friday—Venus, Saturday—Saturn, Sunday—Sun. Find the corresponding Tarot Trump and work with that card on the corresponding day.

4. The above may be applied to the "hours" of the day and the zodiac calendar.

5. With inexpensive printing available, some of the cards could be enlarged and placed somewhere in the home on the appropriate day.

6. See if there are any Tarot cards you instinctively "like" or "dislike" more than the others. Try to explore and understand why.

7. Meditate upon placing yourself "in the card" as the central figure(s). Imagine all the other symbolism, furniture, landscape around you in space. What would you be wearing? How would you feel?

8. Create a fantasy by "walking into the card" as an observer. Imagine a conversation with the central figure(s). Describe the landscape vividly. How would you relate to the figure(s) in the card? Would they ask anything of you? Would you ask anything of them?

9. Painting the cards is of inestimable value.

The study of Tarot is complex. Its intricacy can appear baffling....at first, until we realize that its information is already contained within us. And after patient work and exploration, it grows gradually and gently within us, showing its hundreds of thousands of faces, angles, attitudes, until we can experientially appreciate the words of Israel Regardie in the *Tree of Life*:

> *Within himself latent unfolding spiritual faculties will be felt, and the faint memory of experience gained in time long since past and dead will gradually arise to illuminate the mind and pulse anew in the heart, expanding the horizon of consciousness. So to-day his feet stand in that place which yesterday, when contemplating the august nature of the work, his eye could scarcely see. Beyond him in the Invisible will be his next day's resting place. And he will be like unto Ra himself, a Sun of light and radiance and celestial nourishment to all those with whom he comes into daily contact.*

Divination is an ancient art. It is a promise of bold vision in a world predominantly shackled by the senses. But the diviner must be worthy to perpetrate so erudite an approach to the future, must be prepared to the utmost to avoid error, arrogance, or any delusion which stings of charlatanism or theatrics. The "future" is a part of each of us now if we are wise enough to recognize it, farsighted enough to determine it, and gracious enough to embrace it.

Through persistent use of divination, one's latent psychic inclination emerges with a refined intuitive faculty. This is not something which occurs in spurts, but gradually, until the student begins slowly to realize that he is perceiving life with another sense. The consistent use of the Tarot can do nothing but transform the inner world. This is no article of faith, but can be tested by anyone who takes the time and effort to experience deeply this phenomenal tool. The Tarot unlocks potential and occasions regeneration. It is the promise of ultimate renewal beyond all conceivable limitation, the Key to consciousness of self. But *work* with it! Beyond all inertia and lassitude, beyond confusion, disappointment, and even apparent failure, work with it and come to know who you are. Renew your consciousness with it and become all you want to be.

ABOUT THE AUTHOR

Cris Monnastre, born April 2, 1946, is currently finishing a doctoral program in psychology with a specialty in clinical psychology. She is a therapist in the Los Angeles area and combines traditional therapy with Golden Dawn techniques. She is a poet, musician, and composer, and lives with her two sons, Aaron and Adam. Cris is the author of the Introduction to the Fifth Edition of Regardie's *The Golden Dawn* (Llewellyn 1986).

The Abbey Theatre Tarot Readings*

Mary K. Greer

One hundred years ago, a member of the Hermetic Order of the Golden Dawn built and funded Ireland's famed Abbey Theatre as the result of a Tarot reading. The struggles in Ireland to win independence from England gave rise to a group of writers who characterize what is now known as the Irish Literary Renaissance. At the forefront of this phenomenon was the Abbey Theatre, the first and only subsidized national theatre in an English-speaking country until the 1960's.

In the early 1900's an amateur theatre group called the Irish National Theatre Society produced plays by Irish writers on Irish subjects, hoping to "discover and stimulate new work." Members of the group included William Butler Yeats, Maud Gonne, Lady Gregory, George Russell (A.E.), J.M. Synge, Padraic Colum, and the actors William and Frank Fay. The literary and historical turn of their plays, and their daring usage of Irish-English and Gaelic in serious drama instead of stock comedy, resulted in innovative, even shocking performances that usually did not make enough money to cover expenses.

But the person who actually built a permanent theatre for this daring company was an Englishwoman named Annie Elizabeth Fredericka Horniman, who hated Irish nationalism, and who was hated by the Nationalists. Annie, the poet William Butler Yeats, and Ireland's "Joan of Arc," Maud Gonne, had been early members of the Hermetic Order of the Golden Dawn which used the Tarot as the basis of their rituals and levels of initiation.

The roots of our modern English Tarot decks lie in the Golden Dawn, for the Rider-Waite-Smith Tarot, and the

---

* Adapted from her forthcoming book: *Magical Women of the Golden Dawn: Rebels and Priestesses.* (Rochester: Park Street Press / Inner Traditions, 1994).

Crowley-Harris Thoth deck came directly from their teachings, and the correspondences they made between the Major Arcana and Hebrew letters, the Tree of Life, and Astrology.

By 1903 the Golden Dawn, having gone through several major struggles, was beginning to fragment. Annie had been a major figure in the Order and was skilled in Astrology, Tarot and "scrying in the spirit vision." She had been working closely with Yeats to try to hold the Golden Dawn together. Now, disappointed at the turn of events, Yeats did not quit the G.D. but turned his full attention to the literary revival that was finally gaining recognition. Annie would never compromise; she left the Order when it differed from her standards. As she was wealthy from inheritances, primarily from her grandfather, the founder of Horniman Tea, she spent much of each year touring Europe: attending theatrical performances, operas, and art gallery openings. She had also anonymously funded Yeats's and George Bernard Shaw's first publicly performed plays in 1894. The British public was both notoriously conservative, and extraordinarily plebeian in their play-going interests. While music hall entertainment and Gilbert and Sullivan drew huge crowds, the new forms of drama, epitomized by Ibsen and Shaw, scandalized society. Annie was determined to promote an English art theatre in which young playwrights could develop their abilities and skills through professional productions. Back to back with quality performances of the best of the classics, she wanted to see both old and new plays performed by an egalitarian acting company without "stars". Annie additionally recognized Yeats's literary genius, and was eager to make his dramatic vision, based on a vision of the Celtic mysteries, available to the world. Annie began by volunteering her services to Yeats as a part-time secretary and organizer, helping him with his correspondence and periodically clearing out his rooms, but she ached to do something more creative.

It was in 1903 that Annie did a series of four Tarot readings that resulted in the "birth of the modern English Theatre." Fortunately she sent these readings and her interpretations to Yeats, because they are now held in the National Library of Ireland, and so are available to dumfounded theatrical and literary scholars.

Theatre historian James Flannery in *Miss Annie F. Horniman and the Abbey Theatre* noted with obvious amazement that the interpretation of all four of her Tarot readings presented the actual sequence of events that were to happen: "It is perhaps even more remarkable that some of the predictions themselves are extraordinarily accurate, particularly those concerning the new directions which Yeats was to take in his life and art, the conflicts with the Fay brothers which were to develop, and the final quarrel with Miss Horniman herself."[1]

Since Annie was meticulous in her methods, the readings follow precisely MacGregor Mathers' book *The Tarot*, published in 1888, and his *Manuscripts N and O of Book "T" – The Tarot* published in *An Introduction to the Golden Dawn Tarot* by Robert Wang and also in *The Complete Golden Dawn System of Magic* by Israel Regardie. Each card had a precise divin-atory meaning. Reserving the esoteric significance of symbols exclusively for rituals and for "entering the card" as astral explorers, it was never considered in mundane spreads.

I discovered from photographs in Kathleen Rain's *Yeats, the Tarot and the Golden Dawn* that Yeats's personal Tarot deck exactly resembled a facsimile deck published by Menegazzi in 1985, called *The Tarocco Italiano Made by Dotti, Milano, 1845*. It is likely that Annie Horniman, who went to Italy nearly every year, brought back an original Dotti deck for Yeats, and, since it was one of the most artistically detailed and graceful of the decks available at that time, must have owned one herself. Mathers himself recommended the Italian Tarot cards over all others. The cards reproduced here are from this Dotti reprint.

On March 1, just days after resigning from the Golden Dawn, Annie asked the Tarot for advice about Yeats and herself. She always used Yeats's G.D. motto, *Demon est Deus Inversus* (The Devil is God in Reverse), calling him "Demon," while she was *Fortiter et Recte* (With fortitude and righteousness) or FeR. She wrote: "D(emon) and I spoke to-day of a current and plans of working in it. The plans are to be the cutting, the cards of our Significators Q and Prince S (Queen and Prince of Swords, signifying their Sun signs of Libra and Gemini respectively) to tell the results." It is only in the fourth and most important reading that I will present the techniques and card interpretations in depth.

Annie began by cutting of the deck into the four stacks representing the four Elements and the Tetragrammaton. The

---

[1] Flannery, 1970 #35, p. 8.

cards at the bottom of each of the four stacks signified Annie and her Demon's plans. These cards were Yod/Fire = Princess of Cups, Heh/Water = Six of Swords, Vav/Air = Prince of Swords (Yeats), Heh Final/Earth = Ten of Pentacles. To Annie these cards indicated that Yeats's intellectual plans (P of S), being firm and solid (10 P), could earn success with effort (6S), once he recovered from a loss of joy (Princess C, debilitated by being Water in a Fire position.)

The second step in the reading involved spreading the cards into a horseshoe shape and interpreting them in groups of three determined by an elaborate counting technique (given later), and then interpreting the cards again in pairs. The reading was quite positive.[2] Both Annie and Willie were about to begin an exciting and productive period—that is—once he got over his unrequited love for Maud Gonne (here, the Princess of Cups) who was the all-too-obvious subject of almost all his poems and plays. Just as the previous week, on February 21, Maud had suddenly married John MacBride, the Irish hero of the Boer War against the British in South Africa, dashing Yeats's hopes of making her his own wife. Annie passed lightly over Yeats's "remaining anxious about giving up Princess S (Maud)," who, from the adjacent cards, was in great trouble, for Maud discovered on her honeymoon that she had a conventional, madly jealous, alcoholic and violent husband.

At the beginning of May 1903 the Irish National Theatre Society performed five one-act plays in London at the Queen's Gate Hall. Three of these plays were by Willie. The day before the first performance Annie spread the cards again asking, "How will the result of to-morrow's performances of his plays affect the Prince of S?" She cut the cards into four stacks: Yod/Fire = Six Pentacles, Heh/Water = Seven Wands, Vav/Air = Ten Wands, Heh Final/Earth = Empress. The result of the entire reading was again encouraging, including a "gain of

---

2 Annie did complete readings from two of the four stacks. The Heh/Water stack, containing her Queen of Swords Significator, when spread from right to left in a horseshoe were: 6 of Swords, 2 of Cups, 3 of Pentacles, Devil (7*), Empress, Queen of Cups (looking sun-wise), 8 of Swords, 4 of Wands, 7 of Pentacles (6*), Hierophant (4/8*), 2 of Wands (3*), Star, Fool (2*), Death, 4 of Pentacles, Queen of Swords (1*) (looking sun-wise), Wheel of Fortune (4*), 4 of Cups. Annie also read the cards from the Vav/Air stack as indicating the effects specifically on Yeats. These cards when spread from right to left in a horseshoe were: Prince of Swords (1*) (looking sun-wise), 9 of Pentacles (9*), 3 of Cups, Queen of Wands (no direction indicator), High Priestess, Strength, Tower, Moon (4*), Emperor, 9 of Wands (8*), 6 of Wands (center singleton when pairing), Hermit, King of Pentacles (7*) (looking sun-wise), Magician, 8 of Wands (3/10*), King of Wands (6*) (looking deosil), 7 of Swords, Hanged man (5*), 5 of Pentacles (2*), Princess of Swords (looking deosil), King of Cups (looking sun-wise). (*The numbers in parenthesis indicate the results of a "count" as described in the fourth reading.)

authority about his dramatic affairs."[3] Yeats would profit swift-
ly and find success. With "Mercury (The Magician) governing
all" (it was the odd card in the middle of the horseshoe spread
after pairing cards from both ends), the outlook was excellent
for his success as a writer to spread.

Annie was, of course, trying to encourage Yeats, and
therefore, as with all the readings, she tended to slant her
interpretation as she wanted it. A pair of cards (2 of Pentacles
and 7 of Swords) that Annie felt meant a "happy change
brought about by a journey" (he was soon to make his first trip
to America) could as easily have meant "happy change which is
unstable and untrustworthy." But, as with many contrary
interpretations, both meanings did apply, for Yeats returned
from America with a vastly inflated ego caused by his tremendous welcome there.

The plays were a huge success, the critics delighted, and
the houses packed. On the other hand, the cards said Yeats
would have to face some antagonism to the carrying out of his
plans, possibly through the opposition of the production man-
ager, William Fay. They were "not harmonious characters"
though they would work together. In the long run, Willie Fay
would be both the blessing and the bane of the Society. Upon
his return to Ireland, Yeats found other members of the Society
jealous of his London success.

Soon Annie offered to help with Yeats's ambitious new
historical play called *The King's Threshold.* It would necessi-
tate more elaborate costumes than ever before and Annie
wanted to create them. A month before the production, on
September 13, as she researched period costumes and sewed
beautiful brocades and velvets in her London flat, Annie
dashed off a third, amazingly accurate reading, asking: "D's
affairs in connection with theatre?" The four stacks indicated
that: Yod/Fire = Four Wands, and so, "all is now settled," yet,
because Heh/Water = Ace of Wands was an unlucky combination of Water and Fire, there were still the remains of an upset.
Vav/Air = Three Cups showed Yeats's thoughts turning toward
his friends. While Heh Final/Earth = Ten Cups reassured

[3] From right to left the cards of the second reading (taken from the second stack) were: 7 of Wands,
Prince of Pentacles (2*) (looking sun-wise), 3 of Swords, 2 of Wands, 8 of Wands (3*), World (7*),
Ace of Pentacles, 3 of Cups, Chariot, 7 of Swords, Magician (central singleton), 2 of Pentacles (4*),
King of Cups (5*) (looking sun-wise), 2 of Cups (8*), 2 of Swords (9*), Lovers (6/10*), Princess of
Wands, Fool, 7 of Cups, Prince of Swords (1*) (looking deosil), and Temperance (*The numbers in
parentheses indicate the results of the count.)

Annie, the prospective financier, with "material prospects very happy and good."[4]

In Annie's reading of the triads within the horseshoe we find that "Ireland (represented by the Hierophant since Ireland's Sun is in Taurus) is between some wish and the Queen S (Annie herself)" which could only mean that it was the Irish themselves that stood between Annie and what she wanted to do for Yeats.

But Princess S (also Annie) "makes a final fateful decision, and Prince S is inspired in his efforts to new energy leading to fame and gain of power." As Annie was to describe her decision to buy a theatre for Yeats: "I sat alone here in my flat making the costumes for the Irish Players to wear in *The King's Threshold*. I was thinking about the hard condition in which they were working, and the idea struck me that if and when enough money were to turn up, I would spend it on hiring or building a little hall where they could perform in fair comfort." This was her dream and since the most outspoken Nationalists had recently quit over disagreements about a play, the possibility lay clear before her.

On October 8, 1903, only days after her 43rd birthday, *The King's Threshold* opened with costumes by Annie Horniman that were lauded by the press as "inspired by rare intelligence and a poetic imagination," while criticized by the Nationalists as too gaudy and ornate.

The following day Annie did her fourth and final Tarot reading asking, "What is the right thing for me to do in regard to the I.N.Th. now?" She sent the result to Yeats, writing him:

> *Oct. 9th / 03*
> *Dear Demon,*
>   *Read this Tarot please. I am so anxious to help effectually as best I may & it seems as if it were already ordained. I'll stay on here during the next week to see what I am to do. Do you realize that you have now given me the right to call myself "artist"? How I thank you!*

---

[4] The cards when spread from right to left were: 4 of Wands, Queen of Swords (looking sun-wise), Hierophant (3*), 6 of Cups, 8 of Swords, Princess of Swords (looking sun-wise), Worlds, Emperor, 7 of Swords, Queen of Wands (looking sun-wise), Devil, 5 of Cups (central singleton), 8 of Pentacles, Princess of Wands (4*) (looking deosil), 10 of Wands, Sun, Lovers, Judgment (5*), 6 of Swords, Prince of Swords (1*) (looking deosil), Moon, 5 of Pentacles, and King of Pentacles (2*) (looking deosil). (*The numbers in parenthesis indicate the results of the count.)

Annie had spent many years at the Slade School of Art
and supported the artistic endeavors of others with her gen-
erosity. But at last she had done something creative herself,
fulfilling a deeply hidden need.

With the encouragement of this fourth Tarot reading, and
the fact that her Hudson Bay stocks had almost doubled in
value giving her an influx of unexpected funds, Annie decided
to purchase a building that would be the permanent home for a
national drama in Ireland. Officially she would not make her
offer until the following year but there is no doubt that the
decision was made by the time she mailed Willie this reading.

Sitting in her room at her modest, "temperance" hotel in
Dublin, Annie shuffled her Tarot cards and cut them into four
stacks. She interpreted the bottom card of each:

Yod/Fire = High Priestess:
Some change is directed by the Highest.

Heh/Water = Seven Swords:
Irresolution as to the course of action.

Vav/Air = Ten Wands:
Anger in the Mind.

Heh Final/Earth = Devil:
Most solid Materiality needed.

Annie now took all the cards in the third stack which con-
tained her Significator, the Queen of Swords (marked on the
page by a cross), and placed them in a horseshoe from right to
left beginning with the Ten Wands. The cards in this reading
were, from right to left: Ten Wands, Four Pentacles (5), Five
Wands, Two Pentacles, Wheel of Fortune (6), Three Pentacles,
Princess of Wands (9) (facing sun-wise), Eight Pentacles,
Emperor, Chariot, Queen of Swords (1) (looking deosil), Three
Cups, Three Wands (7/10), King of Wands (2) (looking deosil),
Justice (8), Prince of Cups (looking deosil), Two Swords (3),
Four Swords (4), Fool. Annie indicated the Major Arcana by
their Astrological associations, and the cards selected by the
"count" are numbered here in parenthesis. I suggest strongly
that the reader lay out their own cards (preferably using an
Italian or Marseilles deck) in order to follow the interpretation.

Commencing with an overview of the cards in the horseshoe, Annie discovered that there were 19 cards in all, which

was considered a "bad" indicator, but, as we shall see, had little substantive effect. Counting the cards in each suit she found five Trumps or Major Arcana meaning that the reading was "within my own Will." If there had been a majority of Trumps then the situation would have been fated—outside her Will to control. Among the minor Arcana cards there was a majority of Wands, which she indicated as meaning that "Energy must prevail." It was obviously up to her to exert her own will as her decision would determine all that was to come.

Annie then counted how many numbers were repeated. There were three 3's, which according to Mathers pointed out to some kind of deceit. "I think something now which is not <u>fact</u>," she noted. She believed she could be an equal part of this creative enterprise, working harmoniously with Yeats and the others to build the theatre of their dreams. This was her greatest delusion.

Next she read the cards in triadic groups. These triads were determined by a complex method of counting beginning with the Significator (Queen of Swords) and *counting in the direction the Significator faced*. For every Ace she was to count 5 cards, for every Princess—7, for any other Court Card—4, for every Trump corresponding to an element—3, for every Trump corresponding to a Zodiac sign—12, for every Trump corresponding to a Planet—9, and for every small card the number of its pips. The only significance given to reversed cards was that the count proceeded in the direction the Significator then faced, and in a triad showed the "coming or going of a matter." For her interpretation of the triads she wrote:

1 – (Queen of Swords with 3 Cups and Chariot) =
I am in a happy friendly successful current

2 – (King of Wands with Justice and Three Wands) =
Which will carry me on if I decide with a certain amount of self-assertion

3 – (Two Swords with Four Swords and Prince of Cups) =
That will restore peace & be well for a youngish man.

4 – (Four Swords with Fool and Two Swords) =
All will change for the better and quarrels will pass away.

What is the right thing for me to do in regard to the I. N. Th. row? Oct. 9th/03.

Some change is directed by the Highest
Irresolution as to the course of action
Anger in the mind
Most solid materiality needed.

19 cards bad.

5 Trumps - within my own Will.

Energy must prevail.

Three 3's - deceit - I think something now which is not _fact._

I am in a happy friendly successful current, which will carry me on if I decide with a certain amount of self-assertion. That will restore peace & be well for a youngish man. All will change for the better & quarrels will pass away. Some gift will cause quarrels & anger but it will bring good fortune & gain whilst away from home - self-assertion is absolutely necessary.

5 – (Four Pentacles with Five Wands and Ten Wands) =
Some gift will cause quarrels and anger.

6 – (Wheel of Fortune with Three Pentacles and Two
Pentacles) =
**But it will bring good fortune & gain whilst
away from home.**

7/10 – (Three Wands with King of Wands and
Three Cups) =
Self-assertion is absolutely necessary.

For some reason she didn't comment on the last two
triads, but she might have interpreted them like this:

8 – (Justice with Prince of Cups and King of Wands) =
**I am in a good current to make a decision con-
cerning a fair young man.**

9 – (Princess of Wands with Eight Pentacles and Three
Pentacles) =
**A fair young woman is moving away from pru-
dence and towards a business transaction.**

We can see from the events in her life just how accurate
her interpretation was. Annie (the Queen of Swords) had just
made her first "artistic" contribution to the theatre by designing and making the costumes for *The King's Threshold*—she
was riding a wave of happiness and success. She foresaw such
opportunities continuing if she asserted herself to do so, and
she did design costumes for two more plays. Yeats was obviously concerned over the ability of the I.N.Th.S. to continue and
thus her assistance would bring him peace of mind. The quarrels referred to in the fourth triad might have come from the
fact that she had quit the golden Dawn in anger over the internal bickering while Yeats stayed on, but they could also refer to
the public uproar over the morality of J.M. Synge's first play
for the Abbey, *In the Shadow of the Glen.* One other quarrel
that was smoldering, this between Yeats and Annie, was that
Yeats wanted very simple designs for the stage and costumes,
while Annie insisted on a "historical correctness," that required
that they be elaborate and bright in color. Yeats wrote Frank
Fay on Jan. 20, 1904: "Miss Horniman has to learn her
work...and must have freedom to experiment. I have told her
that old stages permitted elaborate dress though not elaborate

scenes, and this combined with the fact of its being a Court, mislead her into overdoing colour and the like in certain parts." Arguments with Yeats over their differing vision finally resulted in her giving up all artistic aspirations.

The gift that could cause quarrels and anger definitely foreshadows the long-term result of her gift of free use of the Abbey Theatre for the I.N.Th.S., for her alliance with the Directors was to be choleric and end in great bitterness.

The good fortune and gain that she achieved "away from home" in Ireland was the experience and reputation she attained that was to serve her so successfully elsewhere. The "self-assertion necessary" implied that it was time to take action and go ahead with her decision.

So she turned her back on fiscal prudence, although with an income of £700 a year, she was in the upper 3 percent of the population income. She had not only the money but the creative vision to make an investment in culture rather than commerce. Like her 1894 theatrical season, the Abbey Theatre proved to be a financial disaster. By 1907 when she began looking to Manchester, England for a possible new theatre, she was sure that the Abbey would never survive and she did everything in her power to persuade Yeats to allow her to produce his plays abroad. Yet all her enterprises, backed as much by her innovative ideas and enthusiasm as by her money, ultimately proved their worth as major events in the formation of the modern English theatre.

Annie's next step, according to the Book "T", was to pair cards from either end of the horseshoe moving in toward the center, and then to interpret these pairs. The strength or weakness of each pair depended upon whether their elemental energies were congenial or not. Below I have given the paired cards with Annie's interpretation, and an indication of how "strong" each pair is:

Fool + 10W =
   Passing away of strife. (Moderate)

4S + 4P =
   Gift brings change for the better. (Weak)

2S + 5W =
   Quarrel brings peace. (Moderately Strong)

Prince C + 2P =
Happy change or visit for youngish man.
(Moderately strong)

Justice + Wheel of Fortune =
Decision brings good fortune. (Moderately Strong)

King W +3P =
Many small expenses in strong current.
(Moderate)

3 W + Princess W =
Annoyance of fair young woman. (Very Strong)

3C + 8P =
Prudence in a matter of friendship.
(Moderately Strong)

Queen S + Emperor =
Queen S with Aries, a new beginning of life.
(Moderately Strong)

Chariot =
Victory and success crowns all. ("One card at the end of the pairing signifies the partial result of that particular part of the Divination.")

This part of the reading rounds out the story; but, even more than in the first section, Annie interpreted these pairs so that they shone with a positive light on her intention. The Fool can act foolishly or can indicate the highest spiritual wisdom. Annie was moving directly into strife like a fool, but guided by a Divine Intent. Annie's gift of the Abbey Theatre certainly brought a good change, but also introduced new problems—as the Four of Swords, which can represent illness, should have told her. Because they faced a common enemy in "that Englishwoman," quarrels with Annie often led to strange alliances and a suspension of animosities among the members of the Society. Yeats, this time as the Prince of Cups, left in November on his first trip to America—a sea voyage—as the 2 Pentacles can mean in addition to a "happy change."

Annie's decision was truly a fortunate one. But she could never leave any bill unaccounted for including the "small expenses" of everyday overhead, which annoyed the managers to no end. Annie was a good business woman, as Justice together with the Wheel of Fortune indicated, and all her transactions were carried out through legal contracts or letters of intent. Although she made the Abbey the home of the I.N.Th.S., it remained legally hers until she severed contact with them and sold it to the Society for a nominal sum in 1910. A final quarrel did result in legal arbitration to which both parties acceded.

Annie's interpretation of the 3 Wands as "annoyance" in relation to Princess W arises not from the meaning of the 3 Wands, which has more to do with trade and enterprise, but from her jealousy of Maud Gonne (who was Princess W in the other readings), and who, as a rabid Nationalist, was more bothered by Annie's decision, than she was pleased. Princess W could have also referred to Lady Gregory. Lady Augusta Gregory was one of the Directors and a writer of plays based on Irish folklore, who was to become Annie's greatest rival for the patronage of Yeats. Neither Gonne nor Gregory was happy to have "their" theatre owned by an Englishwoman, yet neither had the resources nor inclination to buy a theatre themselves. According to Maud Gonne in her autobiography, *A Servant of the Queen*: "Miss Horniman had the money and was willing to spend it, but Lady Gregory had the brains...they both liked Willie too well. Lady Gregory won the battle; Miss Horniman's money converted the old city morgue into the Abbey Theatre, but it was Lady Gregory's plays that were acted there. Miss Horniman brought back Italian plaques to decorate it but Lady Gregory carried off Willie to visit the Italian towns where they were made." It is Lady Gregory's name that is etched on the plaque honoring the founders of the Abbey Theatre, and she blatantly (and enterprisingly) claims the entire credit in her autobiography, while Annie is deemed a pathetic shrew by most historians.

Yet, despite all the problems—which Annie preferred to overlook, there was the chance for a "new beginning of life" which she desperately needed since she had quit the Golden Dawn. Since the Emperor also meant "realization," she moved quickly to realize" a theatre by spring of the following year—when the Sun was in Aries!

The concluding card was a singleton indicating the final, though only partial, result of the question—the victory of the Chariot. But the Chariot is seen as ultimately unstable in itself because it is essentially adolescent. In the long run, the Abbey Theatre was only a training ground for Annie Horniman. It was at her Gaiety Theatre in Manchester, England that she was able to build the Art Theatre of her dreams that established a reputation for both quality and daring, playing not only superb performances of the classics from Greece to Shakespeare to English Restoration comedy to the finally-lauded Ibsen and Shaw, but also encouraging young playwrights to develop their talents. It was at Manchester that she would earn her title: "Founder of the Modern English Repertory Movement." Thus, like the Charioteer, there would come a time when she would move on.

ABOUT THE AUTHOR

Mary K. Greer, M.A., teaches Tarot, women's mysteries, and magical writing through her organization Tools And Rites Of Transformation (T.A.R.O.T.). She is the author of four books on the Tarot including *Tarot for Your Self: A Workbook for Personal Transformation,* and *The Essence of Magic: Tarot, Ritual and Aromatherapy*. It took five years to research and write her biography of four original members of the Golden Dawn called *Magical Women of the Golden Dawn: Rebels and Priestesses* (Wingbow Press, 1994). She has been an editorial assistant, typesetter, graphic designer, astrologer, and a college administrator, professor, and Director of Women's Studies at New College of California in San Francisco. Having lived in Japan, Germany, London, Mexico and six states in the U.S., Mary now makes her home with her husband, Ed Buryn (travel-writer, photographer and creator of the *William Blake Tarot Deck*), and their daughter Casimira, in the Sierra foothills.

BIBLIOGRAPHY

Fay, Gerard. *The Abbey Theatre: Cradle of Genius*. (Dublin: Clonmore & Reynolds, 1958).

Flannery, James W. *Miss Annie F. Horniman and the Abbey Theatre*. (Dublin: The Dolmen Press, 1970).

Frazier, Adrian. *Behind the Scenes: Yeats, Horniman, and the Struggle for the Abbey Theatre*. (Berkeley & L.A.: Univ. of CA Press, 1990.)

Gooddie, Sheila. *Annie Horniman: A Pioneer in the Theatre*. (London: Methuen, 1990).

Horniman, A.E.F. "The Origin of the Abbey Theatre" in *The Abbey Theatre: Interviews and Recollections,* E.H. Mikhail, ed. (London: Macmillan, 1988).

MacBride, Maud Gonne. *A Servant of the Queen: Reminiscences.* (1938. Reprt: Woodbridge, Suffolk: The Boydell Press, 1983).

Mathers, S.L. MacGregor. *The Tarot: Its Occult Signification, Use in Fortune-Telling, and Method of Play, Etc.* (1888. Reprt: New York: Samuel Weiser).

National Library of Ireland, Dublin. *Ms 18,312.*

Pogson, Rex. *Miss Horniman and the Gaiety Theatre, Manchester.* (London: Rockliff Press, 1952).

Raine, Kathleen. "Miss Horniman's Letter to W.B. Yeats Offering to Subsidize the Abbey Theatre." in *The Noble Drama of W.B. Yeats* by Lian Miller (Dublin: Dolmen, 1977).

Raine, Kathleen. *Yeats, The Tarot and the Golden Dawn.* (Dublin: Dolmen, 1972, 1976).

Regardie, Israel. *The Complete Golden Dawn System of Magic.* (Phoenix: Falcon Press, 1984).

Rowell, George and Anthony Jackson. *The Repertory Movement: A History of Regional Theatre in Britain.* (Cambridge, Cambridge Univ. Press, 1984).

Saddlemeyer, Ann, ed. *Theatre Business: The Correspondence of the first Abbey Theatre Directors.* University Park, PA: Pennsylvania State Univ. Press, 1982).

Menegazzi, O. *The Tarocco Italiano Made by Dotti, Milano, 1845.* (Milan: Meneghello, 1985).

Wade, Allan, ed. *The Letters of W.B. Yeats.* (New York: Octagon/Farrar, Straus & Giroux, Inc., 1980).

Wang, Robert. *An Introduction to the Golden Dawn Tarot.* (New York: Samuel Weiser, 1978).

Spiritual Tarot
and Circle Spread Divination
Frater P.C.

ivination is the art, practice, or method that helps us to foresee or foretell future events, or to discover some hidden knowledge or understanding through the infusion of Divine aid and guidance. The Tarot is an outer tool designed to help the aspirant achieve inner spiritual awareness. Like all the other outer vehicles for spiritual attainment, such as religion, magick, education, mantras, holy books, etc., a Tarot divination's first and primary purpose is to act as an aid in elevating us to our Higher and True Divine Self. The ultimate goal of anyone seeking knowledge and conversation with their Higher Genius (Holy Guardian Angel-Divine aspect) is to eliminate all forms and all outer vehicles of divination. This would include Geomancy, Tarot, Runes, pendulums, Ring and Disk, tea leaves, Astrology, Palmistry, or any and all other exterior methods. In other words, the Higher Self really has no need for these exterior tools such as Tarot cards, because the Higher Self is a compilation of the Tarot. It is our mundane self that has this need for exterior vehicles of divination. A person united with the Higher Self would find a Tarot reading predicting the future of their life's events totally unnecessary, because conversation with the Higher Self is clearer, more succinct, and more accurate than any exterior vehicle could possibly be.

An individual who needed to discover water, oil or gold beneath the surface of the Earth, and who was in total integration with their Higher Self, would have little need for a dowsing rod or geological survey. Other questions that arise in life that often require the need for divinations, such as jobs, careers, finances, love, health and marriage, would also be easily answered by the Higher Self, the Divine Genius; and the need for exterior tools to help in the revelation of these questions would really be a moot point. If what we are doing in a divinatory act is really tapping into our Higher Selves, or at least in a small way, a portion of our Divine Aspect (which is intimately tapped into the Cosmos), then it would stand to reason that if we want to increase our skills, ability, and accuracy with the Tarot, we need first to learn how to provide for ourselves a clear and distinct connection with our Higher Genius. The actual spread itself, the size of the cards, and the color become secondary to the actual process of raising ourselves to the Higher. It is through this invisible link, called the subconscious mind, that extends to the Higher Genius that we are able to understand the nature of an act or the answer to a question.

The prime reason for developing and understanding the spiritual Tarot is to carry us to the summit above. It is from the vantage point of one standing up high on the summit looking down over the valley, that we can see with greater clarity and distinction, the results of any particular action or question that the divination process may be attempting to answer. For as long as we remain safe in the valley below, our line of vision and our insight into the natural and orderly flow of the Universe will be limited to that which is before our nose. Through the knowledge and conversation with our Higher Genius (Holy Guardian Angel, Divine Aspect), we learn our True Will. Our True Will is the purpose for our existence, our reason for physical incarnation. Put simply, it is the reason that we're here to begin with. It is through the process of deep spiritual Tarot study and divination that we can have a greater understanding of the nature of any act or action in our lives as it pertains or relates directly to our True Will. From this standpoint, even the so-called mundane questions become spiritual questions. Questions that deal in terms of love, finances, money, jobs, careers, and education can and perhaps should be answered with our True Will in mind. Spiritual Tarot divination becomes like a road map, giving us a more clear-cut direction in our lives and putting us in sync with the flow of the Universe, rather than at odds with it. The poet Thoreau said: "To affect the quality of the day, this is the highest of arts," and it is directly through the art and practice of the spiritual Tarot that we can better learn to affect the quality of our lives by following the axiom of the Golden Dawn which states, *"Quit the night and seek the day."*

There are a few things we should keep in mind. First, Tarot divination should never be taken lightly. It should always be looked at as a very high spiritual practice. When the process of Tarot divination is done correctly, the mind eases into opening itself to the higher and clears a pathway through the subconscious mind to the Divine Genius, which, as stated earlier is intimately linked to the infinite. I am not going to emphasize the methods of preparing oneself for serious spiritual Tarot, as these methods can be found in a number of good books. The point is that preparation for spiritual Tarot is essential. In my personal preparation, before a serious Tarot divination, it is not uncommon to take a spiritual cleansing bath followed by some basic ritual work, such as the Lesser Banishing Ritual of the Pentagram, the Banishing Ritual of the Hexagram, and the Middle Pillar Ritual. These all help prepare the mind and place it in a consciousness less directed by ego and personal desires and more directed by higher influences.

Secondly, calling on the highest Divine Name before any working can begin is an absolute essential part of the Golden Dawn system; and in studying the mystical systems of other cultures, the same is basically true. An elaborate prayer invocation is not essential. It can be as simple as, *"Oh Lord of the Universe, the Vast and Mighty One, look now with favor upon me. Open my mind unto the Higher so that I may know the secrets of Thy wisdom and of Divine Light."*

Thirdly, we need to bring to the forefront of our mind the Law of Cause and Effect, *karma*. Every action or in-action in our lives has a specific karmic consequence. Karma is neither good nor bad, it just is. In the process of developing ourselves into higher spiritual beings with greater spiritual awareness, some decisions and actions will be in harmony with our True Will, others will not. There is definitely a price to be paid karmically for not being true to one's self or one's True Will. The Tarot in its highest and most spiritual forms can be used to unveil the path leading unto our True Will.

Fourth, like religion and the other outer vehicles of spiritual attainment, the art of Tarot can become corrupt and mundane. It can serve little purpose other than to amuse and entertain. It is really quite silly to believe that some pretty pictures on pasteboard could somehow miraculously foretell the future on their own, or in any way give us guidance in any area of our lives. A person who would rely on a pack of cards to guide their life would be naive and foolish, or at best, someone avoiding personal responsibility.

So if it is not the Tarot cards that provide us with this hidden knowledge of future events in our lives, then what is it exactly that does this? It is the Higher Genius, the Divine Self, the Holy Guardian Angel that reveals itself through the process of divination. In other words, the tool itself is not as important as the person who is using the tool. A paint brush in the hands of an unskilled or untrained artist is merely a stick with a bunch of bristles at the end; but in the hands of a trained and skilled artist, it becomes a tool to create a work of art. So it is the same with someone who has practiced and is trained to understand the nature of the Tarot and has learned to open themselves to the higher aspect, to the Divine Self, and allow that energy to feed through the images of the Tarot (or other forms of divination) through the understanding of its influence and symbology as it relates to the question at hand.

I would never hint or suggest that a person become addicted to divination. Personally, I have met such people. These people oftentimes lead crippled lives because every movement, every direction, every question, and every decision requires a divination of some sort. There are crucial points in a person's life when Divine guidance from one's Higher Genius can be essential to the fulfillment of one's True Will. It is at these cross-roads in our life that the spiritual Tarot can be an invaluable aid. On the other hand, performing a divination from a non-spiritual vantage point may actually serve to deceive us rather than to enlighten us.

Understanding the Spiritual Tarot

One of the most effective ways to learn how to use the Tarot from a spiritual stand point is to eliminate the Minor Arcana and work only with the Major Arcana. The Major Arcana are the spiritual cards of the pack. For those of you who are used to working with all seventy-eight cards, you will find that you can develop a very complete understanding of influences, energies, problems and opportunities that exist in any situation by using the Major Arcana only. My personal experience is that a person starting with the Tarot should use and study only the

Major Arcana for an extended period of time before even attempting to blend in the Minor Arcana into the reading technique. Working strictly with the Major Arcana will also help you to develop greater spiritual insight and a deeper understanding of the subtle influences and forces that operate in your life. In addition, understanding the Major Arcana is really a self exploratory voyage. So as we learn more about the nature of each Major Arcana card in the Tarot, we are really learning about ourselves.

Each one of the Major Arcana cards is a specific influence or energy. In the context of a Tarot reading, it is oftentimes an influence or energy applied to our lives or a specific situation. Understanding this spiritual influence and energy becomes more clear and succinct when we see how the Major Arcana—the spiritual cards of the Tarot—relate to the *Sepher Yetzirah*, often called the *Book of Formation*. The *Sepher Yetzirah* is an esoteric Qabalistic document that highlights the energy structure of the Universe and the cosmology of creation. We can say that the Tarot describes in pictures what the *Sepher Yetzirah* describes in words. The twenty-two Major Arcana are pictorial symbols of the twenty-two Hebrew letters. These Hebrew letters have been applied to the paths on the Qabalistic Tree of Life. Modern Hermetic Qabalists have also applied the Tarot to the twenty-two paths on the Qabalistic Tree of Life. These paths are transitional roadways between various states of consciousness. They are Microcosmic, meaning that they are inter-

nal or part of our subconscious make-up. The Sephiroth are
Macrocosmic, and thus relate more to the Minor Arcana. They
are the influences outside our personal sphere of sensation or
personal being.

In addition, through an esoteric understanding of the
Major Arcana, as it applies to the Qabalistic Tree of Life, the
twenty-two spiritual cards of the deck can even be sub-divided
into Planetary, Elemental and Zodiacal influences. This is a
great aid, because in understanding the twenty-two Major
Arcana, we have a greater understanding of Planetary and
Zodiacal influences in our life; and in understanding Zodiacal
and Planetary influences, we develop a better understanding of
the nature of each card of the Major Arcana. This provides for
an integrated understanding of the Universe that acts in an
integrated way.

Those who study and devote themselves to this science
and art have concluded that the better a particular divinatory
method or divination spread simulates an aspect of the
Universe, the more accurate that particular method will be.
According to this theory, working with the Tarot should be a lot
more accurate than flipping a coin. Again, the person doing the
reading is always more important than the method being
employed. The method used can greatly aid or hinder a person
in opening to the Higher. This is one reason why the use of the
twenty-two Major Arcana is being employed in the following
spread. As one begins to work with the Major Arcana, particularly in the area of divination, one can begin to see these subtle
spiritual influences manifesting into one's life. This teaches us
on a regular basis the axiom of the Emerald Tablet which
states, *"As above so below."* This explains the nature of working
only with the spiritual cards of the Tarot, and how they work.
For the things that are above must manifest into our world
below. The energies that are in us and above us, are influential
and predominant in our lives. In understanding the premise of
the Emerald Tablet, it becomes increasingly clear that the
Minor Arcana of the Tarot do not need to be employed at all for
most divinatory situations. In the hands of a trained and
skilled Tarotist, though, they can be an added aid and guide.

The Circle Spread Spiritual Divination

The Circle Spread is a spiritual divination using only the Major Arcana cards of the Tarot. This spread is designed to help us better understand our spiritual situation and the influences within us as well as around us. It cannot be too strongly emphasized that these influences will manifest in our lives for good or for bad. For as the spiritual influences work their way down from the higher realms of spiritual existence, they begin to take on physical manifestation in our daily lives. What we are really looking at here is karmic influences. The spread does not necessarily show what these influences are or where they are coming from, but in the long run it is appropriate to say that all karmic influences come from ourselves.

This is a very practical spread for regular use. Here are some of the questions that the Circle Spread Divination is designed to answer.

1) Karmic consequences of a pivotal decision.
There are several times in our lives when we have a pivotal decision to make and we're concerned about the karmic consequences of that decision. We also benefit by knowing the influences around us; especially the effect these influences have concerning a pivotal decision. The Circle Spread Divination will show us the influences around us as well as the influences around any particular situation.

2) What energies are around you.
Many times it's not good enough to know whether a decision is the right decision or will be financially rewarding or emotionally fulfilling. Often we want to know what kind of influences surround us. Remember, even though a particular situation in our lives can look positive now, better understanding of the influences that are around us can help us better prepare for the inevitable manifestation of the spiritual into the physical. An example of this is a friend of mine in Chicago. She called and asked if I would perform a reading in regard to a move she was about to make. It was for a new job in Tucson. She had been promised a great deal of money and financial support in the act of making the move. It seemed like a win/win situation. After laying out the Circle Spread Divination, I noticed that the influences around her, were in fact very positive. I also

noticed the influences around the situation (in this case, the move itself), seemed very positive. However, the final outcome card was the Blasted Tower. My interpretation was for her to go ahead and make the move; that the influences around her in the situation were extremely positive and that she should expect tremendous change in her life. Not just the changes that she was expecting, for those were obvious, but there would be additional changes that would work out in a very positive way. Within forty days of beginning her job in Tucson, she was already in the process of quitting for a better job with more freedom, more travel and more money.

3) The energies around the situation.

This is a look at the Macrocosmic influences, the energies outside of our sphere of sensation. Because these energies *are* outside of our sphere of sensation, they appear foreign to us. It is at this point that the novice will say, "I must be involved in a false reading, or I must have done something wrong." Since we are limited to our own sphere of sensation, we often cannot see outside influences. In addition, these are the influences around the situation or the question itself, not around us. You might say that every decision has a karmic consequence and these are the influences around a particular decision.

4) Probable outcome of a decision.

It is here that the Circle Spread Divination helps guide us in what will probably happen if we do something, or what will probably happen if we do not do something.

5) To determine the probable karmic consequence of any magickal operation.

Not all magickal acts, regardless of how well intended have a positive karmic consequence or a positive outcome. The Circle Spread Divination, can help you zero in on the outcome of any act, be it magickal or physical.

6) Uncovering trouble areas.

The Circle Spread Divination will also help in better understanding areas of trouble. These areas of trouble can be either Macrocosmic or Microcosmic. This layout is based on the Elements of Fire, Water, Air and Earth. Each one of these Elements is a direct aspect of our personality. This spread can then aid us in better understanding our own psychological strengths and weaknesses.

The Layout

The Circle Spread Divination is based on two primary rituals of the Golden Dawn. These two rituals are the Lesser Banishing Ritual of the Pentagram, and the Banishing Ritual of the Hexagram. In Golden Dawn symbology, the pentagram is the signet star of the Microprosopus or the Microcosm, our sphere of sensation. The Banishing Ritual of the Hexagram with its integrated symbols of Fire and Water is the signet star of the Macroprosopus or Macrocosm. Together, the formulae of these two rituals are combined into one divinatory Tarot layout, to provide us with a spiritual portal for understanding a spiritual situation, on an internal level, (L. B. R. P. Microcosm), and on an external situation, (B. R. H. Macrocosm).

Begin by formulation of the question, and always be specific: "What is the probable outcome if I _____;" or "What are the influences around me and around _____ situation." After you have formulated the question, close your eyes and allow your mind to relax and perform your invocation to the Higher. Ask for guidance and understanding in regard to the question at hand. In Golden Dawn symbology, we would also invoke the great Angel HRU. An outline of that invocation can be found in the book, *The New Golden Dawn Ritual Tarot* by Chic and Sandra Tabatha Cicero.

Upon the formulation of the question, you should begin to shuffle the twenty-two Major Arcana. Any method of shuffling is acceptable. My personal preference is to lay them on a floor or table and mix them thoroughly. The cards, after they have been shuffled are cut into four piles. The four piles signify the Tetragrammaton, Y. H. V. and H final. Be sure to cut the cards from right to left as this is the way that Hebrew is written. After you have cut the cards into four piles, from right to left, take the right pile and place it on top of the left pile next to it. Place that pile on top of the next pile and place that pile on top of the final pile. Traditionally, the Golden Dawn did not use reverse keys. There are only a few cards that are employed in this spread, so we suggest the use of reverse cards. The choice, however, is yours.

The Circle Spread Divination

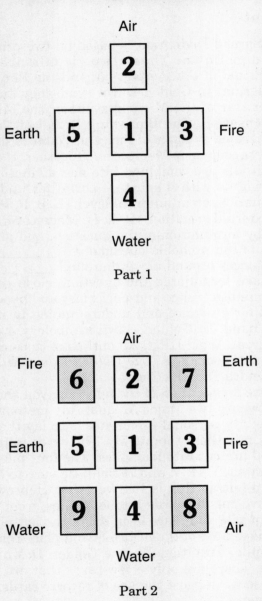

Air

2

Earth **5** **1** **3** Fire

4

Water

Part 1

Air

Fire **6** **2** **7** Earth

Earth **5** **1** **3** Fire

Water **9** **4** **8** Air

Water

Part 2

You are now ready to lay out the cards. Turn over the first card. Place it in the center of the table. This first card is called the *Significator.* The Significator card is the card that best represents you at this particular time and in regard to this particular situation.

The next card that you turn over is the beginning of the formation of the Microcosmic portion of the spread. These are the spiritual influences surrounding you within your own sphere of sensation. This card goes directly above the Significator card. This is the spiritual influences affecting you now through the Element of Air. Air primarily represents your mental or thinking operation; thus this card is said to have an influence on your thoughts.

The next card is placed to the right of the Significator card. This card represents the spiritual influences upon you through the Element of Fire. Fire governs the lower emotions or raw energy aspects of the personality. This is a very powerful position in that it represents raw energy life force. This card tells you what kind of influences are about you right now through your lower emotions.

The next card is placed directly below the Significator card. This is the Element of Water. This card shows the spiritual influences about you, filtered through the Element of Water. Water is attributed to higher spirituality and to higher forms of love, compassion and sympathy. Using Greek terminology, we would say that Water is more akin to Agape than to Eros.

The final card of the first part of this operation is placed to the left of the Significator. This particular card explains the spiritual influences around you, filtered through the Element of Earth. In essence, this card sums up the Elements of Air, Fire and Water. It also gives you some idea of the energies around you from a more mundane aspect.

Now you have laid five cards out before you. You will also notice that the cards form the equal arm cross which is the magickal tool of the path of Tav, the Hebrew letter that represents the Universe card of the Tarot. It is through the Universe card and the path of Tav that we enter higher realms of spirituality. It is also the path influences of the spiritual plane manifesting into our mundane and physical lives. The first part of this operation, now simulates the Lesser Banishing Ritual of the Pentagram in movement. This shows us the influences as they affect us internally.

The second part of this operation will show us the influences around the situation or question at hand from a Macrocosmic level. Because the Banishing Ritual of the Hexagram is Macrocosmic, it is based on Zodiacal positions in the heavens and thus the Elements will be arranged differently. So the next card that we turn over will go just to the left of the card representing Air. However this card represents Fire, raw emotional energy on a Macrocosmic level. The next card is placed in the upper right hand corner; again in accordance with the Banishing Ritual of the Hexagram which is now the position of Earth. Here we have Macrocosmic or outside influences around the situation itself filtered through Earth. This card gives us a more mundane perspective of the situation. The next card is placed in the lower right hand corner. This card is the outside influence of the Element of Air.

The final card of this operation is placed in the left lower hand corner. This card highlights the spiritual aspect to the higher forms of spirituality and love on a Macrocosmic level; it is the outside influence of the Element of Water around the situation or the question at hand. Now we have what appears to be a cube. The cube is significant in that the Qabalistic document, the *Sepher Yetzirah* calls the Universe "Cubical." For spiritual advice on a particular matter and to better understand the influences within us and outside us, no other cards need be turned over. Looking at these cards and meditating on them in their positions and influences can tell us a lot about ourselves; where we are and what is influencing us. (Several good books will be listed at the end of this chapter that give in depth information as to the actual interpretation of the twenty-two Major Arcana cards.) If you wish to know the final outcome to a particular decision, you must then turn over an additional two cards. One card is turned over first on the left side of the spread; the other card is turned over on the right side of the spread. The card to the left indicates the probable outcome if no action is taken; if you let things go on as they currently are or have followed the present course.

The card on the right side of the reading will indicate the probable outcome if you take the action that your question was directed to. This card will tell you karmically the probable outcome. It will also give you some idea of the mundane effects. For example, the Star card would indicate a very positive outcome in most situations, both on the physical and on the spiritual plane. If in your judgment, you are being totally honest with yourself, both cards seem to be equally positive and both are interpreted as part of the final outcome if you take the particular action that your question was directed to.

If both cards are extremely negative, then it will require you to study the influences that are surrounding you at this time. Through meditation and contemplation, the influences can be changed after a significant amount of time by changing internal attitudes, through meditation, prayer, ritual work and/or contemplation.

The Circle Spread Divination is a very intuitive spread. One word of caution; please do not read this over and then begin laying out the cards and expect to make a snap judgment on your life. Divine divination is too serious and your life is too important to make major decisions without adequate practice and training in regard to divination, particularly the Tarot. Through practice, meditation, study and through reading, you can, however, develop very positive skills. These skills can be applied to your life with great effectiveness. More importantly they can aid and guide you in the acquisition of serious spiritual knowledge that will help you develop a deeper understanding of your True Will and your Higher Self.

The spiritual and the physical are intimately interlinked. As we become more aware of the spiritual, we can develop a better relationship with the physical. In the words of a Golden Dawn ceremony, *"Quit the physical, seek the spiritual."*

ABOUT THE AUTHOR

Frater P.C. has been aware of the Hermetic systems since he was a young child. A very influential Aunt exposed him to Rosicrucianism at the age of twelve. He found that astral projection, scrying, and traveling in the Spirit Vision were things that came easily to him.

Frater P.C. studied human psychology for several years, attending various universities. He studied the art of hypnosis under one of the leading hypnotists in the world, Jimmy Grippo.

Frater P.C. is one of the founders of the Hermetic Order of the Eternal Golden Dawn (the EGD), and spends his time in intensive study on the Qabalah, Enochian, Egyptian, and most other western esoteric systems. He is also one of the developers of a healing system called Ruach Healing.

SUGGESTED READING:

The New Golden Dawn Ritual Tarot
by Chic and Sandra Tabatha Cicero
Llewellyn Publications

The Qabalistic Tarot
by Robert Wang
Samuel Weiser Inc.

The Golden Dawn
by Israel Regardie
Llewellyn Publications

**The Sepher Yetzirah —
The Book of Creation: In Theory and Practice**
by Aryeh Kaplan
Samuel Weiser Inc.

The Divination of the Rose Cross

Donald Michael Kraig

he system of Tarot divination described in *The Golden Dawn*, called "The Opening of the Key", is daunting for several reasons. First, it has several errors in it which makes it confusing. Second, to do a thorough reading requires a deep knowledge of the Tarot, the Kabalah and Astrology. Third, it has several parts that seem disjointed and separate, but which must be united by the diviner into a unified whole (what is called "synthesis" in Astrology). While few Tarot systems come close to its accuracy and depth, its learning curve is very long. While spending the time to decipher it and make the necessary corrections to the errors which have occurred in print (and different books that describe it have different errors!) is worthwhile, it is regrettable that few people practice the method. Even Aleister Crowley rarely used it, preferring instead the Yi King.

I have another problem with the system which is actually based more on sociology than metaphysics. In the late 1800s, the time when the Golden Dawn's explanation of the Tarot was revealed, people lived in a static, Newtonian world. It was decades later that this was shattered by Einstein, Schrödinger and others. The late 1800s was a static world while ours is constantly changing. (Curiously, it was the beliefs of occultists which helped to make this modern and more accurate interpretation of reality, but that is another story.)

Thus, I personally found "The Opening of the Key" to be static. My personal challenge was to develop a dynamic (in the sense of being able to deal with change) Tarot spread that would remain in the tradition of the Golden Dawn. The answer came to me while attending a lecture by Chic Cicero and

Sandra Tabatha Cicero. I jotted down some notes which were to become *The Divination of the Rose Cross*.

The symbol of the Rose Cross is an important part of the Golden Dawn. Within it are revealed the mysteries of the Kabalah, alchemy, magick and much more. Many people and groups use it, frequently without giving credit to its origination in the Golden Dawn.

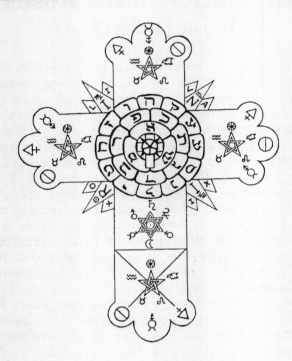

The Rose Cross used by the Rosicrucians (AMORC) of San Jose, California, is much simpler, being a simple cross with rose petals at the center. They say that the rose represents the *unfolding* of the soul. It was this notion of the rose being an unfolding which I wanted to include in a new spread. I also wanted to allow the diviner to be able to use the cards in a way which permits more access to the realms of the subconscious; a notion omitted from many spreads.

The Divination of the Rose Cross is clearly explained in the following descriptions. Each of its seven steps is a development in the formation of the Rose Cross used as a basis for this divination.

STEP ONE: The Wand of Power
Divination means "to make divine." Therefore, the first move is to unite the Macrocosm with the Microcosm. This is done by the row of cards which represents the Middle Pillar of the Kabalistic Tree of Life with an added, external view of the problem.

STEP TWO: The Cross of Time
The horizontal bar that completes the cross part of the figure allows you to look at the past, recent past and present as it relates to your question.

STEP THREE: The Bud of the Rose
A bud is that part of a plant which will become a flower. Here you create the bud that will become the rose by dealing three circles of cards around the juncture of the bars of the cross. Although somewhat difficult to describe, if you try it you will see that it is actually quite easy to do.

STEP FOUR: The Unfolding of the Rose, Part One
Here we begin to see the rose of information burst into bloom. Interpret the newly revealed cards as described. Note that the "horizon," or horizontal bar of the cross, separates those things in our conscious, from those that are in our subconscious. Note, too, that there are dynamic cards which are "crossovers" and show the vitality of spirit along with changes that can occur as things move from our subconscious to our conscious.

STEP FIVE: The Unfolding of the Rose, Part Two
In this step another row of petals is formed. Here is described what will come about as a result of the action(s) suggested by the question for which this divination is being performed. Note that there is no either or aspect to this step. You are informed of things which will occur and which are likely to occur and given crossover cards that link the two. With this information you should be able to determine a choice of action.

Diagram 1

The Wand of Power

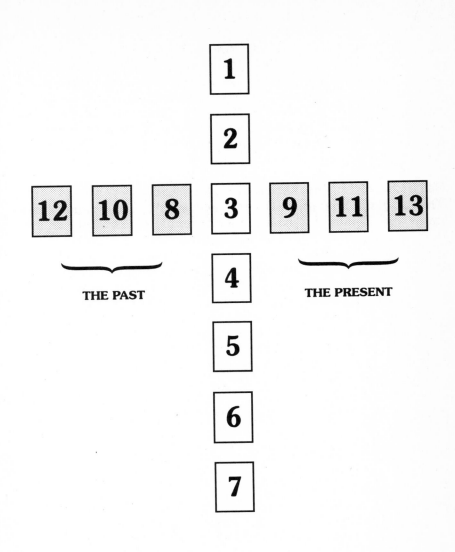

Diagram 2

The Cross of Time

STEP SIX: The Unfolding of the Rose, Part Three
This set of petals deals with deep psychological information and includes changes which will occur and have an effect on your psyche. If you are reading for another person it is not only important to be completely honest at this step, but also to understand the limitations of your client. If he or she is unprepared for this information it could devastate the client psychologically. Be aware of your client's needs. If you are doing the divination for yourself be sure that your interpretation is honest and you do not delude yourself.

STEP SEVEN: The Thorns and the Crown
This is an optional step. The previous six steps will usually give more than enough information for a completely accurate and in-depth reading. It should be noticed that through step six there is no "final outcome". This was omitted on purpose to show that the universe is changing. The "final outcome" of one situation in our lives is the beginning of other situations in our lives.

However, after experimenting with this reading many times, several people felt they needed a more static answer. Thus were born the Thorns and the Crown. The thorns are added at an angle at the base of the vertical bar, which is now seen to represent the stem of the rose. The two cards, thorns, indicate problems which may yet develop.

The Crown, a set of five cards arcing over the entire spread, can be interpreted as a final outcome.

The Divination of the Rose Cross

STEP ONE: The Wand of Power
Begin this reading by determining the question you wish to deal with. Make sure that the question is an open question, not one that can be answered with a simple yes or no. Rather than asking if you should do this or that, ask what the outcome will be if you do a particular action. In this way you will get added information but the choices, the decisions, will remain yours.

Once the question is determined, ask for guidance in this reading. You may ask that the great angel HRU watch over it, or you may focus on another archangel, god or your Holy Guardian Angel. Take as long as you feel is appropriate. There is no rush.

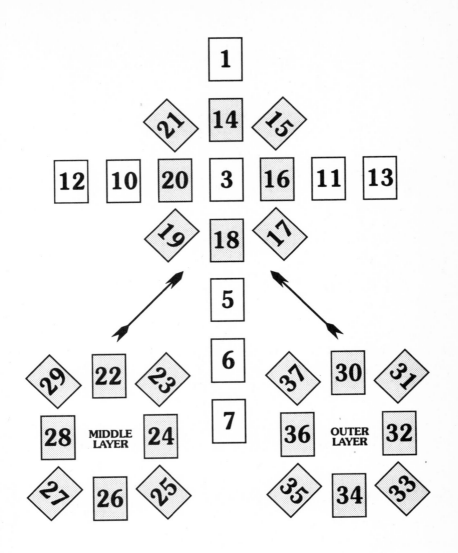

Diagram 3

The Bud of the Rose

113

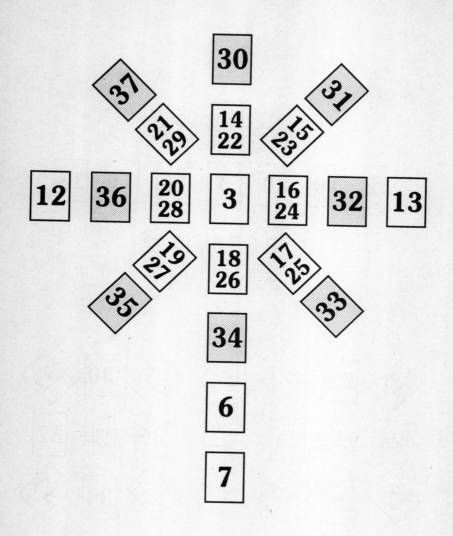

Diagram 4

The Unfolding of the Rose, Part One

114

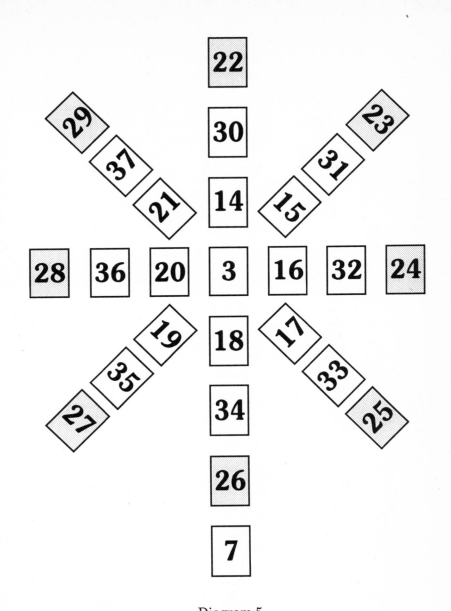

Diagram 5

The Unfolding of the Rose, Part Two

As you look at each card, consider its meaning in relationship to the position in the spread where it falls. Then consider it in relation to all of the cards you have already interpreted in the reading. *There should be no contradictions!* If the meanings of cards in particular positions in the spread seem contradictory you simply have not understood the cards in context. Pause, think about what is going on and ask for additional guidance if necessary.

You may find that as more cards come up they will give a deeper meaning to earlier cards. You may have to reinterpret the earlier cards, adding to them or even altering your original interpretation. This is perfectly normal and positive. This reading is designed to give information and aid in decision making; not prove what psychic powers you may or may not have.

Lay down a row of seven, face down cards as shown in Diagram 1. Then turn card one over and interpret it according to the position meaning as given below. When you are complete with this card, move to the second card. Continue in this manner through the seven cards.

Card 1. AIN SOPH: The first card represents the highest spiritual aspect of this question.

Card 2. HEAD: This refers to what is on your conscious mind concerning this question.

Card 3. DAH'AHT: This concerns an inner secret about the question. Alternatively, it may deal with how the client communicates with others concerning this question.

Card 4. TIFERET: Cuts through to the heart of the matter. Deals with emotional links to the question. May give a key for meditation.

Card 5. YESODE: The power and force behind the question. Where it draws its energy from and possibly how to deal with that energy if a positive conclusion is not evident.

Card 6. MAHL-KOOT: Why the client is tied to the problem. Possibly what the client can do about the tie to overcome it by altering his or her behavior rather than trying to alter the external world.

Card 7. GAIA: An external view of the problem. How other people might view it. Its real importance in your life once you get out of being so deeply involved with it.

STEP TWO: The Cross of Time

Lay out six more cards, face down, in the order shown in Diagram 2. Turn over cards 12, 10 and 8. Interpret them as the past. Follow this by turning over cards 9, 11, and 13 and interpret them as the present.

THE PAST: Cards 8, 10 and 12 represent those past events, experiences, emotions and thoughts which have a direct bearing on the question at hand. Card 8 happened the most recently while card 12 happened furthest in the past. Card 10 describes that which links the distant with the recent past concerning this matter.

THE PRESENT: Cards 9, 11, and 13 describe events, experiences, emotions and thoughts about the question at hand which have either recently occurred, are occurring or will occur shortly. Card 9 is the most influencing card on this arm, while card 13 is currently having the least effect. This may change within a week. Card 11 describes that which links cards 9 and 13, and, if card 13 seems negative, provides advice on how to overcome its effect.

STEP THREE: The Bud of the Rose

Forming the Bud: Deal out the circle of cards which forms the innermost layer of the bud of the rose by laying out the cards *face down* as in Diagram 3. Note that card 14 lies on top of card 2, 16 is on top of 9, 18 is on top of 4 and 20 is on top of 12.

Deal out two more circles of cards, as shown in the diagram (the Middle and Outer layers of the bud) face down, *on top* of the circle of cards (numbers 14 - 21) already formed.

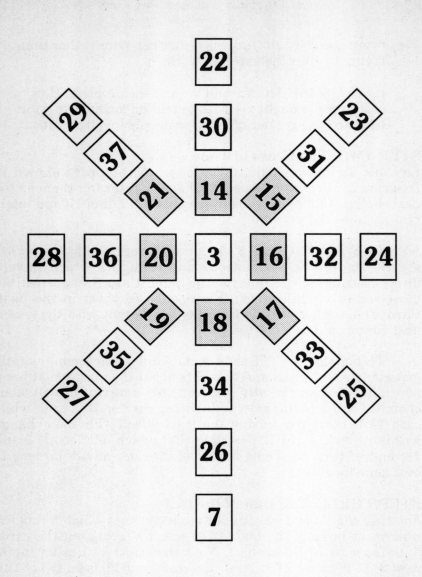

Diagram 6

The Unfolding of the Rose, Part Three

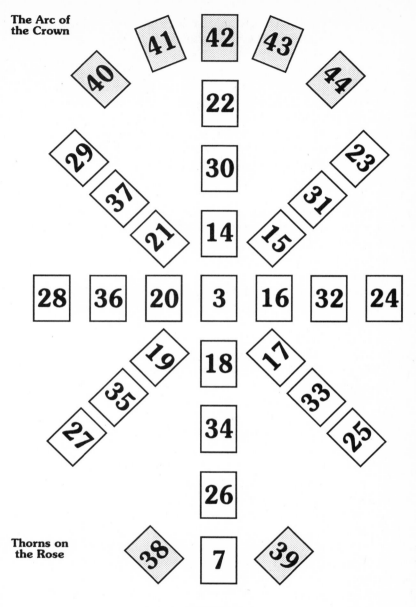

Diagram 7

The Thorns and the Crown

119

STEP FOUR: The Unfolding of the Rose, Part One
Turn over the topmost layer of the rose, forming the face-up
circle shown in Diagram 4. It will give a general picture of the
situation and should be interpreted with those things above
the horizon dealing with the consciousness and those things
below the horizon dealing with the subconscious. The cards on
the horizon, numbers 36 and 32, can be viewed as crossovers
between the conscious and the subconscious, especially with
those cards immediately above and below each (i.e., card 36 is
most closely related to cards 35 and 37 while card 32 is most
closely related to cards 31 and 33).

STEP FIVE: The Unfolding of the Rose, Part Two
Turn over the next layer of the rose, cards 22 - 29, and form a
second row of face-up rose petals outside of the circle already
formed. This will be the outermost circle of petals and will
describe in detail those things which will come about as a
result of the action suggested by the question asked. Cards
above the horizon deal with the developments sure to come
while those below the horizon, being linked to other external
forces not directly discussed in this reading, are *likely* to come
to pass, but one should not be surprised if events unknown to
you at this time prevent them from taking place. The cards on
the horizon, numbers 28 and 24, should be linked to the cards
above or below the horizon at the discretion of the reader.

STEP SIX: The Unfolding of the Rose, Part Three
Turn over the last layer of the rose, cards 14 - 21, and place
them in the same position where they were, as shown in
Diagram 6. This will be the innermost circle of petals and will
describe in detail either the changes that will occur to you as a
result of taking the action described by the question or will
explain those changes which must take place in you before the
desired events will occur. This can be very deep psychological
information, so be sure that the client is ready to hear the
information. If you are reading for yourself, be sure that you
are being honest in your interpretation. Cards below the horizon have deeper, more hidden information than those cards
above the horizon.

STEP SEVEN: The Thorns and the Crown

Steps one through six provide enough information for most readings. For more information, two cards, 38 and 39 may be placed next to the bottom card, card seven. These "thorns" indicate problems which may develop blocking success. Three to five cards may arc over the rose. This "crown" is interpreted as the so-called "final outcome" of the reading. (See Diagram 7.)

I would like to add in closing that I have purposely not included ultra-specific instructions for this reading and for giving interpretations. It is hoped that you will take this information and experiment with it. For example, how exactly should you interpret the Arc of the Crown? I leave that up to you. I do not want you to perform my divination. I would hope that you would make it yours.

Just as the idea of dynamism and change is a part of this reading, it is my hope that *The Divination of the Rose Cross* will evolve. This can only happen if people share their ideas. After you experiment with this reading for a while I hope to hear from you. You can write to me in care of Llewellyn Publications.

ABOUT THE AUTHOR

Donald Michael Kraig is the author of *Modern Magick*, one of the most popular books on the subject ever written. He is also the former Editor of *The Llewellyn New Times* and *FATE* magazine, and is a regular contributor to several metaphysical publications. He has been a student and teacher on a variety of metaphysical topics for over 20 years. After intense study Don became a Certified Tarot Master (CTM), an honor bestowed upon him by The Associated Readers Of Tarot, an international, not-for-profit educational organization. He has been a student of the Golden Dawn system for over 15 years.

Taro-strology:
The Tarot Wheel of the Year
Thom Parrott

The Four Knaves (Princesses) rule the celestial Heavens from the North Pole of the Zodiac to the 45° of Latitude North of the Ecliptic. They form the Thrones of the Four Aces, who rule in Kether. The Four Kings, 4 Queens, 4 Princes rule the Celestial Heavens from the 45° of North Latitude down to the Ecliptic. The 12 Tarot Keys attributed to the 12 Signs of the Zodiac rule the Celestial Heavens from the Ecliptic, down to the 45° of South Latitude. The 36 smaller cards of the Suits (from two to ten) rule the Celestial Heavens from the 45° South of the Ecliptic to the South Pole, or the Malkuth place therein. And all calculation arises from the Star "Regulus," the 0° of our Leo.

— from Israel Regardie's *The Golden Dawn*

The system of correspondences between the Tarot and Astrology, as put forward in *Book T* of the Golden Dawn, quoted above, is a complex and beautiful construction which illuminates both. While this subject deserves a book to itself, a brief overview of the relationships of the Aces and Court Cards applied to the Wheel of the Year is both possible and, I hope, beneficial.

Although I assume most of us are conversant with the Tarot and with Astrology, I feel it is important to go over some basic information. This will both introduce the fundamentals to the newcomer and put them into the context appropriate to the task at hand for all of us.

Basic Elemental Concepts

The Elements, as put forward in Hermetic Science, are the four fundamental states of matter, ruled by the Quintessence, the fifth Element. Earth is the state of matter wherein molecules

---

[1] Sixth edition, page 596.

tend to cling to one another—*solid*. Air is the state of matter wherein molecules tend to fly apart—*gas*. Water is the state of matter wherein molecules tend to flow over one another—*liquid*. Fire is the quality of matter wherein molecules transmit vibration to one another—*electro-magnetism*. The Quintessence is the ruling force which coordinates the other four—*Spirit* or *Soul*.

In both Astrology and the Tarot, the common attributes of Fire are energy, enthusiasm and Yang emotions; of Water, receptivity, sensitivity and Yin emotions; of Air, intellect and communication; and of Earth, practicality and stability. The Quintessence exhibits transcendence and the archetypal power that arises from it.

Elements and the Tarot

The Quintessence is represented in the Tarot by the Major Arcana or Trumps in the deck as a whole. Within each subordinate Element or Suit, the Quintessence is represented by the Ace.

Fire is represented by the Wands as a whole and by the Kings in each Suit. Within the Trumps, Fire is symbolized by the card of Judgment.

Water is represented by the Cups as a whole and by the Queens of each Suit. Within the Trumps, Water is symbolized by the Hanged Man.

Air is represented by the Swords as a whole and by the Princes or Knights of each Suit. Within the Trumps, Air is symbolized by the Fool.

Earth is represented by the Disks or Pentacles as a whole and by the Princesses or Pages of each Suit. No Trump is assigned to Earth.[2]

Regarding the association of all Wands and all Kings with Fire (and so forth through the Royals and Suits), there are *two types or levels* of Fire, and for each of the other Elements, at work. These are derived from the presence in each of the Elements of all the other Elements—nothing is completely separate from anything else and everything is a composite of all the influences that go into its existence, to the limits of the Universe—Creation is a hologram, therefore, each component

---

[2] The Tarot Trump of The Universe, although primarily attributed to the planet Saturn, does have a dual set of correspondences associated with it -- one for Saturn and one for the Element of Earth.

(no matter how small) contains within itself the Whole, viewed from its own personal perspective.

The Suit is the primary representation of the Element while the title of the Court Card is the secondary representation.[3] In a sense, the Suit is the Sun Sign while the Title is the Ascendant. These are sometimes referred to as Specific Fire (or whatever Element is involved) and *Primal* Fire; *Specific* being the Title and *Primal* being the Suit.

Elements and Astrology

In Astrology, the Elements appear as the Triplicities of the Signs of the Zodiac. These are the initiating, fructifying and closing representations of each Element, called Cardinal, Fixed and Mutable. The Fire Signs are Aries (Cardinal Fire), Leo (Fixed or Kerubic Fire) and Sagittarius (Mutable Fire). The Water Signs are Cancer (Cardinal), Scorpio (Kerubic) and Pisces (Mutable). The Air Signs are Libra (Cardinal), Aquarius (Kerubic) and Gemini (Mutable). The Earth Signs are Capricorn (Cardinal), Taurus (Kerubic) and Virgo (Mutable).

The Elements also appear as rulers of the Seasons. By definition, each Season begins at 0º of a Cardinal Sign. In the Northern Hemisphere, Spring begins at 0º of Aries, Summer at 0º of Cancer, Autumn at 0º of Libra and Winter at 0º of Capricorn. These points are called the Vernal Equinox (when day and night are each 12 hours), the Summer Solstice (longest day), the Autumnal Equinox and the Winter Solstice (longest night), respectively.

(Since the Seasons are created by the changing angle of the Earth's axis to the Sun, in the Southern Hemisphere the Seasons are reversed. Therefore Spring begins at 0º of Libra, Summer at 0º of Capricorn, Autumn at 0º of Aries and Winter at 0º of Cancer—in the Southern Hemisphere. Many of the correspondences used in Astrology, and applied to the Tarot here, will be invalid South of the Equator—particularly the Elemental associations with the Signs and Seasons. Perhaps someone from "down under" can rectify this system for application to the Southern Hemisphere in a subsequent volume.)

---

[3] This is often referred to as a Sub-element.

Taro-strogy

Taro-strology is a combined name signifying the union of Tarot and Astrology. Several sets of allocations have been put forward for this purpose. The one we will be dealing with here derives from the Golden Dawn as described by Israel Regardie —the paragraph quoted at the beginning of this article sets out the primary relationships.

Because of space limitations, among other things, we will be dealing here almost exclusively with the Aces and Princesses, and the Kings, Queens and Princes. The 12 cards assigned to the Signs will be discussed briefly. The cards assigned to the Decans will be conspicuous by their absence.

The Seasons: Aces and Princesses

The Ace rides over the Fixed or Kerubic Sign of its own Element along with the two Signs on either side of it, ruling them through the personality of the Princess of its Suit.

The Ace is the pure, unformed, *potential* of the Element of its Suit. It is beyond gender or personality. In a reading, it must rely on other cards or position for its specific significance.

The Princess is the most material and human *expression* of the Element of her Suit. She is the Throne of the Ace—that is, she is the manifesting personality of her Element, transmitting and transforming its energy for application on our Earthly plane.

This partnership spans the full length of the Tree of Life, reaching from Kether to Malkuth in a single leap which clarifies, and is clarified by, the equations 1=10 (the Zelator Grade of the Golden Dawn) and 10=1 (the Ipsissimus Grade). In essence, it is impossible to separate the Source from its mode of expression. Or, as Marshall McLuhan put it, "the medium is the message."

The Cusps: Queens, Princes and Kings

The Queens (Cardinal Cusps) represent the *forces that impel the change of Seasons* and the intensity of the equinoxes and solstices. They harness the revolutionary forces of the Kings, initiating new realities from the fruit of the old. Their reality is blended with experience of the Season just passed.

The Princes (Kerubic Cusps) arise out of their Mother's Energy to express their own with assertion, power and clarity. They manifest the *heart of the Season* which is, neither looking back nor forward.

The Kings (Mutable Cusps) are Princes who have matured into wiser and more spiritual men. Their reality is blended with experience and they *look forward to the Season yet to come.*

The Signs: 12 Trumps

The Signs divide the plane of Earth's orbit into twelve arcs of 30° each. These are each referred to by the name of a constellation which appears to be stationary within the arc. The Signs provide a backdrop against which the Planets move. The

Planets represent aspects of personality while the Signs represent ways of expressing these aspects.

The Signs of the Zodiac are listed below with the title of the Tarot Card to which they are attributed:

Aries—The Emperor
Taurus—The Hierophant
Gemini—The Lovers
Cancer—The Chariot
Leo—Strength
Virgo—The Hermit
Libra—Justice
Scorpio—Death
Sagittarius—Temperance
Capricorn—The Devil
Aquarius—The Star
Pisces—The Moon

The Cards in the Wheel

SPRING: Aries, Taurus, Gemini

Spring extends from the Vernal Equinox to the Summer Solstice. It consists of the Cardinal Fire Sign—Aries, the Fixed Earth Sign—Taurus and the Mutable Air Sign—Gemini. Spring is ruled by Earth. In Astrology, Earth stands for *practicality, sensuality* and *caution*.

The Ace of Disks:

Elemental Earth

The Ace of Disks is the power that manifests Spring— although Spring is actually initiated by the restless instability of Winter as transmuted by the Queen of Wands in the last 10 degrees of Pisces.

As Spring, the Ace of Disks represents *physical growth* and *fertility*—green things rising out of the ground and out of the skeletons of last year's growth, birds and most animals giving birth, the celebration that the most life-threatening weather of the year has passed and all other things which may be analogous to these. While all the other Seasons tend to elicit a collective "why?" Spring inspires joyful acceptance—it is, therefore, at once the most material and the most spiritual of Seasons, for when we are truly feeling one with the Divine, we ask no questions but accept what is.

The Princess of Disks:

Earth of Earth

The Princess of Disks rules, as the Throne of the Power of the Ace, Spring—Aries, Taurus and Gemini. She is Earth of Earth and the Planet Earth in Assiah.

The Princess of Disks is the transmuting and transmitting personality necessary to bring the power of the Ace of Disks into manifestation on the earthly or material plane. She is Mother Earth, per se, applying her energies to warming and refreshing, healing and nurturing her earthly sphere and its inhabitants. She tills the soil, plants seeds, seeks to procreate (May Day) and find a partner (June weddings). She is the most *physical* personality among the Court Cards.

The Queen of Wands:

Mutable Water to Cardinal Fire
PISCES (Moon) to ARIES (Emperor)

The Queen of Wands rules the last Decan of Pisces and the first two Decans of Aries; and two of these are assigned to Mars, whose heat restores the vibrancy necessary to turn Winter to Spring.

The Queen of Wands uses the powers of *choice and intention* of the Ace of Swords (Winter) applied with the mystical understanding of the Moon (Pisces) to initiate the change of Seasons. While she begins this process in her mind (Air, Swords), she carries it out on the material level (Earth, Disks) under the power of the Ace of Disks and the authority of the Princess of Disks.

The Queen of Wands transmutes the energy raised by the King of Cups, balancing *desperation with adaptable force*. In the course of invoking Spring, the Queen of Wands raises the fiery and initiatory energies of the Emperor (Aries).

ARIES: The Emperor

March 21—April 20

The Emperor represents the *egoistic force* necessary for a seed to push its sprout up through the covering mulch and its root down through frozen earth—or for a baby bird to batter a hole in the walls that enclose it—or for a human child to pass through the birth canal contracting upon it with a force capable of breaking adult bones. The aggression of Aries is based on the struggle to survive.

The energy of the Emperor is dominated by the *emotional intensity* of the Queen of Wands (Water of FIRE) moderated by the *conscious materialism* of the Prince of Disks (Air of EARTH). The presence of all four Elements shows both *immediate fecundity* and the *potential for growth and productivity*.

The Prince of Disks:

Cardinal Fire to Kerubic Earth
ARIES (Emperor) to TAURUS (Hierophant)

The Prince of Disks rules the last Decan of Aries and the first two Decans of Taurus. The energy set in motion by personal *awakening* (Aries) produces an overpowering *momentum* (Taurus). The Prince is Air of Earth and the Sun in Assiah.

The Prince of Disks uses the powers of *stability and manifestation* from the Ace of Disks (Spring) applied with the *single-minded enthusiasm* of the Emperor (Aries) to sustain the momentum established by the Queen of Wands. He works on the material level (Earth, Disks) under the power of the Ace of Disks and the authority of the Princess of Disks.

The Prince of Disks manifests the fruit of the energy of the Queen of Wands, balancing *instability with work*. In the course of manifesting Spring, the Prince of Disks establishes the occult earthiness of the Hierophant (Taurus).

TAURUS: The Hierophant

April 21—May 20

The Hierophant represents the *outward manifestation of hidden things*. It is the green leaves, the newborn creatures, the Spring runoff—but it is not the life force within them. Taurus is the manifesting gardener and the teacher of gardening, but he is neither the garden nor its product.

The energy of the Hierophant is dominated by the *conscious materialism* of the Prince of Disks (Air of EARTH) moderated by the *passionate intellect* of the King of Swords (Fire of AIR). There is, however, no Water in his makeup—he has no emotional receptivity, no compassion and no flexibility.

The King of Swords:

Kerubic Earth to Mutable Air
TAURUS (Hierophant) to GEMINI (Lovers)

The King of Swords rules the last Decan of Taurus and the first two Decans of Gemini. From *stolid materialism* (Taurus) rises the schizophrenic philosophy of *comparison and conflict* (Gemini). Fire of Air and the Zodiac in Yetzirah.

The King of Swords uses the powers of *stability and manifestation* of the Ace of Disks applied with the *studious pragmatism* of the Hierophant (Taurus) to bring the process of Spring to its conclusion. He does his work under the power and authority of the Ace and Princess of Disks.

The King of Swords brings the energy raised by the Prince of Disks to maturity, balancing *materialism with insight*. In the course of understanding or experiencing Spring, the King of Swords impels the intuition of the Lovers (Gemini).

GEMINI: The Lovers

May 21— June 20

The Lovers represent the transition from the single minded *creative forces* of the Emperor and the Hierophant into the more *dualistic energies* of late Spring and early Summer. In Spring, the Earth and the weather and the growing things arising out of the one through the agency of the other all seem to be one thing. In Gemini, the potential for conflict between life and that which supports it becomes apparent, along with the need for mediation and harmony to further the aims of both.

The energy of the Lovers is dominated by the *passionate intellect* of the King of Swords (Fire of AIR) moderated by the *emotional fluidity* of the Queen of Cups (Water of WATER). With no Earth in its makeup, the Lovers tends to be too idealistic and unstable to bring its dreams into manifestation (hence the 8, 9 and 10 of Swords as the Decans ruled by the Lovers represent frustration in various extreme forms).

SUMMER: Cancer, Leo, Virgo

Summer extends from the Summer Solstice to the Autumnal Equinox. It consists of the Cardinal Water Sign—Cancer, the Fixed Fire Sign—Leo and the Mutable Earth Sign—Virgo. Summer is ruled by Fire. In Astrology, Fire stands for *energy, enthusiasm* and *optimism*.

The Ace of Wands:

Elemental Fire

The Ace of Wands is the power that manifests Summer—though Summer is actually initiated by the enthusiastic outpouring of Spring as transmuted by the Queen of Cups in the last Decan of Gemini.

As Summer, the Ace of Wands represents *limits to growth* —the heat of the Sun sears the Earth, leaves become broad and dark to shelter the ripening fruit and to keep the ground shady, cool and moist, humans and other animals seek shade and fluids, those creatures (whether fixed or motile) unable to cool and irrigate themselves parch, burn and die. It is a time when we humans complain of an excess of light and heat.

The Princess of Wands:

Earth of Fire

The Princess of Wands rules, as the Throne of the Power of the Ace, Summer—Cancer, Leo and Virgo. She is Earth of Fire and the planet Earth in Atziluth.

The Princess of Wands is the transmuting and transmitting personality necessary to bring the power of the Ace of Wands into manifestation on the material plane. She applies her energies to bringing Spring's product to maturity and beginning the ripening process. She is the most material of the *spiritual* personalities.

The Queen of Cups:

Mutable Air to Cardinal Water
GEMINI (Lovers) to CANCER (Chariot)

The Queen of Cups rules the last Decan of Gemini and the first two of Cancer. It is the *dual nature* of the Twins (Gemini) producing the *sidestepping* Crab (Cancer). She is Water of Water and Saturn in Briah.

The Queen of Cups uses the powers of *durability and manifestation* of the Ace of Disks (Spring) applied with the *alchemical transmutation* of the Lovers (Gemini) to initiate the change of Seasons. While she begins this process on the material level (Earth, Disks, Spring), she carries it out on the level of the Yang emotions (Fire, Wands, Summer) under the power of the Ace of Wands and the authority of the Princess of Wands.

The Queen of Cups transmutes the energy raised by the King of Swords, balancing *intellect with imagination*. In the course of invoking Summer, the Queen of Cups raises the maternal and possessive energies of the Chariot (Cancer).

CANCER: The Chariot

June 21— July 22

The Chariot is the intentional exertion of *either more or less* coercive power to bring order and productivity out of conflict. To prevent the new growth of Spring from withering in the Summer Sun, irrigation must be provided. To prevent a shortage of water, artificial shade and companion planting must be used. Cancer must sidestep between Sun and shadow, choosing, weeding, containing—supporting the strong and letting the weak decline.

The energy of the Chariot is dominated by the *emotional fluidity* of the Queen of Cups (Water of WATER) moderated by the *explosive enthusiasm* of the Prince of Wands (Air of FIRE). The absence of Earth in the Chariot's makeup shows an inability to ground its intense but unstable forces.

The Prince of Wands:

Cardinal Water to Kerubic Fire
CANCER (Chariot) to LEO (Strength)

The Prince of Wands rules the third Decan of Cancer and the first two of Leo, the *ambiguity* of the Crab resolving itself into the *dominating personality* of the Lion. He is also Air of Fire and the Sun in Atziluth.

The Prince of Wands uses the powers *of intensity and expansion* of the Ace of Wands (Summer) applied with the *nesting and nurturing qualities* of the Chariot (Cancer) to sustain the momentum established by the Queen of Cups. He works on the level of the Yang emotions (Fire, Wands) under the power and authority of the Ace and Princess of Wands.

The Prince of Wands manifests the fruit of the energy of the Queen of Cups, balancing *dreaminess with drive*. In the course of manifesting Summer, the Prince of Wands establishes the spiritual love shown by the card Strength (Leo).

LEO: Strength

July 23—August 22

Strength arises out of understanding which, in turn, arises out of *compassion*. Simply railing about the intensity of the forces arrayed against the maturing harvest will produce only frustration. To overcome our enemies, we must learn to see them as companions, if not as friends. We must do our best to perceive as they perceive, to think as they think. In this way, we can plan our counter-attack, if necessary, with insight and skill— but if we are truly able to get into their shoes, we may find that a win-win solution of our problems is not only pos-sible but also the easiest solution and the one that best meets our needs.

The energy of Strength is dominated by the *explosive enthusiasm* of the Prince of Wands (Air of FIRE) moderated by the *desire for consolidation* of the King of Disks (Fire of EARTH). The absence of Water in Strength's personality echoes the potential aridity of the height of Summer.

The King of Disks:

Kerubic Fire to Mutable Earth
LEO (Strength) to VIRGO (Hermit)

The King of Disks rules the last Decan of Leo and the first two Decans of Virgo. Our *aggressive efforts* to manifest our highest Selves (Leo) require occasional rest periods for *consolidation* (Virgo). The King is Fire of Earth and the Zodiac in Assiah.

The King of Disks uses the powers of *intensity and expansion* of the Ace of Wands applied with the *compassionate aggression* of Strength (Leo) to bring the process of Summer to its conclusion. He does his work under the power and authority of the Ace and Princess of Wands.

The King of Disks brings the energy raised by the Prince of Wands to maturity, *balancing hysteria with application*. In the course of experiencing Summer, the King of Disks impels the spiritual guidance of the Hermit (Virgo).

VIRGO: The Hermit

August 23—September 22

The Hermit has turned the corner from the creative intensity of Spring and Summer. This last of the Signs of Summer is looking forward to the harvest of Autumn—indeed, the harvest has already begun. Standing in his desert place, he holds aloft the lamp of guidance and inspiration: "Here is fulfillment. Here is rest."

The energy of the Hermit is dominated by the *desire for consolidation* of the King of Disks (Fire of EARTH) moderated by the *compassionate intellect* of the Queen of Swords (Water of AIR). Here are the four Elements in relative balance once again—that which has survived the heat of Summer is ready for the coming harvest.

AUTUMN: Libra, Scorpio, Sagittarius

Autumn extends from the Autumnal Equinox to the Winter Solstice. It consists of the Cardinal Air Sign—Libra, the Fixed Water Sign—Scorpio and the Mutable Fire Sign—Sagittarius. Autumn is ruled by Water. In Astrology Water stands for *emotion, sensitivity* and *fluidity*.

The Ace of Cups:

Elemental Water

The Ace of Cups is the power that manifests Autumn—though Autumn is actually initiated by the ripening heat of Summer as transmuted by the Queen of Swords in the last Decan of Virgo.

As Autumn, the Ace of Cups represents the *harvest*, the results of the processes of new growth and ripening of Spring and Summer. Like Spring, the weather is moderate and enjoyable, but where Spring showed us how warm we felt at relatively low temperatures, Autumn shows us how cold we can feel at relatively high temperatures.

The Princess of Cups:

Earth of Water

The Princess of Cups rules, as the Throne of the Ace, Autumn —Libra, Scorpio and Sagittarius. She is Earth of Water and the Planet Earth in Briah.

The Princess of Cups is the transmuting and transmitting personality necessary to bring the power of the Ace of Cups into manifestation on the material plane. She applies her energies to completing the ripening process and manifesting the harvest. She is the most material of the *emotional* personalities.

The Queen of Swords:

Mutable Earth to Cardinal Air
VIRGO (Hermit) to LIBRA (Justice)

The Queen of Swords rules the last Decan of Virgo and the first two Decans of Libra. Dissatisfaction with the *limits of Earth* (Virgo) leads to analysis of perceived options and, therefore, to *judgment* (Libra). She is Water of Air and Saturn in Yetzirah.

The Queen of Swords uses the powers of *intensity and expansion* of the Ace of Wands (Summer) applied with the *guiding spirituality* of the Hermit (Virgo) to initiate the change of Seasons. While she begins this process on the level of the Yang emotions (Fire, Wands, Summer), she carries it out on the level of Yin emotions (Water, Cups, Autumn), under the power and authority of the Ace and Princess of Cups.

The Queen of Swords transmutes the energy raised by the King of Disks, balancing *pragmatism with perception*. In the course of invoking Autumn, the Queen of Swords raises the karmic energy of Justice (Libra).

LIBRA: Justice

September 23—October 22

With Justice, the wheel of karma turns to the *balance point* once more (Autumnal Equinox), then turns again; initiation, growth, harvest...and soon to rest. In Autumn, we take in the results of the seeds we sowed in Spring and the nurturing we gave them in Summer. The energy of Justice is dominated by the *compassionate intellect* of the Queen of Swords (Water of AIR) moderated by, or in this case, augmented by the *expressive poetry* of the Prince of Cups (Air of WATER). Justice contains neither spiritual Fire nor grounding Earth—it reaches its decision on the basis of intellect and emotion alone, swayed by neither inspiration nor practicality.

The Prince of Cups:

Cardinal Air to Kerubic Water
LIBRA (Justice) to SCORPIO (Death)

The Prince of Cups rules the last Decan of Libra and the first two Decans of Scorpio. The impartial, intellectual *Justice* of Libra causes the emotional Death of Scorpio. He is Air in Water and the Sun in Briah.

The Prince of Cups uses the powers of *sensitivity and fluidity* of the Ace of Cups (Autumn) applied with the *karmically cleansing energies* of Justice (Libra) to sustain the momentum established by the Queen of Swords. He works on the emotional level (Water, Cups) under the power and authority of the Ace and Princess of Cups.

The Prince of Cups manifests the fruit of the energy of the Queen of Swords, balancing *perfectionism with artistry*. In the course of manifesting Autumn, the Prince of Cups establishes the intense transition of Death (Scorpio).

SCORPIO: Death

October 23—November 22

As the night lengthens and the cold grows, the *harvest is gathered in* and the perennial plants wither and fall. In traditional pastoral cultures, the herds were culled during Scorpio—with Samhain at its head, Scorpio was the month of slaughter. (Is there enough to last through the coming Winter? Or shall we, too, fall in the coming darkness?)

The energy of Death is dominated by the *expressive poetry* of the Prince of Cups (Air of WATER) moderated by the *ferocious spirituality* of the King of Wands (Fire of FIRE). In the absence of Earth, Death uproots all living things—if not literally, by turning our attention away from growth and toward survival.

The King of Wands:

Kerubic Water to Mutable Fire
SCORPIO (Death) to SAGITTARIUS (Temperance)

The King of Wands rules the last Decan of Scorpio and the first two Decans of Sagittarius. From Death (Scorpio) arise the fiery arrows of the Centaur (Sagittarius). Fire of Fire. The Zodiac in Atziluth.

The King of Wands uses the powers of *sensitivity and fluidity* of the Ace of Cups applied with the *dispassionate spirituality* of Death (Scorpio) to bring the process of Autumn to its conclusion. He does his work under the power and authority of the Ace and Princess of Cups.

The King of Wands brings the energy raised by the Prince of Cups to maturity, balancing *emotional thinking with creative intensity.* In the course of experiencing Autumn, the King of Wands impels the spiritual growth of Temperance (Sagittarius).

SAGITTARIUS: Temperance

November 23—December 21

Autumn draws to a close under the dominion of Temperance, ending on the longest night of the year. We have done all we can of a material nature and must now look to the Divine for our survival. In the growing darkness, we prepare to celebrate the rebirth of Light at Yule.

The energy of Temperance is dominated by the *ferocious spirituality* of the King of Wands (Fire of FIRE) moderated by the *manifesting fertility* of the Queen of Disks (Water of EARTH). Lacking Air, Temperance is concerned with the direct understanding (intuitive as opposed to analytical) and acceptance of the Unity of Kether and Malkuth—the Creator and the Created are one—as above, so below.

WINTER: Capricorn, Aquarius, Pisces

Winter extends from the Winter Solstice to the Vernal Equinox. It consists of the Cardinal Earth Sign—Capricorn, the Fixed Air Sign—Aquarius and the Mutable Water Sign—Pisces. Winter is ruled by Air. In Astrology, Air stands for *communication, relationship* and *intellect*.

The Ace of Swords:

Elemental Air

The Ace of Swords is the power that manifests Winter—though Winter is actually initiated by the contracting emotionalism of Autumn as transmitted by the Queen of Disks in the last Decan of Sagittarius.

As Winter, the Ace of Swords represents the *threat of death and the intelligence necessary to prevent it*; death from cold and the foresight to gather firewood—death from starvation and the knowledge to store food—death from despair— and power to focus the mind on the invisible Spring yet to come.

The Princess of Swords:

Earth of Air

The Princess of Swords rules, as the Throne of the Power of the Ace, Winter: Capricorn, Aquarius and Pisces. She is Earth of Air and the Planet Earth in Yetzirah.

The Princess of Swords is the transmuting and transmitting personality necessary to bring the power of the Ace of Swords into manifestation on the material plane. She applies her energies to winnowing, to breaking rock, to inspiring the thoughts that drive away fear. She is the most material of the *intellectual* personalities.

The Queen of Disks:

Mutable Fire to Cardinal Earth
SAGITTARIUS (Temperance) to CAPRICORN (Devil)

The Queen of Disks rules the last Decan of Sagittarius and the first two Decans of Capricorn. ("I shot an arrow into the air [Sagittarius] but it fell and hit my derriere [Capricorn].") She is Water of Earth and Saturn in Assiah. And she has an earthy sense of humor.

The Queen of Disks uses the powers of *sensitivity and fluidity* of the Ace of Cups (Autumn) applied with the *manifesting idealism* of Temperance (Sagittarius) to initiate the change of Seasons. While she begins this process on the level of Yin emotions (Water, Cups, Autumn), she carries it out on the intellectual level (Air, Swords, Winter), under the power and authority of the Ace and Princess of Swords.

The Queen of Disks transmutes the energy raised by the King of Disks, and of Autumn, balancing *passion with pragmatism*. In the course of invoking Winter, the Queen of Disks raises the materialistic backlash of the Devil (Capricorn).

CAPRICORN: The Devil

December 22— January 20

Following the Winter Solstice, we face the coldest, darkest time of year, and here the Devil rules. Waiting for Spring, we have, if anything, too much time to think—about our selves, our *material needs*, the restrictions and burdens of our lives. And we distract ourselves with drunkenness (or curse the lack of drink), with sex (or curse our unfulfilled desire), with food (or curse our hunger and our lack).

The energy of the Devil is dominated by the *manifesting fertility* of the Queen of Disks (Water of EARTH) moderated by the *active hopes and fears* of the Prince of Swords (Air of AIR). Devoid of Fire, the Devil is all thoughts and feeling about our material condition (this is, of course, pure hell)—beginning with the longest night of the year, Capricorn leads the Signs in suicides—the heart of darkness.

The Prince of Swords:

Cardinal Earth to Kerubic Air
CAPRICORN (Devil) to AQUARIUS (Star)

The Prince of Swords rules the last Decan of Capricorn and the first two of Aquarius. The reaction to *material work* (Capricorn) causes the *Waters of Life* to be meted out to us proportionately (Aquarius). He is Air of Air and the Sun in Yetzirah.

The Prince of Swords uses the powers of *intelligence and objectivity* of the Ace of Swords (Winter) applied with the *material sensuality* of the Devil (Capricorn) to sustain the momentum established by the Queen of Disks. He works on the mental level (Air, Swords, Winter) under the power and authority of the Ace and Princess of Swords.

The Prince of Swords manifests the fruit of the energy of the Queen of Disks, balancing *fatalism with analysis*. In the course of manifesting Winter, the Prince of Swords establishes the conscious faith in the Divine Source shown by the Star (Aquarius).

AQUARIUS: The Star

January 21—February 20

Under the Star, we first notice that night is not so long—that new light grows. Once again, our *faith in the Light* appears to be rewarded. Winter is not forever. Our needs are met from Divine Sources, as well as from material resources. We turn from our personal compulsions to the sparkle of the One Light. We burn the boughs of Yule at Candlemas.

The energy of the Star is dominated by the *active hopes and fears* of the Prince of Swords (Air of AIR) moderated by the *exalting grace* of the King of Cups (Fire of WATER). Ungrounded and vaporous, the Star rules over the coldest part of the year, but the day lengthens and hope is reborn in the mind—though evidence of the validity of hope is still hidden.

The King of Cups:

Kerubic Air to Mutable Water
AQUARIUS (Star) to PISCES (Moon)

The King of Cups rules the last Decan of Aquarius and the first two Decans of Pisces. From the airy conceptions of the Water Bearer (Aquarius) flow forth the oceans rich in Fishes (Pisces). Fire of Water. The Zodiac in Briah.

The King of Cups uses the powers of *intellect and objectivity* of the Ace of Swords applied with the *spiritual faith* of the Star (Aquarius) to bring the process of Winter to its conclusion. He does his work under the power and authority of the Ace and Princess of Swords.

The King of Cups brings the energy raised by the Prince of Swords to maturity, balancing *judgment with compassion*. In the course of experiencing Winter, the King of Cups impels the occult processes which lead to pure spiritual understanding of the Moon (Pisces).

PISCES: The Moon

February 21—March 20

At the end of Winter we look both backward and ahead, trying to find the underlying sense of things—the meaning of life. Death has come in plenty and we have only the *promise of new life*, though we must plant seeds now in the faith that they will take root when warm weather comes. (Will the Light truly return, or is this hint of Spring a jest perpetrated by evil spirits? Will the monster that has swallowed the warmth of our Sun be persuaded to eject it again, or will our Source of Light and Life be lost forever? No, look, the Sun comes once again [knock wood].)

The energy of the Moon is dominated by the *exalting grace* of the King of Cups (Fire of WATER) augmented by the *emotional intensity* of the Queen of Wands (Water of FIRE). At the end of Winter, the first two Elements flow within and through each other, preparing the emulsion out of which mediating Air shall produce Earth.

Conclusion

Here ends a very brief over-view of the way the Tarot cards are assigned to the Astrological Signs, Cusps and Seasons. I hope it sheds some illumination on the manner in which these components influence each other. Remembering, for instance, that Death is supervised by the Prince of Cups with the King of Wands under the influence of the Ace and Princess of Cups, should give insight into the meanings of each of these cards and the way they function in a reading.

ABOUT THE AUTHOR

Thom Parrott, born in Washington, D.C., on the 21st of July, 1944 at 7:30 PM, began reading the Tarot in 1980 while taking a class in Wicca from Oz in Albuquerque, NM. The ritual beginning his initiation into the Craft was performed the evening John Lennon was killed.

In the intervening years, Mr. Parrott has studied various occult arts and sciences including Astrology and Ceremonial Magick, always focusing on the Tarot as his preferred method of Divination and as an explication of the Unity of All Things within a Single Divine Whole.

Thom is an award winning songwriter and performer with two albums in release. With A.A. MacGregor, he co-authored the award winning and successfully produced play: "The Murder Game".

By the Signs of the Earth:
Geomancy in the Golden Dawn

Mitch & Gail Henson

Perhaps more than any other method of divination Geomancy lends itself to the style of magical evocation as taught by the Hermetic Order of the Golden Dawn. In spite of this it has never gained the same degree of popularity as the Tarot and the other systems of second sight that the Order has made available to its initiates.

It should be kept in mind that the Golden Dawn was not nor is it now a school for fortune tellers. It teaches several systems of divination with the express intent of defining an individual's progress along his/her chosen path.

In spite of its affinity with evocation, Geomancy seems to be the most neglected method of divination taught by the Order. There are several reasons for this. The most prominent, is its seeming complexity. Like other methods taught by the Order, this guarantees great accuracy with little room for self delusion, though it must be admitted that, unlike other divinatory methods, Geomancy offers the greatest chance of misinterpretation. Stephen Skinner, in his well-presented study *The Oracle of Geomancy*, points out that since we are dealing with the Geomantic spirits, we should take care how our questions are asked, because the answers are only going to reflect the most literal form of the question.

The guiding principles for the divination are the entities known as *Geomantic Spirits*. According to a theory promoted by Aleister Crowley, these are separate and distinct from our intuitive faculties, they are a sentient order of beings with a life unto themselves. As he points out, "We postulate the existence of intelligences, either within or without the diviner, of which he is not immediately conscious. (It does not matter whether the communicating spirit so called is an objective entity or a concealed portion of the diviner's mind.)"

This being the case the system is unlike others in that the psychic awareness of the diviner is of no importance one way or the other. It is the magician's ability to evoke the spirit that becomes the focus of consideration for a successful Geomantic divination.

Israel Regardie states, "All previous works dealing with Geomancy are defective in this one particular area at least, the omission of that procedure which is an initiated technique.

"Geomancy is divination through the Element of Earth. In one of the rituals of the Hermetic Order of the Golden Dawn the initiate is sworn to invoke, in his workings, the highest name of God that he knows. In this way, whatever he does will come under the guidance and benediction of the highest spiritual force that he knows. Thus the ruler of the Element of Earth has to be magically invoked so that it may truly govern this work of prognostication."

From that point, invoking the God-name *Adonai ha-Aretz*, we follow the hierarchies to the Geomantic spirit most concerned with the question at hand. Though it is nowhere explained in the existing literature, it is at least implied that a full ceremony of evocation should be conducted to insure the success of the operation. So there, we've just further complicated the system. Be that as it may, this should be an incentive to entice the magician to seriously consider Geomancy as a viable form of divination. Later we will give the details for proceeding with a Geomantic evocation.

As stated by Regardie, Geomancy is divination through the Element of Earth. It is defined by a binary system of dots in odd or even points. As taught by the Golden Dawn, this may be done with a pencil and a piece of paper; but for such a significant operation, we suggest the use of a consecrated box of earth and a wand designed for that purpose. For the construction and consecration of these tools see Chic and Sandra Ciceros' *Secrets of a Golden Dawn Temple* pp. 508-517 (Llewellyn Publications, 1992).

At first glance, as stated earlier, the system seems somewhat complex. This should not deter the magician from applying him/herself to the discipline. The following chart notes the various Elements of the Geomantic system:

No.	Geom. Fig.	Name	Sign	Element	Ruler	Planet
1	● / ● / ●● / ●	**Puer**	Aries	Fire	Bartzabel	Mars
2	● / ●● / ● / ●●	**Amissio**	Taurus	Earth	Kedemel	Venus
3	●● / ●● / ● / ●●	**Albus**	Gemini	Air	Taphthar-tharath	Mercury
4	●● / ●● / ●● / ●●	**Populus**	Cancer	Water	Chasmodai	Moon
5	●● / ●● / ● / ●	**Fortuna Major**	Leo	Fire	Sorath	Sun
6	●● / ● / ● / ●●	**Conjunctio**	Virgo	Earth	Taphthar-tharath	Mercury
7	● / ●● / ● / ●	**Puella**	Libra	Air	Kedemel	Venus
8	●● / ● / ●● / ●●	**Rubeus**	Scorpio	Water	Bartzabel	Mars

No.	Geom. Fig.	Name	Sign	Element	Ruler	Planet
9		**Acquisitio**	Sagittarius	Fire	Hismael	Jupiter
10		**Carcer**	Capricorn	Earth	Zazel	Saturn
11		**Tristitia**	Aquarius	Air	Zazel	Saturn
12		**Laetitia**	Pisces	Water	Hismael	Jupiter
13		**Cauda Draconis**		Fire	Zazel/ Bartzabel	Saturn/ Mars
14		**Caput Draconis**		Earth	Hismael/ Kedemel	Venus/ Jupiter
15		**Fortuna Minor**	Leo	Fire	Sorath	Sol
16		**Via**	Cancer	Water	Chasmodai	Luna

At this point we append the Sigils of the Rulers:

Ruler	Sigil
Bartzabel	
Kedemel	
Taphthartharath	
Chasmodai	
Sorath	
Hismael	
Zazel	

Since the divination deals solely with the Element of Earth only the following divine names should be used when invoking the appropriate Geni:

Sphere	Divine Name	Archangelic name	Choir of Angels
Malkuth	**Adonai ha-Aretz**	**Auriel**	**Ashim**

Depending on the Ruler (Spirit) to be invoked the following planets and beings should be used when appropriate:

Planet	Angel	Intelligence	Spirit (Ruler)
Saturn	Cassiel	Agiel	Zazel
Jupiter	Sachiel	Iophiel	Hismael
Mars	Zamael	Graphiel	Bartzabel
Sol	Michael	Nakhiel	Sorath
Venus	Hanael	Hagiel	Kedemel
Mercury	Raphael	Tiriel	Taphthartharath
Luna	Gabriel	Malkah be Tarshism ve-ad Ruachoth Schechalim	Schad Barschemoth ha-Shartathan

Table of Planetary or Magical Hours

	Sunday	Monday	Tuesday	Wednesday	Thursday	Friday	Saturday
Sunrise							
1st hr	☉	☽	♂	☿	♃	♀	♄
2nd hr	♀	♄	☉	☽	♂	☿	♃
3rd hr	☿	♃	♀	♄	☉	☽	♂
4th hr	☽	♂	☿	♃	♀	♄	☉
5th hr	♄	☉	☽	♂	☿	♃	♀
6th hr	♃	♀	♄	☉	☽	♂	☿
7th hr	♂	☿	♃	♀	♄	☉	☽
8th hr	☉	☽	♂	☿	♃	♀	♄
9th hr	♀	♄	☉	☽	♂	☿	♃
10th hr	☿	♃	♀	♄	☉	☽	♂
11th hr	☽	♂	☿	♃	♀	♄	☉
12th hr	♄	☉	☽	♂	☿	♃	♀
Sunset							
1st hr	♃	♀	♄	☉	☽	♂	☿
2nd hr	♂	☿	♃	♀	♄	☉	☽
3rd hr	☉	☽	♂	☿	♃	♀	♄
4th hr	♀	♄	☉	☽	♂	☿	♃
5th hr	☿	♃	♀	♄	☉	☽	♂
6th hr	☽	♂	☿	♃	♀	♄	☉
7th hr	♄	☉	☽	♂	☿	♃	♀
8th hr	♃	♀	♄	☉	☽	♂	☿
9th hr	♂	☿	♃	♀	♄	☉	☽
10th hr	☉	☽	♂	☿	♃	♀	♄
11th hr	♀	♄	☉	☽	♂	☿	♃
12th hr	☿	♃	♀	♄	☉	☽	♂

The Sigils for the above chart can be determined by using the Kameas associated with the planets. These can be found in *The Golden Dawn* by Israel Regardie (Llewellyn Publications, 1989) and *The Magician's Companion* by Bill Whitcomb (Llewellyn Publications, 1992).

Because the spirits are of a planetary order, the day and hour for the evocation must be observed for the divination to be effective. The following table should be consulted prior to a Geomantic ritual and divination:

The correct hour for the ritual is found by dividing the total time between sunrise and sunset by twelve. You will then have the length for the magical hours of the day. The same applies by dividing the time between sunset and sunrise to get the length of the planetary hours at night.

The following list of Geomantic figures gives the general meanings to the characters.

Geomantic Figure	Latin Name	English	Divinatory Meaning
1	**Puer**	Boy	Boy, yellow, beardless, inconsiderate, good rather than bad.
2	**Amissio**	Loss	A bad figure. Loss or that which is taken away.
3	**Albus**	White	Fair, wisdom, clear thought. Good.
4	**Populus**	People	Indifferent, congregation.
5	**Fortuna Major**	The Greater Fortune	Greater fortune, Success, protection. Very good.
6	**Conjunctio**	Conjunction	Union, assembling, good.
7	**Puella**	Girl	A girl, pretty face, not very good.
8	**Rubeus**	Red	Very bad. Red, vice, fiery temper.

9	●● ● ●● ●	**Acquisitio**	Gain	Obtaining, success, absorbing, receiving. A good figure.
10	● ●● ●● ●	**Carcer**	Prison	Bound. Good or bad depending on the nature of the question.
11	●● ●● ●● 	**Tristitia**	Sorrow	Damned, sorrow, grief, a bad figure.
12	● ●● ●● ●●	**Laetitia**	Joy	Joy, laughing, a good figure.
13	● ● ● ●●	**Cauda Draconis**	Dragon's Tail	The dragon's tail, exit, a bad figure
14	●● ● ● ●	**Caput Draconis**	Dragon's Head	The head, dragon's head. entrance, a good figure.
15	● ● ●● ●●	**Fortuna Minor**	Lesser Fortune	Lesser aid, safeguard, external figure, a good figure.
16	● ● ● ●	**Via**	Way	Way, street, neither good nor bad.

Aleister Crowley wrote the following mnemonic rhyme for his magical son (Charles Stansfeld Jones) in June of 1918:

> *Caput Draconis: Strong and fierce*
> *Of whorls—which Acquisitio beginning keeps spinning.*
> *Puer's a boy, with all a boy's endeavour;*
> *Puella's rather good but not to clever.*
> *Fortuna Minor means a lucky touch;*
> *Fortuna Major more, maybe too much.*
> *Via means change, apart from Querent's action.*
> *Populus, settling down, with satisfaction.*
> *Rubeus always gives a nasty jar,*
> *And Carcer tends to keep you where you are.*
> *Conjunctio brings about completion; Albus*
> *Is whiter than the walls once built by Balbus.*
> *Tristitia lags, with heavy antic motion:*
> *Laetitia is like the laughing ocean.*
> *Amissio: loves come, and goods diminish.*
> *Cauda Draconis means—a sticky finish.*

If we place the figures side by side in the following table, the student should find it a little easier to assimilate the characters:

Acquisitio	⣏	**Amissio**	⣏
Albus	⣏	**Rubeus**	⣏
Puella	⣏	**Puer**	⣏
Laetitia	⣏	**Tristitia**	⣏

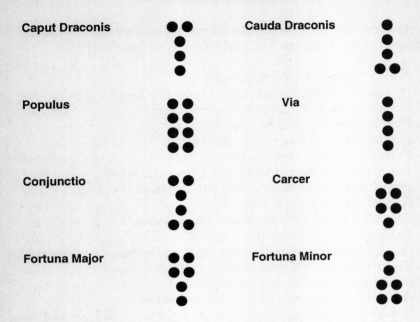

Caput Draconis

Cauda Draconis

Populus

Via

Conjunctio

Carcer

Fortuna Major

Fortuna Minor

Please note that the Geomantic figures DO NOT have an independent existence nor should they be confused with the spirits. In point of fact, the spirits, so named are the Planetary Rulers. To suggest that the figures are sentient would be something like stating an independent awareness for the sign of Scorpio in Astrology. It should also be noted that the angels invoked are planetary because of Geomancy's association with Astrology.

In essence the same method for the consecration of the Box and Wand discussed in Chic and Sandra Cicero's *Secrets of a Golden Dawn Temple* (Llewellyn Publications, 1992) applies to the following invocation.

The terms evocation and invocation are used almost interchangeably within the context of Geomancy because as a method of divination its main focus resides within the purview of invocation. On the other hand the context is one of ceremonial magic which relies exclusively on evocation.

Let's look at a sample Geomantic evocation/divination. The nature of the question will determine the Ruler and consequently the hierarchy to be followed. In the following example the question pertains to how long the Querent will be able to afford his/her present address. Since this is a question involving finances the planet consulted will be Jupiter and the Ruler is Hismael.

GEOMANTIC EVOCATION

The magician is fully robed. A black candle and any incense associated with the Element of Earth is placed on the altar. Place the consecrated box in the North of the Temple.

Perform the Lesser Banishing Ritual of the Pentagram and the Lesser Banishing Ritual of the Hexagram.

Next perform the Supreme Invoking Ritual of the Pentagram for Earth. Draw the Invoking Pentagram of Spirit (Passive) and the Invoking Earth Pentagram while vibrating **"NANTA, AGLA"** and **"EMOR DIAL HECTEGA, ADONAI."** Do this in all four quarters. Trace a circle with the consecrated Wand in the dirt contained in the box. Inside the circle trace the Invoking Pentagram of Earth. Inside the Pentagram trace the Sigil of the Ruler; in this case, Hismael.

Stand facing north and vibrate the name **"ADONAI HA-ARETZ"**, light the black candle then light the incense. Trace the sign of Taurus over the box.

Standing in the 1=10 grade, the sign of Zelator and say, **"In the divine name of ADONAI HA ARETZ, I invoke the mighty and powerful Archangel, AURIEL, come forth and invest this divination with Truth. I invoke thee choir of Angels ASHIM, thou souls of flame, I invoke thee SACHIEL, thou Angel of Malkuth who rules the day and hour of Jupiter."**

Trace the Sigil of SACHIEL over the consecrated box. **"Come thou forth IOPHIEL to manifest the spirit HISMAEL."**

Trace the Sigils of IOPHIEL and HISMAEL over the box. **"Come forth I say and invest this working with the truth of what I perceive."**

At this point begin the actual divination by allowing the wand to tap the consecrated Earth. When you have intuitively determined the number of dots, stop and count them. On a piece of paper retained for this purpose, make two marks if the number is even. If the number of dots had been odd you would make one mark. Smooth out the area in the box taking care not to deface the circle and pentagram. Begin the procedure with the wand, marking the consecrated Earth as before. After you're finished, count the number of dots and depending on whether it is even or odd, place your mark on the paper under the first dot or dots. Do this a total of four times. The result is a Geomantic figure. Follow this by creating three more figures in the same manner. These four figures are called the *Mothers*. Write the figures down on the paper from right to left in the order obtained. (Note: if the Second Mother {Ascendant} happens to be the Rubeus or Cauda Draconis, scrap the divination and try again after a couple of hours have passed.) To the left of the top row write the word *Head*. In the next row down write the word *Neck*. For the next row write down the word *Body* and the bottom row write down the word *Feet*. Your figures should appear something like this:

Mothers	IV	III	II	I
Head	●	● ●	●	● ●
Neck	● ●	●	●	● ●
Body	●	●	●	●
Feet	● ●	●	● ●	●

At this point you can banish and close the Temple. You are ready to proceed with the basic mechanics of determining a Geomantic chart.

Geomancy uses groupings usually referred to as **Mothers, Daughters, Nephews, Witnesses,** and a **Judge.** We have already generated the Mothers; next we will generate the four *Daughters*. This is done by taking the dots from the four heads of the Mothers and laying them on top of one another from I to IV:

Heads of Mothers

	IV	III	II	I		
	●	● ●	●	●	=	●
						●
						● ●
						●

Do the same with the necks :

Necks of Mothers

	IV	III	II	I		
	● ●	●	●	● ●	=	● ●
						●
						●
						● ●

With the bodies :

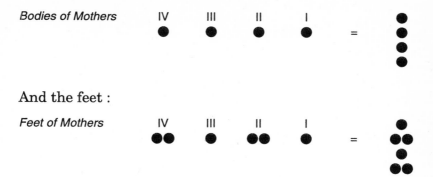

And the feet :

Thus from the four Mothers, we have just created the four Daughters. Before we proceed to generate the Nephews we will begin our spread:

Daughters   **Mothers**

VIII   VII   VI   V   IV   III   II   I

The *Nephews* are generated in a somewhat different manner. By adding the dots of two figures together you will get an odd or even number. If the number was even you would put down two dots. If it were odd you would put down one dot. In our example to get Nephew IX we will take Mothers I and II, add the two dots labeled *Heads* which gives you an even number. Put down two dots. Add the three dots labeled *Necks* giving you an odd number. Put down one dot. For the *Bodies* you will get an even number or two dots and finally for the *Feet* you will get an odd number or one dot:

Nephew IX

Following the same procedure with Mothers III and IV you should be able to generate:

Nephew X

We now obtain Nephews XI and XII by following the same procedure with the two sets of Daughters:

Nephew XII   **Nephew XI**

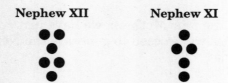

From the four Nephews we will now obtain the two *Witnesses*. Follow the same formula as before to acquire the following:

Witness XIV   **Witness XIII**

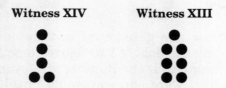

The final step is obtain the *Judge* from the two Witnesses:

Judge XV

You are ready to lay the spread and interpret. Note, if the answer is not clear you have the option to clarify the response by combining Mother I and Judge XV to obtain the *Reconciler* XVI. This does not hold true if you simply do not like the response. Do not insult the oracle.

Our spread is laid down in this manner:

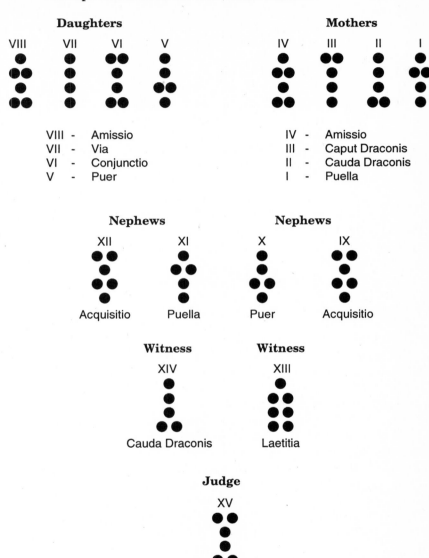

Daughters

| VIII | VII | VI | V |

VIII - Amissio
VII - Via
VI - Conjunctio
V - Puer

Mothers

| IV | III | II | I |

IV - Amissio
III - Caput Draconis
II - Cauda Draconis
I - Puella

Nephews

| XII | XI |

Acquisitio   Puella

Nephews

| X | IX |

Puer   Acquisitio

Witness

XIV

Cauda Draconis

Witness

XIII

Laetitia

Judge

XV

Conjunctio

For a quick reading all we need to do is examine the Judge and the two Witnesses. Relative to our example question, the answer from the Judge is positive since Conjunctio deals with assembling, union, and coming together. Well aspected, it is considered good. Next we look at the Left Witness—Cauda Draconis is not good. We will reserve judgment until we have examined the Right Witness—Laetitia. This is a good figure associated with joy and is quite healthy. Pulling these three figures together we might conclude that in the normal course of getting the rent or mortgage together we could see some rough times ahead but will never really have any major difficulties affording our present dwelling. If the answer were ambiguous we would add Mother I with Judge XV to get the Reconciler to further clarify the answer. Since the answer is clear it would be pointless to try to elucidate the reading with the Reconciler. If more detail is desired we would refer back to the First Mother for the beginning of the matter. Figure IV gives us the termination of the matter and ends the interpretation.

Astro-Geomancy

It is interesting to note that there are striking similarities between Astrological Geomancy as practiced by the Dahomey tribe in Africa, in Arabic speaking countries and Europe.

Stephen Skinner suggests that European Geomancy originated in the Middle East. It traveled by parallel routes to Africa and the western continent. This explains the Astrological association between Geomancy as practiced in the Middle East, Europe and Africa. Though speculative, Skinners' theory seems the best possible model for us to use. We are fairly certain that the house system developed in Europe and came to fruition through the work of Cornilius Agrippa.

The following diagram is an older version of the Astrological wheel. It is used here to distinguish between Astrology and astro-Geomancy. The houses are numbered counterclockwise rotating down the square.

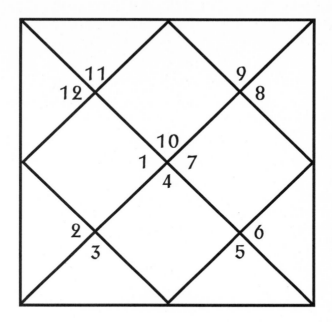

Once the Geomantic figures are placed in their respective houses we might find it convenient to add the number of points contained in the figures then divide them by twelve. The remainder will tell us where the Part of Fortune ⊕ is to be placed. The *Part of Fortune* refers directly to ready cash belonging the Querent.

It is important to remember that Astrology and Geomancy are two separate and distinct fields of divination and although Geomancy blends with Astrology, it is a marriage of convenience. It would be the gravest error to run an Astrological chart to compare to your Geomantic chart.

Please note that in a Geomancy chart the figures are placed according to *angular, succedent* and *cadent* houses. These are angular 1, 10, 7 and 4; the succedent 2, 11, 8 and 5; and the cadent houses are 9, 6, 3 and 12.

Angular means those houses placed on the angles, the horizon in the East and West, at the midheaven and directly below the Earth. Those houses following the angular houses are called the succedent and those furthest from the angular houses are the cadent houses.

The basis for using an Astrological chart in Geomancy is the meanings contained within the house structure. The following defines the meaning of the each house:

1st House: Personality of the Querent, his life, health, habits, behavior and other personal characteristics.

2nd House: Money, property, finances, possible theft through negligence or loss.

3rd House: Communication, relatives by blood, letters, news, short journeys, writing, other pursuits associated with Mercury.

4th House: Home, inheritance, possessions, hidden treasure, environment, retirement, the conclusion of any matter. Information about theft or thieves.

5th House: Women, luxury, drinking, procreation, creation, artistic work. Gambling and speculation.

6th House: Employees, sickness, which body parts are most likely to suffer illness or injury. Domestic animals and close relatives other than immediate family.

7th House: Love, marriage, prostitution, partnerships. Public enemies, lawsuits, war opponents, thieves and dishonor.

8th House: Death, Wills, legacies. Poverty.

9th House: Long journeys, relationships with foreigners, science, the church, art, religion dreams and divinations.

10th House: Fame, reputation, honor, mother, trade authority.

11th House: Friends, social contacts, altruistic organizations.

12th House: Sorrow, hospitals, intrigue, prisons, restrictions, unseen dangers, fears.

The figures are placed in the houses according to the following chart:

Mothers:		Daughters		Nephews:	
I	House 10	V	House 11	IX	House 12
II	House 1	VI	House 2	X	House 3
III	House 4	VII	House 5	XI	House 6
IV	House 7	VIII	House 8	XII	House 9

The Second Mother is placed in the *ascendant* or the first house. Our example has produced Cauda Draconis. If either Cauda Draconis or Rubeus comes up as the ascendant the chart must be forfeit and a new reading done. Under such circumstances, a minimum of two hours must pass before a new reading is commenced.

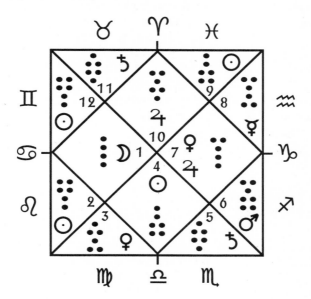

The astro-Geomantic chart above contains the newly generated Geomantic figures and the Zodiacal signs. These are placed by taking the corresponding sign for the second Mother and placing it next to the ascendant or the first house and following the sequence of houses in the same manner that a standard horoscope is erected. After we insert the signs we can add the ruling planets for our Geomantic figures.

The following set of tables is taken from Israel Regardie's *The Golden Dawn* (Llewellyn Publications) and denotes the essential integrity of the Geomantic figure in their relationship to the houses.

ACQUISITIO
Generally good for profit and gain.

Ascendant	Happy, success in all things.
Second House	Very prosperous.
Third House	Favor and riches.
Fourth House	Good fortune and success.
Fifth House	Good success
Sixth House	Good - especially if it agrees with the 5th.
Seventh House	Reasonably good.
Eighth House	Rather good, but not very. The sick shall die.
Ninth House	Good in all demands.
Tenth House	Good in suits.
Eleventh House	Good in all,
Twelfth House	Evil,[1] pain and loss.

AMISSIO
Good for loss of substance and
sometimes for love; but very bad for gain.

Ascendant	Ill in all things but for prisoners.
Second House	Very Ill for money, but good for love.
Third House	Ill end-except for quarrels.
Fourth House	Ill in all.
Fifth House	Evil except for agriculture.
Sixth House	Rather evil for love.
Seventh House	Very good for love, otherwise evil.
Eighth House	Excellent in all questions.
Ninth House	Evil in all things.
Tenth House	Evil except for favor with women.
Eleventh House	Good for love, otherwise bad.
Twelfth House	Evil in all things.

FORTUNA MAJOR
Good for gain in all things where a person
has hopes to win.

---

[1] Since the above was written, attitudes have changed regarding the nature of evil as the idea per-
.tains to Magic. We have no intention of degressing but would advise the reader to substitute
"Unfavorable" for "Evil."

Ascendant	Good save in secrecy.
Second House	Good except in sad things.
Third House	Good in all.
Fourth House	Good in all, but melancholy.
Fifth House	Very good in all things.
Sixth House	Very good except for debauchery.
Seventh House	Good in all.
Eighth House	Moderately good.
Ninth House	Very good.
Tenth House	Exceedingly good. Go to superiors
Eleventh House	Very good.
Twelfth House	Good in all.

FORTUNA MINOR
Good in any manner in which a person wishes to proceed quickly.

Ascendant	Speed in victory and in love, but choleric.
Second House	Very good.
Third House	Good - but wrathful.
Fourth House	Haste; rather evil except for peace.
Fifth House	Good in all things.
Sixth House	Medium in all.
Seventh House	Evil except for war or love.
Eighth House	Evil generally.
Ninth House	Good, but choleric.
Tenth House	Good, except for peace.
Eleventh House	Good, especially for love.
Twelfth House	Good, except for alternation, or for serving[2] another.

LAETITIA
Good for joy, present or to come.

Ascendant	Good, except in war.
Second House	Sickly.
Third House	Ill.
Fourth House	Mainly good.

---

[2] In the Fourth, Fifth, and Sixth Editions of *The Golden Dawn* from Llewellyn and all editions of *The Complete Golden Dawn System of Magic* from New Falcon this word had been "Suing." In Crowley's "A Handbook of Geomancy" published in *The Equinox Vol I No. 2* we find the word "Serving." Crowley's work is a slightly edited version of the MacGregor Mathers original.

Fifth House	Excellently good.
Sixth House	Evil generally.
Seventh House	Indifferent.
Eighth House	Evil generally.
Ninth House	Very good.
Tenth House	Good, rather in war than in peace.
Eleventh House	Good in all.
Twelfth House	Evil generally.

TRISTITIA
Evil in almost all things.

Ascendant	Medium, but good for treasure and fortifying.
Second House	Medium, but good to fortify.
Third House	Evil in all.
Fourth House	Evil in all.
Fifth House	Very Evil.
Sixth House	Evil, except for debauchery.
Seventh House	Evil for inheritance and magic only.
Eighth House	Evil, but in secrecy good.
Ninth House	Evil except for magic.
Tenth House	Evil except for fortifications.
Eleventh House	Evil in all.
Twelfth House	Evil. But good for magic and treasure.

PUELLA
Good in all demands, especially in those relating to women.

Ascendant	Good except in war.
Second House	Very good.
Third House	Good.
Fourth House	Indifferent.
Fifth House	Very good, but notice the aspects.
Sixth House	Good, but especially for debauchery.
Seventh House	Good except for war.
Eighth House	Good.
Ninth House	Good for music. Otherwise only medium.
Tenth House	Good for peace.
Eleventh House	Good, and love of ladies.
Twelfth House	Good in all.

PUER
Evil in most demands, except in those relating to War or Love.

Ascendant	Indifferent. Best in War.
Second House	Good, but with trouble.
Third House	Good fortune.
Fourth House	Evil, except in war and love.
Fifth House	Medium good.
Sixth House	Medium.
Seventh House	Evil, save in War.
Eighth House	Evil, save for love.
Ninth House	Evil except for War.
Tenth House	Rather evil. But good for love and War. Most other things medium.
Eleventh House	Medium; good favor.
Twelfth House	Very good in all.

RUBEUS
Evil in all that is good and Good in all that is Evil.

Ascendant	Destroy the figure if it falls here! It makes the judgment worthless.
Second House	Evil in all demands.
Third House	Evil except to let blood.
Fourth House	Evil except in War and Fire.
Fifth House	Evil save for love, and sowing seed.
Sixth House	Evil except for bloodletting.
Seventh House	Evil except for war and fire.
Eighth House	Evil.
Ninth House	Very Evil.
Tenth House	Dissolute. Love, fire.
Eleventh House	Evil, except to let blood.
Twelfth House	Evil in all things.

ALBUS
Good for profit and for entering into a place or undertaking.

Ascendant	Good for marriage. Mercurial. Peace.
Second House	Good in all.

Third House	Very good.
Fourth House	Very good except in War.
Fifth House	Good.
Sixth House	Good in all things.
Seventh House	Good except in all things.
Eighth House	Good.
Ninth House	A messenger brings a letter.
Tenth House	Excellent in all.
Eleventh House	Very good.
Twelfth House	Marvelously good.

CONJUNCTIO
Good with good, or evil with evil.
Recovery from things lost.

Ascendant	Good with good, evil with evil.
Second House	Commonly good.
Third House	Good fortune.
Fourth House	Good save for health; see the eighth.
Fifth House	Medium.
Sixth House	Good for immorality only.
Seventh House	Rather good.
Eighth House	Evil, death.
Ninth House	Medium good.
Tenth House	For love, good. For sickness, evil.
Eleventh House	Good in all.
Twelfth House	Medium. Bad for prisoners.

CARCER
Generally evil. Delay, binding,
bar, restriction.

Ascendant	Evil except to fortify a place.
Second House	Good in Saturnine questions; else evil.
Third House	Evil
Fourth House	Good only for melancholy.
Fifth House	Receive a letter within three days. Evil.
Sixth House	Very evil.
Seventh House	Evil.
Eighth House	Very evil.
Ninth House	Evil in all.

Tenth House	Evil save in hidden treasure.
Eleventh House	Much anxiety.
Twelfth House	Rather good.

CAPUT DRACONIS
Good with good; evil with evil.
Gives good issue for gain.

Ascendant	Good in all things.
Second House	Good.
Third House	Very good.
Fourth House	Good save in war.
Fifth House	Very good.
Sixth House	Good for immorality only.
Seventh House	Good especially for peace.
Eighth House	Good.
Ninth House	Very good.
Tenth House	Good in all.
Eleventh House	Good for the church and ecclesiastical gain.
Twelfth House	Not very good.

CAUDA DRACONIS
Good with evil, and evil with good. Good for loss,
and for passing out of an affair.

Ascendant	Destroy figure if it falls here! Makes judgment worthless.
Second House	Very evil.
Third House	Evil in all.
Fourth House	Good especially for conclusion of the matter.
Fifth House	Very evil.
Sixth House	Rather good.
Seventh House	Evil, war, and fire.
Eighth House	No good, except for magic.
Ninth House	Good for science only. Bad for journeys. Robbery.
Tenth House	Evil save in works of fire.
Eleventh House	Evil save for favors.
Twelfth House	Rather good.

VIA
Injurious to the goodness of other figures
generally, but good for journeys and voyages.

Ascendant	Evil except for prison.
Second House	Indifferent.
Third House	Very good in all.
Fourth House	Good in all save love.
Fifth House	Voyages good.
Sixth House	Evil.
Seventh House	Rather good, especially for voyages.
Eighth House	Evil.
Ninth House	Indifferent. good for journeys.
Tenth House	Good.
Eleventh House	Very good.
Twelfth House	Excellent.

POPULUS
Sometimes good and sometimes bad;
good with good, and evil with evil.

Ascendant	Good in marriages.
Second House	Medium good.
Third House	Rather good than bad.
Fourth House	Good in all but love.
Fifth House	Good in most things.
Sixth House	Good.
Seventh House	In war good; else medium.
Eighth House	Evil.
Ninth House	Look for letters.
Tenth House	Good.
Eleventh House	Good in all.
Twelfth House	Very evil.

The following table denotes the values of the Geomantic figures in the astro-Geomancy square or wheel.

Table of Essential Dignities

Sign	Ruler	Element	Exaltation	Fall	Detriment	Strong
♈	♂	🜂	☉	♄	♀	♃
♉	♀	🜃	☽	—	♂	♃
♊	☿	🜁	—	—	♃	♄
♋	☽	🜄	♃	♂	♄	☿
♌	☉	🜂	—	—	♄	♂
♍	☿	🜃	☿	♀	♃	♄
♎	♀	🜁	♄	☉	♂	♃
♏	♂	🜄	—	☽	♀	☉
♐	♃	🜂	—	—	☿	♀
♑	♄	🜃	♂	♃	☽	☿
♒	♄	🜁	—	—	☉	☿
♓	♃	🜄	♀	☿	☿	—

In Astrology the aspects are defined as the number of degrees between planets. In astro-Geomancy the aspects are defined only in terms applicable to mundane Astrology. This eliminates the degrees and the orbs. The reason for this is that astro-Geomancy borrows from Astrology and loses some of Astrology's conciseness in the process. It is not the degrees nor orbs that concern us but the degrees between houses. There are 30 degrees for each house.

The following denotes the aspects between houses:

Conjunction	☌	and is 0 degrees	Planets reinforce each other.
Semi-sextile	⊻	and is 30 degrees	Minor influence.
Sextile	✳	and is 60 degrees	Harmonious, all things being equal.
Square	☐	and is 90 degrees	Discord resulting in frustration.
Trine	△	and is 120 degrees	Harmonious.
Quincunx	⊼	and is 150 degrees	Same as Sextile.
Opposition	☍	and is 180 degrees	Tension or hostility between Planets.

The student has enough information to interpret the example chart and create a chart of his/her own. We leave that to the individual reader as an exercise. Space limitations permit us that luxury. Before embarking upon the next section, however, we have listed a summary of rules necessary to complete and interpret an astro-Geomancy chart:

1. If Rubeus or Cauda Draconis shows up in the ascendant, destroy the figure.

2. Determine in which house the question belongs (the house that relates to the question being asked). This house is known as the Significator. Also note if the same figure appears in another house.

3. Interpret the chart according to sextile, trine, square and opposition.

4. Note the figure of the fourth house. This is the end of the matter in question.

5. Form a Reconciler from the Judge and the figure in the house signifying the question.

Geomantic Talismans

The *talisman* is an offensive device used by the magician for a variety of purposes. If one wishes to develop powers and abilities or receive certain goods, one should create a talisman. On the other hand, an *amulet* is a defensive device used for protection. It is not our intention to discuss the properties of amulets in this paper. We leave that for the future.

The Geomantic characters can be turned into Sigils or signatures of the Genii or spirits. This can be done by connecting the dots that form the Geomantic figures. The magician will then draw or paint them on any appropriate inert material. Metals corresponding to the planetary rulers of the spirits are best but wood or paper can be substituted.   The talisman is then charged for a specified purpose; possibly by the use of the Middle Pillar exercise. After the magician circulates the LVX he/she should release the energy with the Neophyte grade signs of the Golden Dawn. These are also known as the Sign of the Enterer and the Sign of Silence. Once the talisman has done its job it must be destroyed.

The following represents some of the shapes that can be made with the figure of Acquisitio:

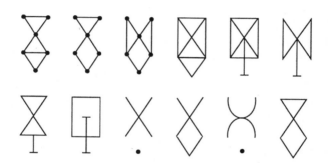

For example we can place the images or Sigils in the Talisman in the following manner.

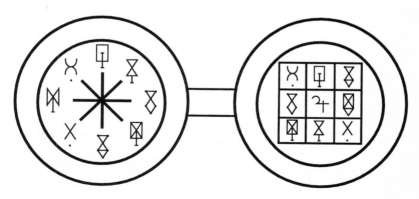

It should be noted here that it is not our intention to describe a complex or complete method for creating Geomantic talismans. That will be covered in a later issue of *The Golden Dawn Journal*.

Finally, the student should keep in mind that what has been presented here is neither to be considered comprehensive nor complete. For further information we refer the reader to the bibliography.

ABOUT THE AUTHORS

Mitch Henson has been interested in Occult topics and alternative religions for over twenty years. He suggested that this might be a reaction to not having been struck dead by the hand of God for cursing out loud as a child.

This interest lead to a love affair with the writings of Aleister Crowley. He was active in an international Thelemic Order for many years. He found that there were some gaps in his knowledge of magic and similar topics and consequently joined the Hermetic Order of the Golden Dawn.

Gail Henson's first love is sewing. It is a rare and unique talent when combined with her second love—Magic.

They met at a lecture given by Mitch on Ceremonial Magic and Qabalah. It has been a strong and healthy magic ever since.

They live in Jacksonville, Florida with their three cats, Tiffani, Morris and Kittles; all of whom are Secret Chiefs in the inner order of the Golden Dawn.

BIBLIOGRAPHY

Agrippa, Henry Cornelius. *Fourth Book of Occult Philosophy.* Kila, MT: Kessington Publishing Company, 1992.

Cicero, Chic & Sandra Tabatha. *Secrets of a Golden Dawn Temple.* St. Paul, MN: Llewellyn Publications, 1992.

Crowley, Aleister. *The Equinox Vol I No 2.* 3rd printing. New York, NY: Samuel Weiser, Inc. 1978.

King, Francis & Skinner Stephen. *The Techniques of High Magic.* Rochester, Vermont: Destiny Books, 1991.

Regardie, Israel. *A Practical Guide to Geomantic Divination.* New York, NY: Samuel Weiser Inc., 1972.

Regardie, Israel. *The Golden Dawn.* 6th edition. St. Paul, MN: Llewellyn Publications, 1986.

Skinner, Stephen. *The Oracle of Geomancy.* San Landro, CA: Prism Press, 1986.

Whitcomb, Bill. *The Magician's Companion.* St. Paul, MN: Llewellyn Publications, 1993.

MYSTERIA GEOMANTICA:
Teachings on the Art of Geomancy
Adam Forrest

Πρῶτον μεν ευχη τηδε πρεσβευω θεῶν
την πρωτομαντιν . . .
Elder Earth, First Oracle, Thee I first invoke with these my prayers...
                                    -Aischylos, *Eumenidês*

ith the teaching and especially the published writing of various alumni of the Hermetic Order of the Golden Dawn (S.L. MacGregor Mathers, W. Wynn Westcott, A.E. Waite, Dion Fortune, Aleister Crowley, Paul Foster Case, etc.), culminating in Francis Israel Regardie's publication of *The Golden Dawn: An Account of the Teachings, Rites, & Ceremonies of the Order of the Golden Dawn* in the 1930s, a vast system of balanced theoretical and practical knowledge regarding the Art of the Magic of Light came into the hands of Western occultists. Geomancy alone of the major components of the G∴D∴ curriculum has so far failed to secure a place of prominence in 20th century magical practice outside the temples and lodges of the established Orders. Why?

I fear that the answer is, quite simply, boredom. Geomantic divination, worked according to the limited information contained in the published Outer Order written lecture, unsupplemented by oral teaching and unenhanced by the expectation of further Geomantic knowledge in the Inner Order, may in all honesty be a tedious experience. Additionally, until the past decade, the Order teaching on Geomancy was one of the most scattered and unintegrated elements in the Rosicrucian system[1]; as late as the period of the AO, the Order

---

[1] Exceeded only by the *Tattvas* (more precisely the *Bhutas*), a conspicuously alien accretion to the G∴D∴ system, introduced in the late 1800s as a result of the infatuation with Tattvas in the London Theosophical circles of the day in which several of the senior Adepts of the Order moved. Tattvas are generally elective, rather than compulsory, study today. The Elemental and Sub-elemental Work is accomplished through the Western symbols of the Spirit Wheel and either the Alchemical Elemental Triangles or the Kerubic Sigils. —APF

Chiefs were circulating additional early Geomantic source material from Cristoforo Cattaneo and John Heydon without integrating it into the Order system.

Within the limited space afforded by this article, I hope to offset the potential for Geomantic tedium and confusion by providing the interested apprentice Geomancer with some of the auxiliary oral teaching appropriate to the Outer Order, and the journeyman diviner with some direction for his or her further development by offering a glimpse of the Geomantic teachings of the Adept Grades.

Geomancy in the Outer Order

A century ago, Geomancy was introduced in the Grade of Practicus, but the curriculum has continued to evolve, and today Geomancy is first taught in the Earth Grade of Zelator.

The basic mechanics of Geomantic divination are widely known and readily available in many other places[2], so I will only summarize them very briefly here.

1. The Geomancer generates 16 random numbers, noting whether each is odd or even.
2. The Geomancer combines these odd and even numbers according to a well-defined procedure, producing eight Geomantic Figures or Tetragrams known as the Four Mothers and the Four Daughters.
3. These eight Tetragrams are then combined to produce four more Tetragrams called the Four Nephews.
4. The Four Nephews are then combined to create the Two Witnesses.
5. The Two Witnesses are combined to generate the Judge or Seal.
6. These Tetragrams are then placed in a chart, most frequently a Zodiacal chart.
7. The Geomancer then interprets the Oracle based on the Elemental, Planetary, and Zodiacal

[2] *The Golden Dawn, The Complete Golden Dawn System of Magic, A Practical Guide to Geomantic Divination, Techniques of High Magic,* etc. If you are unfamiliar with Geomancy, you should consult one of these sources, as the material in this article is intended to suplement the available information, and assumes a reasonable familiarity with it on the part of the reader. —APF

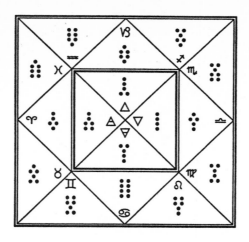

Figure 1: **The 16 Abodes**

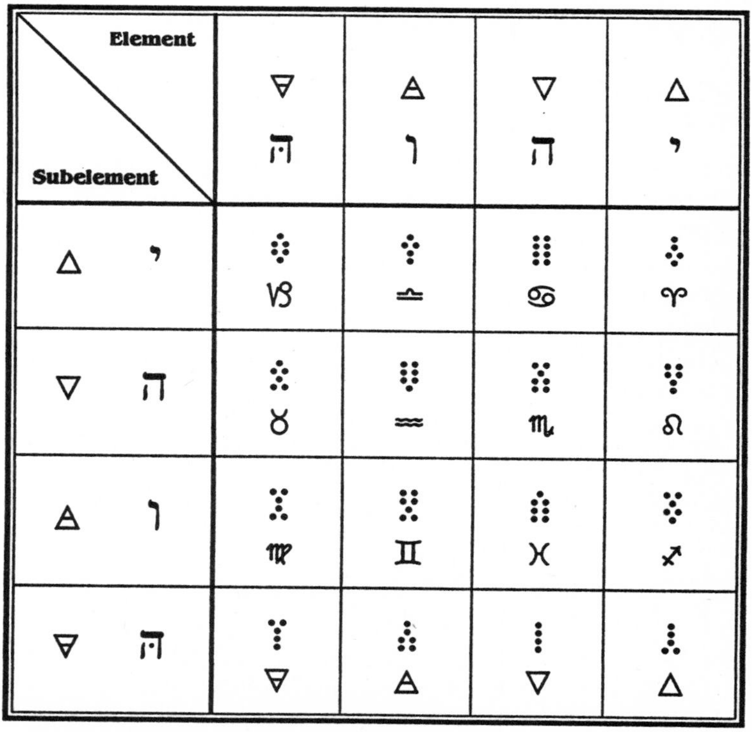

Element	∀ ה	△ ו	▽ ה	△ י
△ י	⠿ ♑	⠿ ♎	⠿ ♋	⠿ ♈
▽ ה	⠿ ♉	⠿ ♒	⠿ ♏	⠿ ♌
△ ו	⠿ ♍	⠿ ♊	⠿ ♓	⠿ ♐
∀ ה	⠿ ∀	⠿ △	⠿ ▽	⠿ △

Figure 2: **Matrix of the Subelements**

179

correspondences of the Tetragrams (see the chart entitled Genii of the Tetragrams) and their relative positions in the chart combined with (as he becomes more experienced in divination) his intuitive and psychic impressions.

Correspondences

An error regarding the Elemental correspondences of the Tetragrams in an early Practicus paper on Geomancy has been frequently reproduced, and is still the source of some confusion today. Figure 2 shows the correct table of Elemental and Sub-elemental correspondences from which the Zodiacal correspondences derive. The Planetary correspondences derive in turn from the Zodiacal correspondences. These basic correspondences are shown in Figure 1 in what might well be the Mother Diagram of Geomancy, the 16 Abodes.

Terminology

An important practical tool not included in the previously published material is the technical vocabulary of Geomancy.

TETRAGRAM: [From Greek *Tetragramma*, "a figure with four parts".] Those of you familiar with the Chinese divinatory system of the I Ching will recall that the six-line figures of that system are called Hexagrams in English. The mechanical structure of the two systems is very similar. From a mathematical standpoint, both are based on binary numbers. The Hexagrams of the I Ching correspond to 6-digit binary numbers, yielding 64 ($=2^6$) possible Hexagrams, and the Tetragrams of Geomancy correspond to four-digit binary numbers, making 16 ($=2^4$) possible Tetragrams.

READING: Like many other forms of divination, a spe-cific Geomantic Oracle is often referred to as a reading.

SQUILL: [From Arabic *shakl*, a Geomantic chart.] To squill is to generate the random numbers from which the *Tetragrams* are derived. It originally referred specifically to the classic Arabic method of using a wand, staff, or finger to make a random number of points or lines in the sand, but has become more generalized in meaning today.

Diviner: _____

Querent: _____

Day, Date, Time: _____

Astrological Conditions:

Question:

House & Genii Governing Question	Major Aspects
Angular Houses	
Domiciles	Reconciliations
Falls	
Exaltations	Notes
Detriments	

Figure 3: **Sample Geomantium** *(with Horoscope)*

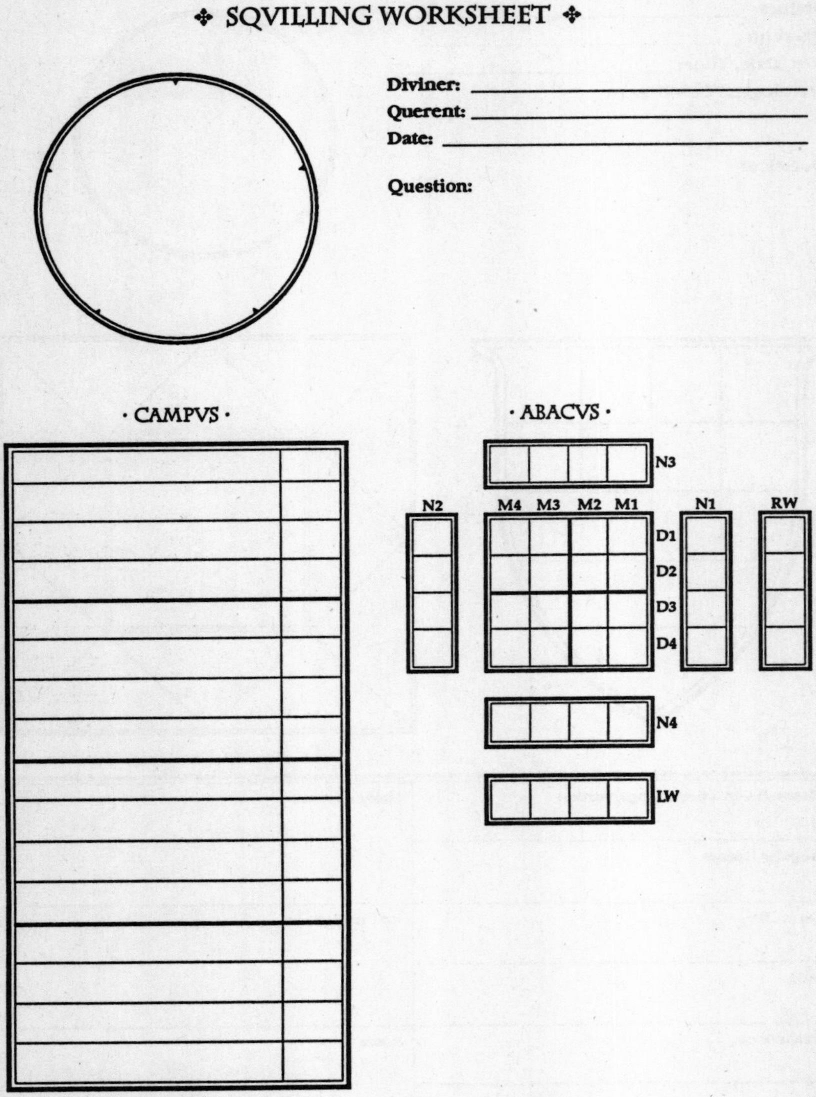

❖ SQVILLING WORKSHEET ❖

Diviner: _____

Querent: _____

Date: _____

Question:

· CAMPVS ·

· ABACVS ·

N3

N2   M4 M3 M2 M1   N1   RW

D1
D2
D3
D4

N4

LW

Figure 4: **Squilling Worksheet**

GEOMANTIUM: [From Greek *Geômanteion*, meaning both "an oracular Geomantic response" and "the location of a Geomantic divination".] The form or Table on which a Geomantic divination is recorded (See Figure 3). A Geomantium may be drawn or printed on paper or card, painted or screened on fabric or wood, chalked or painted on a slate (portable blackboard), or drawn or painted on a marker-board.

A Geomantium almost always includes a *Shield*, a *Chart*, and a *Pentacle*. Some Geomantia include a *Campus* and *Abacus*, though these are often placed on a separate Squilling Worksheet (See Figure 4 for a sample worksheet).

CHART: The diagram on the *Geomantium* on which the *Tetragrams* are placed to provide an interpretive guiding symbol. For the beginning Geomancer, this is most often a horoscope chart, though almost any chart may be used, including most Tarot spreads.

When a horoscope chart is used, it is always the *Square Chart*, the *Charta Quadrata* or *Charta Decussata* (see Fig. 3 —the Geomantium); this is because in Order symbolism the square is Terrestrial and the circle is Celestial, as in G∴D∴ Grade notation (1=10, etc.).

SHIELD: [Sometimes occurs as Latin *Scutum* or Hebrew *Magen*, both simply meaning "shield"] The standard chart in which the Tetragrams of a reading are first recorded (See Figure 5). Some Geomancers interpret directly from the shield, but most transfer the Tetragrams from the shield to a final chart.

PENTACLE: In the context of a *Geomantium*, the term refers to a circle, usually with five equidistant points marked around its perimeter, in which the Geomancer draws an Invoking Pentagram of Earth.

CAMPUS: [Latin, "field"] Originally referred to a smooth patch of earth or sand in which points were made. Now it most often refers to a simple diagram with 16 rectangles in which points are marked for squilling.

ROOT LINES: The 16 random numbers generated by squilling, each of which is recorded as an odd (●) or even (●●) line.

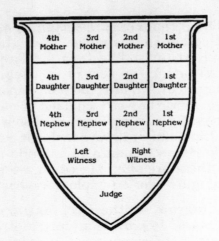

Figure 5: **Placement of the Tetragrams in the Shield**

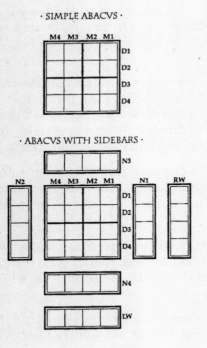

1. *Enter the 16 Root Lines in the Abacus, starting with the upper right hand square, and proceeding down the right hand column (labelled M1), then from top to bottom of column M2, and so on through M3 and M4.*

2. *To find the Mother Tetragrams, read column M1 for the First Mother, M2 for the Second Mother, M3 for the Third Mother, and M4 for the Fourth Mother.*

3. *To find the Daughters, read row D1 from right to left for the First Daughter, D2 for the Second Daughter, D3 for the Third Daughter, and D4 for the Fourth Daughter.*

4. *Combine Columns M1 and M2, putting the result in Column N1 for the First Nephew. Columns M3 and M4 combine in N2 for the Second Nephew. Rows D1 and D2 combine in N3 for the Third Nephew, and D3 and D4 produce N4, the Fourth Nephew.*

5. *N1 and N2 combine to produce RW, the Right Witness; and N3 and N4 yield LW, the Left Witness.*

Figure 6: **The Abacus**

ABACUS: [Latin, "A square board or grid"] A four-by-four grid into which the *Root Lines* are placed. Some *Abaci* also have sidebars to make the derivation of Nephews and Witnesses simpler (Figure 6).

Theory

One question often asked is why there is no *aeromancy, hydromancy,* or *pyromancy* in the other Elemental Grades of Initiation. The principle reason is that the Earth of Geomancy is not primarily Earth as distinguished from the Air, Water, and Fire of the Elemental Tetrad, but the Earth as distinguished from the Heaven of the Cosmic Dyad. Thus, Geomancy encompasses not just Elemental Earth, but all four Elements. In the words of Hermês Trismegistos, "Truly is the Earth the Mother of the Elements; from the Earth do they come, and to the Earth do they return." Indeed, it is probably most accurate to consider Geomancy the Oracle of Malkuth.

Geomancy is the form of divination which most clearly embodies the Hermetic Axiom of "As above, so below". As the *Emerald Tablet* of Hermês states: "It is Truth without falsehood, certain and most true, that that which is below is as that which is above, and that which is above is as that which is below, to execute the wonders of the One."

Interpretation of the Tetragrams

The guides to interpretations provided in the older published Order documents are largely reproduced from Mediæval and Renaissance Geomancies (which are themselves largely derived from Mediæval Astrological handbooks), and are infected with the fatalism and superstition of Mediæval divination. Such interpretations as: *"Rubeus in Eleventh House: Evil, except to let blood,"* have been (I hope) irrelevant since the Middle Ages.

However, the worst offenses are the two superstitious cries of Mediæval alarm: *"Rubeus in Ascendant: Destroy the Figure if it fall here! Makes the judgement worthless,"* and *"Cauda Draconis in Ascendant: Destroy the Figure if it fall here! Makes the judgement worthless."*

These apoplectic directives are based on the crude Mediaeval judgment of Mars and Cauda Draconis as malefic celestial influences, and of Scorpio as "the Sign of Death". They are precisely equivalent to teaching a Cartomancer to destroy a reading and thoroughly frighten the Querent if the Tarot Trumps Death or the Devil turn up as the Significator.

There is insufficient space here to provide contemporary interpretations of the Geomantic Tetragrams in the Houses (there are 192 combinations), but consultation of any decent modern Astrological handbook should set you on the proper course.

Reconciliation

When the Geomancer begins to feel fairly comfortable with the basic procedures, s/he may add the technique of *Reconcilation* to his/her repertoire.

The premise of Reconciliation is that the final Tetragram of a Geomantic reading, the Judge or Seal, represents the influence of the Higher on the question under consideration. This Supernal influence may be considered in further detail by combining the Judge with any of the other Tetragrams in the reading in the same manner in which the Witnesses are combined to produce the Judge. A Tetragram thus formed is called a Reconcilor, and provides additional information about the Divine influence on that particular aspect of the subject of the reading.

The most common Reconcilor formed is the *Initiator*. The Initiator is generated by combining the Judge with the Tetragram in the First House (the second Mother), and represents the influence of the Higher on the Querent in the matter being considered.

Modes of Squilling the 16 Root Lines

The classic method of squilling the Root Lines is that of marking a random number of points either in damp sand or earth, or transferring that method to pen and paper. However, there are a number of alternative methods, which may either be more suited to a particular situation or simply more congenial to your personal style as a Diviner.

PEBBLE-WORKING. I have a bag of beautiful black stones which I often use for squilling. The Geomancer draws a handful of stones from the bag, and sets them aside in pairs until s/he has either one or two stones remaining in his/her hand.

COIN-WORKING. Flipping coins has always been a convenient way to generate yes-no, even-odd, binary responses. One Geomancer of my acquaintance collected a small, smooth, relatively flat stone from a river-bed and painted the Kerubic Earth Sigil (Taurus) on one side, and the triangular Earth Sigil on the other, and uses this for coin-toss squilling of Root Lines. Another, a longtime practitioner of I Ching recently come to Geomancy, uses his I Ching coins, consecrated to divination by long use.

DICE-WORKING. For Geomantic use, get white-on-black dice (white pips on black cubes). Thanks to the burgeoning host of role-playing games in the past twenty years, it is today relatively easy to find dice of many sizes, shapes, and colours. I have a set of dice for use in varying forms of Geomantic computations that include white-on-black 20-, 12-, 10-, 8-, and 4-sided dice, a handful of white-on-black 6-sided dice, and an Elemental set of red, blue, yellow, and black 6-sided dice.

STONE-WORKING. I also use a set of Geomancy Stones (much like the currently popular Rune stones), which look rather like Geomantic dominos. Only ten Stones are needed for a full set, as several of the Tetragrams are inverse images of each other (e.g., the same Stone turned one way is Fortuna Major, but turned the other way is Fortuna Minor). These provide a very fast and simple form of squilling, as you produce not the Root Lines, but the final Tetragrams themselves.

MISCELLANEOUS. As you can see, there are many ways to squill Root Lines and Tetragrams. The most original method I have seen was from a pair of students who took short lengths of heavy copper wire and bent them into the shape of the Kerubic Earth Sigil and placed them in a container. They then lifted one of the wire Sigils from the container, and counted whether it drew an even or odd number of its fellows with it (Remember the childhood game, Barrel of Monkeys?), and this determined the Root Line.

Ritualizing the Geomantic Process

If you prefer a more ritualized form for basic Geomantic divination, incorporate some or all of the following Elements into your Work.

Lay out all your materials for squilling. Trace an Invoking Earth Pentagram over all the materials, saying, **"Except Adonai build the House, they labour in vain that erect it; except Adonai keep the City, the Sentinel waketh in vain."**

Knock 1111-111-111, and say, **"In the Name of Adonai Melekh and of Adonai Malkah, I declare this Geomantic Working open."**

As you mark off or set aside the points in pairs, say with each pair, **"Sandalphon and Metatron watch the Gate of Truth."**

As you set the top line of each Tetragram, say, **"Yod: the Voice of Fire."** As you set the second line of each Tetragram, say, **"Heh: the Voice of Water."** As you set the third line of each Tetragram, say, **"Vav: the Voice of Air."** As you set the bottom line of each Tetragram, say, **"Heh Sophith: the Voice of Earth."**

Before placing the Tetragrams in the Chart, say, **"I come from between the Pillars, and I seek the Light of the Hidden Knowledge in the Name of Adonai."** Then give the Sign of the Zelator[3] over the Geomantium, saying, **"And the Great Archangel Sandalphon said: I am the Reconciler for Earth and the Celestial Soul therein. Form is invis-ible alike in blinding Darkness and in blinding Light. I am the left-hand Kerub of the Ark and the Feminine Power, as Metatron is the right-hand Kerub and the Masculine Power. And I prepare the Way to the Celestial Light."**

At conclusion of Divination, say, **"Adonai, not unto us but unto Thy Name be the glory, Who hath allowed us to penetrate thus far into the Sanctuary of Thy Mysteries."**

Then knock 1111-111-111, and say, **"In the Name of Adonai Melekh and of Adonai Malkah, I declare this Geomantic Working closed."**

The Genii of Geomancy

A variety of terms have been used in Order documents and the books derived from them to describe the Spiritual entities associated with the Geomantic Tetragrams, including Archangels, Angels, Rulers, Spirits, Genii, Dæmones, Dæmonia, and

---

3 Extend the right arm straight ahead, palm perpendicular to the floor, thumb up, then raise the arm straight up to a 45° angle. This Sign is also known as the Sign of Sandalphon, the Sign of Equilibrium, and the Sign of the Middle Path. —APF

Intelligences. All of these terms (or at least their Greek, Latin, and Hebrew originals) are truly ancient, predating Christianity. Greek *Angelos* translates Hebrew *Malakh*, "Messenger". "Ruler" translates Greek *Archon* and sometimes Latin *Angelus Præsidens* ("Ruling Angel"). "Spirit" has been commonly used to translate the Latin *Genius* (source of the Arabic *Djinn*), the Greek *Daimôn* and *Daimonion*, and the Hebrew *Ruach*.

Greek *Daimôn* and *Daimonion*[4] have been Latinized in form as *Dæmon* and *Dæmonium* (as in Agrippa's *De Occulta Philosophia*). Both words generally mean "spiritual being" in the broadest sense, from an Elemental to a God. However, the terms are sometimes used specifically to refer to entities of low rank in the spiritual hierarchy.

"Intelligence" translates Latin *Intelligentia*, Greek *Nous*, and Hebrew *Sekhel*, and refers to a sapient spiritual being, usually of Angelic or Archangelic nature. The term was used by the Pagan Neoplatonists[5], by early Christian writers (Dionysios the Areopagite, St Gregorios Nazianzenos), and by Theurgists from Iamblichos to today. It is significant that Agrippa—principal source of much of the Order's vocabulary of Spirits—specifically describes the Archangels of the Sephiroth as *Intelligentiæ*, and the Angelic Chorus of the *Bene Seraphim* (the "Children of the Seraphim") as the *Intelligentiæ Veneris*, the "Intelligences of Venus".

The Planetary Intelligences and Spirits (*Intelligentiæ* and *Dæmonia*) associated with the Geomantic Work are derived from the system of the Planetary *Qameoth*, or Magic Squares, preserved by Agrippa.

The table entitled *Genii of the Tetragrams* (Figure 7) shows the names of the various Hebrew hierarchies of Spirits associated with Geomancy. Some brief notes are necessary regarding a few of the names.

The Archangels of the Sign for the Lunar Nodes are the Archangels of the Elemental Triplicities corresponding to each Node. For Cauda Draconis, it is the Archangel of the Fire Triplicity, *Shehatsael*,[6] and for Caput Draconis, the Archangel of the Earth Triplicity, *Thuyael*.[7] The Intelligences and Dæmonia for the Lunar Nodes are from the Qameoth. The

---

[4] Daimonion was the term Socrates used to describe his Higher Genius. —APF
[5] The great Neoplatonic Theurgist Iamblichos employed all of the terms in our list. —APF
[6] Shehatsael = Shin (Fire) + Heh (Aries) + Teth (Leo) + Samekh (Sagitt) + Aleph Lamed —APF
[7] Thuyael = Tau (Earth) + Vav (Taurus) + Yod (Virgo) + Ayin (Capricorn) + Aleph Lamed. —APF

Planetary Archangels of the Lunar Nodes may be traced to Solomonic sources familiar to DDCF.

The Intelligence listed for the Moon, *Shelachel*, is an alternate Lunar Intelligence from the Qamea system with a far more manageable name than the usually-listed *Malka beTarshisim voEd Ruachoth Sechalim*.

Some common errors are also corrected here. The name of the Archangel of Venus, *Anael*, has often been wrongly given as Hanael through confusion with Haniel, Archangel of Netzach. The name of the Archangel of Sagittarius, *Adnakhiel*, has been frequently misspelled as Advakhiel, through a scribal error mistaking Hebrew Nun for Vav; interestingly, the same error also occurred in Renaissance Latin typesetting, where the *n* of Ad*n*achiel could easily be set upside-down as a *u*, producing Ad*u*achiel. Finally, the correct name of the Angel of Elemental Fire is *Ariel* ("the Lion of God"), not Aral. An error in Agrippa was long preserved in the Order, in which the two names Ariel and Aral were swapped. This long-lived confusion was only made possible because the four Præfects of the Elements have generally not been recognized as the names of Orders of Angels. Seraph, Cherub, Tharsis, and Aral (more properly Erel) are simply the singular forms of Seraphim, Kerubim, Tarshishim, and Erelim.

Adeptus Minor

In the Adeptus Minor Grade, and particularly in the Subgrade of Theoricus Adeptus Minor, where the Lesser Adept undertakes to explore in depth the formulæ and tools first obtained in the Outer Order Grade of Zelator, the Magician returns to Geomancy in detail.

The Adeptus Minor learns of the history and legend of Geomancy, more tools for Geomantic ritual, Geomantic Talismanic Magic, Egyptian Geomantic correspondences, and some basic applications of Geomancy in the Enochian Work.

We will only have time for a quick look at the historical legends and the known history, a formula for the detailed study of a Tetragram, and two *Qameoth* (Magic Squares) for use in Geomantic Talismanic Magic.

The Legend of Geomancy

The story is told among the Rosicrucian Adepts that the Oracle of Geomancy entered our Tradition in the hands of the Founder, our Greatly Honoured Pater Christian Rosenkreuz. It is said that in his *Itinerarium*, the record of his seminal pilgrimage in search of initiation and enlightenment, CRC tells how on his return from the Sufi *khānqāh* of Damkar in Arabia, he came at length to the Moroccan city of Fez, in the days when Fez was the capital of the Marinid kingdom of the Berbers under Abdallah and Abu Said Uthman. There, by virtue of certain signs and tokens he had learned in Damkar, the young Adept was admitted to the innermost circles of the Magicians and Philosophers of that city. He studied many occult Arts with the Moorish Initiates, but most especially those connected with the Elements. And the Elemental Art in which the marabouts were most skilled was the form of divination that they called *Ilm al-Raml*, the Wisdom of the Sand.

Rosenkreuz recognized *Raml* as the Art of Geomancy, which Hugo de Santalla and Gerardo de Cremona had introduced to Christendom two centuries earlier, but the Art as practiced in Fez was far more subtle and sophisticated than the simple procedures then known in Europe.

The Moorish Adepts said that it was Hermês Trismegistos who first taught the Art of Geomancy to humankind, after having himself received this and many other Secret Arts from the Archangel Gabriel. Hermês travelled the world, teaching Initiates from Africa to India. Finally a great Geomantic Adept named al-Zanāti established a Geomantic Order which preserved the Hermetic Art of Geomancy until their day.

Rosenkreuz studied with the Berbers for two years, until a dream revealed that it was time for him to return to Europe with all the treasures of the Light which he had gathered on his long pilgrimage. And thus did the Hermetic Art of Geomancy come to be one of the precious jewels entrusted to the care of the Rosicrucian Order.

History

The prevailing historical theory is that the earliest form of *Ilm al-Raml* originated in Islamic North Africa in about the eighth or ninth century.

Figure 7: **Genii of the Tetragrams**

Tetragram	Archangel of Sign	Archangel of Planet	Intelligence of Planet	Daemonium of Planet	Archangel of Element	Angel of Element
Puer ⁝∶	♈ Malkhidael מלכידאל	♂ Zamael זמאל	♂ Graphiel גראפיאל	♂ Bartzabel ברצבאל	△ Mikhael מיכאל	△ Ariel אריאל
Amissio ∶⁝	♉ Asmodel אסמודאל	♀ Anael אנאל	♀ Hagiel הגיאל	♀ Qedemel קדמאל	▽ Uriel אוריאל	▽ Phorlakh פורלאך
Albus ⁝⁝	♊ Ambriel אמבריאל	☿ Raphael רפאל	☿ Tiriel תיריאל	☿ Taphthartharath תפתרתרת	△ Raphael רפאל	△ Chassan חשן
Populus ∷∷	♋ Muriel מוריאל	☽ Gabriel גבריאל	☽ Shelachel שלחאל	☽ Chasmodai חשמודאי	▽ Gabriel גבריאל	▽ Taliahad טליהד
Fortuna Major ∶∷	♌ Verkhiel ורכיאל	☉ Mikhael מיכאל	☉ Nakhiel נכיאל	☉ Sorath סורת	△ Mikhael מיכאל	△ Ariel אריאל
Conjunctio ⁝∷	♍ Hamaliel חמליאל	☿ Raphael רפאל	☿ Tiriel תיריאל	☿ Taphthartharath תפתרתרת	▽ Uriel אוריאל	▽ Phorlakh פורלאך
Puella ∶⁝	♎ Zuriel צוריאל	♀ Anael אנאל	♀ Hagiel הגיאל	♀ Qedemel קדמאל	△ Raphael רפאל	△ Chassan חשן
Rubeus ⁝∶	♏ Barkhiel ברכיאל	♂ Zamael זמאל	♂ Graphiel גראפיאל	♂ Bartzabel ברצבאל	▽ Gabriel גבריאל	▽ Taliahad טליהד

Tetragram	Archangel of Sign	Archangel of Planet	Intelligence of Planet	Daemonium of Planet	Archangel of Element	Angel of Element
Acquisitio	♐ Adnakhiel אדנכיאל	♃ Sachiel סחיאל	♃ Yohphiel יהפיאל	♃ Hismael הסמאל	△ Mikhael מיכאל	△ Ariel אריאל
Carcer	♑ Hanael הנאל	♄ Kassiel כסיאל	♄ Agiel אגיאל	♄ Zazel זאזל	▽ Uriel אוריאל	▽ Phorlakh פורלאך
Tristitia	♒ Kambriel כמבריאל	♄ Kassiel כסיאל	♄ Agiel אגיאל	♄ Zazel זאזל	△ Raphael רפאל	△ Chassan חסן
Laetitia	♓ Amnitziel אמניציאל	♃ Sachiel סחיאל	♃ Yohphiel יהפיאל	♃ Hismael הסמאל	▽ Gabriel גבריאל	▽ Taliahad תליהד
Cauda Draconis	☋ Shehatsael שהטסאל	☋ Yakhadiel יחדיאל	☋ Shimdayah שמדיה	☋ Bashbaniah בשבניה	△ Mikhael מיכאל	△ Ariel אריאל
Caput Draconis	☊ Thuyael תויאל	☊ Sophiel סופיאל	☊ Geshion גשיון	☊ Khorbaqiel כרבקיאל	▽ Uriel אוריאל	▽ Phorlakh פורלאך
Fortuna Minor	☉ Verkhiel ורכיאל	☉ Mikhael מיכאל	☉ Nakhiel נכיאל	☉ Sorath סורת	△ Raphael רפאל	△ Chassan חסן
Via	♋ Muriel מוריאל	☽ Gabriel גבריאל	☽ Shelachel שלאכל	☽ Chasmodai חשמודאי	▽ Gabriel גבריאל	▽ Taliahad תליהד

193

The seventeenth century Arabic writer Ahmad al-Rammāl b. Ali b. Zunbul recorded the legendary lineage of the Geomantic Zanātiyya Order: Gabriel to Idris (the Arabic *alter ego* of Hermês Trismegistos) to Tumtum al-Hindi to Halaf al-Barbari (the Berber) to Abu Abdallāh Muhammad al-Zanāti.

Hugo de Santalla (fl. ca. 1125 CE) was responsible for the first European textbook on Geomancy, the *Ars Geomantiæ* ('The Art of Geomancy'), a translation of an earlier Arabic work into Latin. Indeed, we believe that Hugo was also the first to apply the name *Geomantia* ('Geomancy') to this form of divination. He was one of that magnificent fraternity of Latin, Arabic, Greek, and Hebrew scholars in mediæval Spain engaged in the world-changing work of translation. A man of many firsts, Hugo also gave the West the first Latin translation of the *Emerald Tablet* of Hermês Trismegistos.[8]

Following Hugo, other prominent translators rendered Arabic Geomantic texts into Latin, among them Gerardo de Sabionetta, Gerardo de Cremona, and Bartholomeo de Parma.

Geomancy quickly became very popular in Europe, and remained so until the Enlightenment. In a Europe which held a profound belief in the influence of Astrology in daily life, Geomancy seemed to provide a way to erect what amounted to a horoscope with no ephemerides, no astronomical instruments, indeed with no other equipment than a stick and a bit of earth.

Many authors influential in the history of the Western Esoteric Tradition have written on the subject of Geomancy, notably Pietro d'Abano, Robert Fludd, Heinrich Cornelius Agrippa, Simon Forman, Dr Rudd/Peter Smart, John Heydon, Robert Cross Smith (aka Raphael), and in the twentieth century, Franz Hartmann, Aleister Crowley, Francis Israel Regardie, and Stephen Skinner.

Geomancy has been a core part of the Golden Dawn curriculum since the Order's inception, as it is part of the curriculum prescribed by the Cypher MSS.

---

8 The notion has been discussed in Rosicrucian circles that there may be some connection between Hugo de Santalla and Hugo Alverda, and between Abû Adallâh Muhammad al-Zanâti and Elman Zata. Alverda and Zata are two of the legendary eldest Chiefs of the Order. —APF

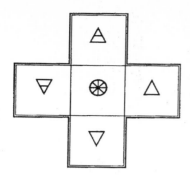

Figure 8:

**Greek Cross
for Testing the Stones**

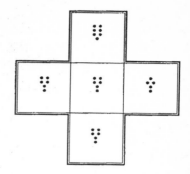

Figure 9:

**Sample Cross Chart
for Testing the Stones**

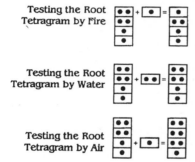

Testing the Root
Tetragram by Fire

Testing the Root
Tetragram by Water

Testing the Root
Tetragram by Air

Figure 10:

Testing the Stones

Figure 11:

**Derivation of the Names
of the Enochian Princes
& Princesses
of the Lesser Angles**

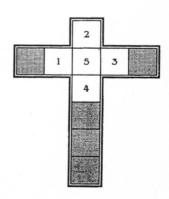

195

Testing the Stones

This is a Formula to be used to analyze a single Tetragram. It
may be used on a one-Tetragram reading, on the Judge of a full
Geomantium, or on a Reconcilor.

Draw a Greek Cross of Five Squares, the centre square of
which answers to Spirit, and the arms to Fire, Water, Air, and
Earth. Place the Tetragram to be analyzed—called the Root
Tetragram—in the central square of the Cross. For the sake of
example, let us say that the Root Tetragram we are analyzing
is Fortuna Major.

Trace the Cross in the Triangle[9] over the Tetragram,
beginning the Triangle at the lower right angle, saying: **"I test
thee with Fire, in the Name of Adonai."** Then squill a
Probation Line (*Qav Bochan*). If it is even, the Fire Line is
unchanged, and you copy the Root Tetragram into the Fire arm
of the Cross. If the Test Line is odd, the Fire Line changes and
a new Tetragram goes on the Fire arm of the Cross. In our
example, say that we get an odd Probation Line on the Fire
Test, so our Fire Tetragram is the Root Tetragram (Fortuna
Major) with a changed Fire Line (Puella).

Trace the Cross in the Triangle over the Tetragram again,
this time starting the Triangle at the lower left angle, saying:
"I test thee with Water, in the Name of Adonai." Then
squill another Probation Line. If it is even, the Water Line is
unchanged, and you copy the Root Tetragram into the Water
arm of the Cross. If the Test Line is odd, the Water Line
changes and a new Tetragram goes on the Water arm of the
Cross. In our example, let us say that we get even on the Water
Test, so the Water line of the Root Tetragram is unchanged and
our Water Tetragram is identical to the Root Tetragram
(Fortuna Major).

Now trace the Cross in the Triangle over the Tetragram
for a third time, this time starting the Triangle at the apex,
saying: **"I test thee with Air, in the Name of Adonai."**
Then squill a Probation Line for Air. If it is even, the Air Line
is unchanged, and you copy the Root Tetragram into the Air
arm of the Cross; if odd, the Air Line changes and a new
Tetragram goes on the Air arm. In our exemplary reading, let
us say that we get odd, and the Air line of the Root Tetragram
is changed, giving us Tristitia on the Air arm of the Cross.

---

9 The Zelator Altar Symbol. —APF

The Line of Earth never changes; it is the strong foundation on which the Tetragram stands. Trace a Circled Cross over the Tetragram, saying: **"Finally, I confirm thee with Earth, in the Names of Adonai and of Yeheshuah Yehovashah."**
Our sample Figure in the Cross of the Five Squares reads:

> *Spirit / Root:* Fortuna Major
> *Fire:* Puella
> *Water:* Fortuna Major
> *Air:* Tristitia
> *Earth:* Fortuna Major

Interpret the Tetragrams in the usual manner, paying special attention to which Elements are in agreement with the Root Tetragram.

Talismanic Geomancy and the Qameoth

The Adept employs a fuller range of Sigils for the Genii of the Tetragrams than the Zelator. He may use the specialized Sigils learned in the Outer Order, or he may sublimate the working by availing himself of Sigils from the Rose, or he may focus on the Elemental, Planetary, or Zodiacal aspect of a particular Geomantic Talisman by using Sigils from the Qameoth.

To emphasize the Planetary energies, he should sigillize the appropriate names using the relevant Qamea of the well-known seven Planetary Qameoth. However, should he wish to focus on the Elemental or Zodiacal Powers, he will derive his Sigils from one of two following Qameoth, which to my knowledge have not been previously published.

The first is the Qamea of Malkuth, and of the Elements. The second is the Qamea haMazzaloth, the Magic Square of the Zodiac. (See figures 12 & 13.)

Adeptus Major

In the 6=5 Grade, the Adept undertakes Enochian Geomancy and Planetary Geomancy. We will restrict ourselves to a brief overview of one aspect of Elemental Enochian Geomancy.

10	92	8	94	5	96	97	3	99	1
11	19	83	17	85	86	14	88	12	90
71	22	28	74	26	25	77	23	79	80
40	62	33	37	65	66	34	68	69	31
51	49	53	44	46	45	57	58	42	60
41	59	48	54	56	55	47	43	52	50
70	39	63	67	35	36	64	38	32	61
30	72	78	24	76	75	27	73	29	21
81	89	13	87	16	15	84	18	82	20
100	2	98	7	95	6	4	93	9	91

Figure 12:

The Qamea of Malkuth and the Elements

12	134	135	9	8	138	139	5	4	142	143	1
121	23	22	124	125	19	18	128	129	15	14	132
109	35	34	112	113	31	30	116	117	27	26	120
48	98	99	45	44	102	103	41	40	106	107	37
60	86	87	57	56	90	91	53	52	94	95	49
73	71	70	76	77	67	66	80	81	63	62	84
61	83	82	64	65	79	78	68	69	75	74	72
96	50	51	93	92	54	55	89	88	58	59	85
108	38	39	105	104	42	43	101	100	46	47	97
25	119	118	28	29	115	114	32	33	111	110	36
13	131	130	16	17	127	126	20	21	123	122	24
144	2	3	141	140	6	7	137	136	10	11	133

Figure 13:

The Qamea of Mazzaloth

Enochian Geomancy

The 16 Enochian Princes and Princesses of the Lesser Angles of the Elemental Tablets answer to the 16 Tetragrams. The five-letter name of the Prince or Princess of each Lesser Angle is derived from a five-letter Whorl at the juncture of the arms of the Sephirotic Cross of that Lesser Angle (Figure 11), much as the eight-letter name of the King or Queen of each Elemental Tablet is derived from the Whorl or Rose at the heart of the Great Cross.

The Names of the Princes and Princesses corresponding to the 16 Tetragrams are:

Albus: Prince of Air of Air: *Arizododa* (Enochian - RIZOD).

Tristitia: Princess of Water of Air: *Alaäl* (Enochian - ALAAL).

Fortuna Minor: Princess of Earth of Air: *Yayai* (IAIAI).

Puella: Prince of Fire of Air: *Elaävo* (LAAVO).

Laetitia: Prince of Air of Water: *Aocagibe* (AOCGB).

Rubeus: Princess of Water of Water: *Menubele* (MNBLE).

Via: Princess of Earth of Water: *Elmala* (LMALA).

Populus: Prince of Fire of Water: *Tipaä* (TIPAA).

Conjunctio: Prince of Air of Earth: *Naäginu* (NAAGN).

Amissio: Princess of Water of Earth: *Oadanu* (OADAN).

Caput Draconis: Princess of Earth of Earth: *Raiabe* (RAIAB).

Carcer: Prince of Fire of Earth: *Eloïmpe* (LOIMP).

Acquisitio: Prince of Air of Fire: *Elnaäo* (LNAAO).

Fortuna Major: Princess of Water of Fire: *Buvada* (BVVDA).

Cauda Draconis: Princess of Earth of Fire: *Yudalo* (IVDLO).

Puer: Prince of Fire of Fire: *Arrefizod* (RRFIZ).

The four lines of each Tetragram are governed by the Kerubic Angels and Archangels of the Lesser Angle to which the Tetragram corresponds. For example, the Tetragram Albus corresponds to the Lesser Angle of Air of Air. The Prince is *Arizododa*. The Fire Line is governed by the Kerubic Archangel *Elarzod* and the Kerubic Angel *Larzoda*, the Water Line by *Ezodalar* and *Zodalare*, the Air Line by *Erzodela* and

Rezodala, and the Earth Line by *Eärezodel* and *Arzodel*. The Divine Names over the Element are *Oro, Ibah*, and *Aozodape*, and over the Sub-element are *Idoigo* and *Ardazoda*.

The Adeptus Major explores the nature of the Tetragrams by Skrying and Travelling in the Spirit Vision, using the Tetragrams as Gates. He encounters the corresponding Enochian Angels, and learns more of the natures and uses of the Tetragrams from these Intelligences, as well as gaining additional insight into specific readings.

Adeptus Exemptus

Geomancy of the Holy Place

The Adept returns once more to the art of Geomancy in the 7=4 Grade of Adeptus Exemptus. Here s/he learns the Geomantic Oracle of the *Sanctum Sanctorum*. We cannot explore the whole operation in detail here, but following is some of the basic symbolism and a general outline of the ritual.

The innermost Adytum of the Hebrew Sanctuary, the Holy of Holies, was named in Hebrew the *Devir*, which is "the Place of the Word, or the Oracle."

The first 12 Tetragrams correspond to the 12 Precious Stones of the Tribes on the Breastplate of Decision anciently worn by the High Priest, the *Kohen haGadol*—who may in modern workings equally well be a High Priestess, *Koheneth haGadolah*—who alone may enter the Devir. Note in the title of the High Priest or Priestess that *Gadol/Gadolah* = Gedulah, i.e., Chesed, the Sphere of the Grade of Exempt Adept.

The last three Tetragrams are the *Panim* (the three aspects which together are the Face of God). The Witnesses are the two *Kerubim* (Sandalphon and Metatron) who are on either side of the Ark, and the Judge or Seal is the *Shekhinah*, the Presence of the Divine.

In this working, even lines are the *Urim* and odd lines are the *Thummim*, which were upon the Breastplate of the High Priest. *Thom* (singular of Thummim) means "perfection, simplicity, completion, integrity". *Ur*, singular of Urim, means simply "light".

The Stones are also the Foundation Stones of *Shalem*, the Holy City, the New Jerusalem, known to the Exempt Adept.

The Oracle of the Sanctum Sanctorum is to be worked

only for questions of great significance. Three Adept Officers are required. The *Adeptus Primus* (Chief Adept) must be an Adeptus Exemptus; the *Adeptus Secundus* (Second Adept) must be at least an Adeptus Major; and the *Adeptus Tertius* (Third Adept) must be at least a senior Adeptus Minor. Adeptus Primus serves as the *Diviner*, Adeptus Secundus as the *Invocator*, and Adeptus Tertius as the *Recorder* of the working. Adeptus Primus is purified by Adeptus Secundus and Adeptus Tertius and him(her)self with Fire, Water, and Air. The Adeptus Primus, at the Black Altar, casts the 16 Root Lines. Calls each line as an Ur or a Thom. The Adeptus Primus derives the first 12 Tetragrams of the reading. Then s/he calls the figures thus:

"The Stone of Zebulun is _____, (Name of First Mother Tetragram). **The Stone of Gad is** _____, (Name of Second Mother Tetragram). **The Stone of Isshakhar is** _____, (Name of Third Mother Tetragram). **The Stone of Assher is** _____. (Name of Fourth Mother Tetragram)."

"The Stone of Reuben is _____, (Name of First Daughter Tetragram). **The Stone of Ephraim is** _____, (Name of Second Daughter Tetragram). **The Stone of Yehudah is** _____, (Name of Third Daughter Tetragram). **The Stone of Dan is** _____, (Name of Fourth Daughter Tetragram)."

"The Stone of Menassheh is _____, (Name of First Nephew Tetragram). **The Stone of Naphtali is** _____, (Name of Second Nephew Tetragram). **The Stone of Benyamin is** _____, (Name of Third Nephew Tetragram). **The Stone of Shimeon is** _____, (Name of Fourth Nephew Tetragram)."

"These are the twelve Stones of the Breastplate of Decision."

Then Adeptus Primus ascends to the White Altar. Parokheth is closed. Behind the Veil, on the White Altar, Adeptus Primus derives the two Witnesses. **"The Kerub Sandalphon proclaimeth** _____, (Name of Left Witness Tetragram). **The Kerub Metatron proclaimeth** _____, (Name of Right Witness Tetragram)."

Behind the Veil, Adeptus Primus enters the Vault. Leaving the door open wide, the Adeptus Primus places the Geomantium on the tripod Circular Altar, and derives the Judge or Seal from the Two Witnesses. From within the Vault, s/he proclaims, **"The Glory of the Shekhinah revealeth *Emeth*, the Seal of God, which is Truth: and it is _____, (Name of Seal Tetragram)."**

From outside the Veil, the Adeptus Secundus invokes the Angelic Intelligence of the Seal Tetragram into the Vault. During the invocation, still standing in the Pastos, the Adeptus Primus harmonizes his/her Middle Pillar Centers with those of the Planetary Wall corresponding to the Intelligence, and as the Divine Brilliance descends from the Spirit Square down the Middle Pillar of the Wall, the Brilliance also descends from the Rose in the Triangle on the Ceiling down the Middle Pillar of the Adeptus Primus. In Vision, the Adeptus Primus sees the Angel manifest at the Wall, and tests the Shining One with the appropriate Signs. The Angelic Intelligence then communicates with the Adeptus Primus, who speaks the Oracle of the Sanctum Sanctorum, with the Adeptus Tertius recording the Oracle.

ABOUT THE AUTHOR

Adam Forrest has been a practicing magician since the age of 16, and a practitioner of the Golden Dawn system of Rosicrucian magic for almost 20 years. He has contributed material to Francis Israel Regardie's *The Complete Golden Dawn System of Magic* (1984), and to Chic and Sandra Tabatha Cicero's *Secret's of a Golden Dawn Temple* (1992). He was co-host, with Dolores Ashcroft-Nowicki, of the first Re-Membering Osiris conference (1993), aimed at re-establishing connections among the diverse branches of the Western Esoteric Tradition. He and his wife and partner Isidora Forrest direct the lecture and ritual program of the Hermetic Society, and present workshops on the Art of Ritual. Adam is also a professional illustrator and graphic designer.

From God to My Soul:
Reading the Auspices
David Godwin

The oath of a Magister Templi is said to be "I will interpret every phenomenon as a direct message from God to my soul." In the case of this high esoteric grade, the consequences of the oath include facing all of your past karma at once—spiritually paying off that huge VISA bill in one lump sum. It also necessarily involves constant attention to and total awareness of your environment, and that includes your spiritual, psychic, astral, mental, emotional, and physical environment—no small feat.

But as an incipient movement in that direction, we mere mortals can make use of the time-hallowed technique of augury and auspice. In ordinary systems of divination, you perform some action—dealing cards, throwing dice, casting yarrow stalks, drinking tea, poking the ground with a stick, or something else—to produce random results which you then interpret in terms of the question at hand. The approach of augury or taking the auspices is entirely different, however, because here you don't do anything to produce random results. You wait for them to come to you; you assume an attentive attitude and wait for the universe to speak to you. In this way, God sends direct messages to your soul at least *some* of the time!

The easiest, safest, and most straightforward way to practice augury today is by a system very similar to that of the ancient Romans. The adepts of the Golden Dawn do not seem to have taken this approach, but it is no real problem to adapt the flexible GD system to the situation. In fact, Roman augury was practiced in such a way that Golden Dawn techniques seem to be tailor made for it.

Roman augurs were officials of the state and members of the college of augurs.[1] They were called upon to deliver forecasts relative to the condition of the empire (or earlier, the republic), the health of the ruler, and, perhaps most frequently, the outcome of a battle or military campaign. Any male patrician could be an augur, although he had to be a member of the official college to perform auspices for the state. Women were apparently barred from the office in the somewhat patriarchal Roman society, but a few found their place as priestesses or oracles. An oracle differs from an augur, however, in that she channels cryptic messages directly from a god rather than observing signs and interpreting them according to the augur's art.

There were also private augurs who did things such as foretell the future of marriages. Any patrician could be a private augur (the office was forbidden, however, to plebeians). Since they usually performed at weddings, their auspices were usually good in order to avoid offending the newlyweds or their relatives, and the functions they actually performed finally degenerated into minor officiating such as witnessing dowries. This class of fortuneteller was condemned by Cicero in *De divinatione*, his great work on divination and augury.

When an augury was to be taken, a sacred place was designated. This could either be a place previously dedicated for

---

1 I am indebted to Donald Tyson for pointing out reference material that was indispensible in writing this article.

the purpose or it could be a space especially created for the augury at hand. If the place was not a Roman land, it had to be consecrated and dedicated as such beforehand.

The augur faced south and used a special, curved wand (*lituus*) to mark off a section of the heavens that he would observe for a certain period of time, usually midnight to daybreak, although certain occasions called for a period during the day. This whole section of the celestial sphere was called the *templum* (temple). The place *from* which the auspices were to be taken—that is, the place where the augur would take his station during the period of observation—was also consecrated and set off by the use of a spoken formula, which varied according to the occasion. The augur would then pitch a tent in this space, with an opening toward the south (or east, in the case of inaugurations).

Once he had the place marked off and consecrated, and his tent put up and oriented, the augur had to specify exactly what signs he was looking for, whether it be the flight or song of birds (*ex avibus*), thunder and lightning (*ex caelo*), or the behavior of four-footed beasts (*ex quadrupedibus*), although the latter method was never used on state occasions, but only for private augury. There was also the observation of the feeding habits of chickens (*extripudiis*), but, inasmuch as that involves the "casting of a lot," in the form of tossing out chicken feed, it is not strictly the sort of auspice that we are considering here. Aside from all these formal divisions, there was also the omen or accident (*ex diris*), such as stumbling, accidental noise, and so on. The augur then sat on a chair in his tent and waited for the signs to appear. During this time, strict silence had to be observed.

At the beginning of the operation, the augur would ask his assistant (if any): "[Name], I wish you to assist me at the auspices." The assistant, who had been chosen beforehand, would answer, "I will." The augur would then say, "Tell me when silence appears to exist" (*dicito, si silentium esse videbitur*). This part of the ceremony was a ritual formality, for the assistant would immediately answer, without moving or looking around, "Silence appears to exist" (*silentium esse videri*).

The augur could use assistants to look for the signs, and there was a strict formula such as the above according to which he asked them if they had seen anything and their reply.

However, the augur was perfectly free to ignore anything that he did not see for himself.

Thunder and lightning on the left side (east) were considered favorable, while these same signs were unfavorable if they occurred in the west (to the right). If there was thunder or lightning in a clear sky, it was regarded as especially important. If there was any phenomenon of this kind at all, the business of the elective assembly (for magistrates) was suspended for the following day. Needless to say, the office of augur came to be abused in order to cause intentional delays in the electoral process.

Divination by birds was either according to song (*oscines*) or flight (*alites*), but only certain kinds of birds were taken into consideration in each classification. *Oscines*, or birds providing auspices by their songs or cries, included ravens, crows, and owls. A raven's call was favorable on the right and unfavorable on the left, but a crow and owl were just the opposite. *Alites* included eagles, vultures, and ospreys. A few birds, such as woodpeckers, were counted as either *oscines* or *alites*, and some, such as eagle owls, were considered unlucky if they were seen at all.

There are special meanings attached to the direction in which the birds are seen, and each of these has a nonsensical-sounding name in Latin and a special meaning. These details are outlined by Henry Cornelius Agrippa in Book I of his *Three Books of Occult Philosophy* (Llewellyn, 1993). Agrippa lifted this section verbatim from Michael Scot's *Physiognomia*, by the way, including at least one obvious omission. As given by Agrippa and applied specifically to *ex oscines*, however, these terms and directions are as follows:

Fernova	–	Alighting upon the left—good
Fervetus	–	Already sitting upon the left, not flying—bad
Viaram	–	Passing on the right and flying toward the left—good
Confernova	–	Alighting upon the right—good
Confervetus	–	Flying from the right—bad
Scimasarnova	–	Passing and then alighting on right side—good
Scimasarvetus	–	Coming up from behind and alighting—good

Scassarvetus	–	Passing and then alighting on left side—bad
Emponenthem	–	Flying left to right and going out of sight—good
Hartena	–	Flying from right to left behind you and then resting—bad

Augury became increasingly corrupt over the passage of time, so that an augur would tell a new magistrate that he had seen lightning on the left, when in fact he had seen nothing at all, just in order to curry favor from the official. It is said that, in the beginning, augurs watched. Later, they prayed for a result. Still later, they demanded it and tried to compel it or bring it about, as with the feeding of chickens. At last, they just made it all up as they wished. The stage of trying to produce a result rather than simply observing the signs or auspices that naturally occurred is equivalent to divination. Although widely accepted and practiced then and now, in the form of astrology, Tarot cards, geomancy, and so on, divination really represents a compromise and a devolution from the "pure" science of augury.

If the modern magician wishes to bring the Roman process up to date, she or he will find the Golden Dawn approach most useful for the purpose:

The first step is to ascertain the place from which you will take the auspices (i.e., observe phenomena). Preferably, this spot should be out of doors, but a roofed porch would be satisfactory, as would an enclosed area with a large picture window. In any event, you must be able to observe a fairly large area that is outside. Preferably, in accordance with the Roman tradition, you should be facing south. One advantage of this orientation if you are taking auspices at night is that you will be facing the Zodiacal belt and will thus have a clear view of the Moon and planets. Shooting stars and comets are also concentrated along this plane, although it is not very likely that you will see a comet.

There is nothing absolute about the tradition of facing south, however. The Greeks, apparently, faced north instead. All you have to remember is that, according to classical augury, east is generally favorable and west unfavorable.

Once the place has been selected, it should be marked off with the Lesser Banishing Ritual of the Pentagram and pos-

sibly the Lesser Banishing Ritual of the Hexagram as well.
Then perform the Supreme Invoking Ritual of the Pentagram
for Air, for all divination and augury falls within the province
of this element, particularly if it is to consist of observed signs
in the sky, such as celestial phenomena, thunderstorms, or the
behavior of birds. (When performing the Supreme Invoking
Ritual of the Pentagram for Air, don't forget to trace the equili-
brating active pentagram of Spirit in each quarter, while
vibrating the divine names; i.e., EXARP and Eheieh. This is
followed by the invoking pentagram for Air, with ORO IBAH
AOZPI and YHVH.)

As in all ceremonial workings on the Golden Dawn model,
you should then invoke higher influences, calling upon the
divine power to bless and oversee the operation. Then formally
state the purpose of the ceremony, the object for which the auspices are to be taken. State what signs you will look for and
how you will interpret them. During this part of the ritual, use
the white end of your Lotus Wand to mark off the section of the
sky (and ground) to which your observations will be confined.
Begin at ground level on the left and proceed clockwise. While
outlining this area, state what you are doing and why; this can
be a simple statement such as: **"Within the quarter of the
heavens thus traced, shall my observations be confined,"** If you want to take a relatively unstructured approach,
which I personally feel is most suitable for this kind of operation, look for any sort of happening whatsoever and interpret it
according to intuition and your knowledge of Qabalistic associations. However, if you are going to do this, that too, must be
formally stated at the beginning of the ceremony.

You must also state the time period involved. If you are
going to stay up all night watching the sky, you must specify
dawn as the termination of the ceremony. Although this was
the normal procedure for Roman augury upon state occasions,
a modern augury for private purposes could be confined to a
period of an hour or even less. The important thing is that you
specify the time limit. If a buzzard comes and stands on your
head five minutes after the time limit has expired, it doesn't
count—at least not for the specific purpose of the augury.

At this point you should again invoke the higher powers,
but this time in a more specific fashion, working your way
down the "chain of command" from a divine name to operative
spirit. The established concluding sentence for this stage of a

Golden Dawn divinatory operation is **"Arise before me clear as a mirror, O magical vision requisite for the accomplishment of this divination."** However, in the present case, I would substitute the word "augury" for "divination."

In the case of taking the auspices, it is probably not necessary to go through all the elaborate steps of the Golden Dawn's Z2 formula for divination. The formula includes a careful consideration of the probabilities involved and two determinations of preliminary results. This procedure, which is designed to emulate the Neophyte ritual, does not seem to apply very well to the passive process of observing auspices.

At the conclusion of the time limit, whether anything has occurred or not, thank the powers involved, dismiss any attracted spirits by the usual formula, and close with the Lesser Banishing Ritual of the Pentagram.

But what should one look for and how should one interpret it? The Romans had books to consult as well as certain ground rules such as left = favorable and right = unfavorable. The modern practitioner may prefer more detail than can be obtained from such a simple binary system. That is where the Golden Dawn system of Qabala and Tarot come in handy. Although he was not writing at the time about the divinatory meaning of the events in the environment, Aleister Crowley provided a good description of associating them with this system in a letter to a follower (reproduced in *Magick Without Tears*). In this letter, Crowley was describing a method of building up the Qabalistic correspondences in your memory by associating everything you see with a chain of connections. For example, the front door of your house reminds you of the Hebrew letter daleth, the fence in your yard calls the letter cheth to mind, and an automobile going down the street reminds you of the Tarot trump, the Chariot, which is associated with the fence through the letter cheth.

In the case of augury, you might want to consider, for example, *how many times* a bird calls. This gives you an immediate connection with the Tree of Life and the Tarot. If you choose to work from the standpoint of the Tarot, what kind of bird is it? Which suit of the Tarot has the closet associations with the bird? If you intend to do an augury using the cries of birds, it would be useful to make out a list ahead of time, giving the types of birds likely to be heard in your area and their elemental associations (and hence Tarot suit). Is a crow Earth,

Air, Fire, or Water (that is, Pentacles, Swords, Wands, or Cups)? How about a pheasant? You must make up your own list based on your own intuitive perception of these birds, because there is very little that is firmly established. I would say that an eagle is traditionally Air, and my feeling is that hawks should be Fire. All water birds such as ducks and cranes are Water. There is a natural tendency of which you should beware, however, and that is to associate *all* birds with Air. Personally, I would say that a crow is Air, but a Pheasant, because it sticks close to the ground most of the time, is Earth.

To take an example, let's say that your question involves changing jobs. Would you be better off to stay where you are or to embark upon uncertain new territory that may prove to be advantageous in the long run? You have determined beforehand (and stated aloud as part of the ceremony) that you are performing an augury by bird cries (*ex avibus*) and that you are going to use a system of Tarot associations that you have worked out beforehand. You hear a pheasant call twice. That indicates the two of Pentacles—the Lord of Harmonious Change. Your question is answered.

If the augury is by bird *flight*, you might want to consider the direction in which the birds are flying. Aside from the data provided by Michael Scot (and Agrippa), which may or may not be authentic (and which is incomplete in any case), you could associate the cardinal points with the elements—or even consider the standard layout of the Tarot on the celestial sphere that surrounds you at all times. Of course, you will have to be aware of the sphere as it exists at that moment; due to the rotation of the earth, it is constantly changing. The first thing you would have to do is to determine toward which star group or constellation the birds are flying—naturally, it helps if you are performing this particular augury on a clear night and are familiar with the constellations.

If you do not already have a clear image built up of the Tarot as projected on the celestial sphere, you can consult MacGregor Mathers' essay, "The Tree of Life as Projected in a Solid Sphere," in Israel Regardie's *The Golden Dawn*. From this, we see, for example, that the Big Dipper is always the Princess (Page) of Wands. If your birds are flying toward Ursa Major, then, it betokens "brilliance, courage, beauty, force, sudden in anger, or love, desire of power, enthusiasm, revenge." Of course, you would also want to consider what kind of birds they were and how many of them were seen. If they are birds of ill omen, the "ill-dignified" reading is indicated. Or, if they are flying *from* that direction to a point upon the earth, you should take the opposite of the normal reading. The number of birds yields additional information through association with the Tree of Life.

Aside from ceremonial augury (*auspicia impetrativa*), one may also attempt to interpret chance events in one's environment as auspices (*auspicia oblativa*), as "direct messages from God to your soul." The augury by accident, or *auspicia ex diris*, falls into this category. This sort of augury, which would have been used only for private purposes in Rome, is probably the most useful for us today, inasmuch as any unusual occurrence can be taken as a sign or omen. Indeed, at the stage of a Magister Templi, it doesn't even have to be unusual; it can be any phenomenon—indeed, *every* phenomenon. The theory is that, if it were not meant to be a personal message for you alone, you would either not be there or you would not notice that particular configuration of time, place, and event.

The types of augury as given by Agrippa are really of this type, because, as he states them, the observation is apparently taken as you are leaving your house on some business; furthermore, either birds or men are equally acceptable as auspices.

Otherwise, as an example of this sort of impromptu augury, let us say that the first thing you notice when you start your day is that a small dog in the neighborhood is annoying a larger dog by trying to initiate some playful tussling, whereas all the big dog wants to do is sleep. This may mean that, at some point during the day, you will be annoyed by someone, or that you yourself will annoy someone (which of these two events is more likely will depend upon which dog you "match" best or feel most closely associated with).

The interpretation of this sort of random event can be as "straightforward" as dream analysis, but it can also become just as elaborate as you care to make it. For example, if you accidentally shut your finger in a door, consider with which Sephiroth that finger is associated. Perhaps the event betokens trouble or danger in the area of life ruled by the associated planet—or perhaps it merely indicates that you should be more careful!

If you do not have all possible phenomena in your environment cataloged and associated with the 32 Paths of Wisdom (and thus the Tarot, Zodiac, and so on), you will have to rely upon your immediate intuitive perception of what an event portends, supplemented with research and reflection later. This is not as hard as it sounds. The more time you spend pondering such associations and the more experience you gain with interpretation, the easier it will become. At the same time, you will be learning a valuable compendium of lore and associations for magical purposes.

ABOUT THE AUTHOR

David Godwin, born in 1939 in Dallas, Texas, and a former resident of Houston, Atlanta, Miami, and New York, is a student of esoteric lore, magic, and the Qabala. He holds a Bachelor of Journalism degree from the University of Texas at Austin and is a 32º Freemason.

The author of *Godwin's Cabalistic Encyclopedia, The Truth About Cabala*, and *Light in Extension*, as well as compiler of the index to the current edition of *The Golden Dawn* by Israel Regardie, Godwin's articles have appeared in *Fate, Gnostica, Llewellyn's Magical Almanac*, and elsewhere.

Godwin has worked as a manual laborer, a newspaper reporter, an editor for a petrochemical magazine, a technical editor for two NASA contractors during the Apollo missions, and a free-lance writer. He is currently senior editor at Llewellyn Publications and lives in Lakeville, Minnesota.

Divination in the
Græco-Egyptian Magical Papyri
M. Isidora Forrest

he Græco-Egyptian Magical Papyri, usually known simply as the Greek Magical Papyri, are a collection of magical texts, written on papyrus rolls in Greek and Demotic which date from the 2nd to the 5th centuries CE (Common Era). I prefer to call them Græco-Egyptian rather than just Greek, for while they were written largely in Greek and they reflect a profoundly hellenized Egyptian culture, they are actually from Egypt (the city of Thebes, modern Luxor) and the magical techniques they employ are almost purely Egyptian.[1] First published in English in 1986 as *The Greek Magical Papyri in Translation including the Demotic Spells* and edited by Hans Dieter Betz, the Magical Papyri are an anthology of ancient 'books' and extracts from books which were translated by an international team of scholars.

The information contained in these texts is extremely rare —a legacy of the coming of the Christian era. Magical books and records, such as those in the Papyri, were systematically destroyed as the Christian religion gained power. We find an example of this kind of destruction in the city of Ephesus in the Christian Bible, *The Acts of the Apostles* 19:19. "Many of them also which used curious arts brought their books together and burned them before all men: and they counted the price of them, and found it fifty thousand pieces of silver."[2] However, we should note that, according to the Biblical record of the incident, this action kicked off an uproar in Ephesus that had the people of the city chanting "Great is Artemis of the Ephesians!" for two solid hours!

---

[1] Betz, Hans Dieter, *The Greek Magical Papyri in Translation including the Demotic Spells* (Chicago and London: University of Chicago Press, 1986), Introduction, p xlvi.
[2] King James version.

Another incident is recorded in 13 CE when the Emperor Augustus ordered the burning of two thousand magical scrolls. Unfortunately, the authorities were not content merely to burn magical books; they also began burning magicians. As a result of this kind of suppression and persecution, magicians took their magic deeply underground. Admonitions to secrecy, such as those found throughout the Magical Papyri, increased.[3]

Before discussing the types of divination found in the Papyri, it is necessary to provide a general introduction to the topic. What is contained in the Magical Papyri? How do they fit in with the religious and magical culture around them? What is the significance of the discovery of the texts which Betz says in the Introduction to his book are as important to the study of Græco-Roman religions as the Nag Hammadi texts were to the understanding of Gnosticism or the Qumran texts to first-century Judaism?[4]

Before the discovery of the Papyri, many historians held a distorted view of the role of magic in the everyday lives of the people. That is, they believed that it *didn't have* much of a role except among very "primitive" people—which the classical civilizations decidedly were not. I have also read authors who seem astounded that most people didn't seem to differentiate between "magic" and "religion." (Ancient Egypt is an example of a culture that didn't make such a distinction; the ancient Egyptian language didn't even have a specific word for religion.[5] It *did* have a specific word for magic: *heka.*) With the discovery of the Papyri, and an increased respect for ancient religions among scholars, many have reassessed their views. Now it is more commonly accepted that magic probably had a larger role in people's lives than previously thought and could even have been an expression of religious feeling.[6]

For religious scholars, the Papyri hold clues and tidbits of hitherto unknown mythological material as well as parts of otherwise lost invocations, prayers, liturgy and rituals. The Papyri also contain what appears to be older Greek material in which the Greek Gods and Goddesses act more as they do in Greek folklore—capricious and even dangerous. On this subject, Betz comments that "strange as it may sound, if we wish

---

[3] Betz, *op. cit.*, p. xli.
[4] *Ibid.*, p. xlii.
[5] Shafer, Byron, ed. *Religion in Ancient Egypt* (Ithaca and London: Cornell University Press, 1991) p. 123.
[6] Betz, *op. cit.*, p. xli.

to study Greek folk religion, the magical papyri found in Egypt are to be regarded as one of the primary sources."[7]

For modern magicians, too, the Papyri are important. The "spells" contained in these Papyri (and others like them now lost) are almost without doubt, the source documents for mediaeval and hence modern magical workings. The Magical Papyri contain formulae for summoning spirit helpers, attracting lovers, creating prosperity in business; as well as many, many workings for divination of various kinds. One has only to compare the texts of the Magical Papyri workings with the texts of mediaeval grimoires such as the *Goetia of the Lemegeton*, the *Grimorium Verum* and the *Grand Grimoire* to see their kinship. (For example, one parallel between them is the technique of repeating invocations several times—in case they don't work the first time. This technique shows up in the Papyri workings, in grimoires, and in modern Golden Dawn teachings.) It is from the Magical Papyri that the much-discussed "Bornless Ritual" is derived.[8] The Papyri can be a rich source of ideas for adaptation to our magical work today.

As is true of so many other important antiquities, the Græco-Egyptian Magical Papyri came to the West through the interest of a collector; in this case, Jean d'Anastasi, a 19th century diplomat who represented Sweden in the Arabian court. His passion was the collection of Egyptian papyri and among those he collected were the magical books from Thebes which we now know as the Greek Magical Papyri. Their exact origin is unknown, although it is likely that these papyri were from a single cache, a tomb, temple or perhaps from a hiding place such as the one in which the Dead Sea Scrolls were found. Whatever their source, they were eventually shipped to Europe and auctioned off to the British Museum in London, the Bibliotheque Nationale and the Louvre in Paris, the Staatliche Museum in Berlin and the Rijksmuseum in Leiden where they remained undisturbed, untranslated, and unpublished for nearly a century.

One reason it took so long for scholars to understand the importance of the material in the Magical Papyri and to translate them was that there was a huge prejudice against the study of "magic." No reputable scholar wanted her or his name

---

[7] *Ibid.*, p. xlv.
[8] See Isreal Regardie's *Ceremonial Magic, A Guide to the Mechanisms of Ritual* (Wellingborough, Northamptonshire: The Aquarian Press, 1980) for more on the Bornless Ritual and its development in the hands of Golden Dawn initiates, including Aleister Crowley.

associated with it. A remark by the *fin-de-siecle* German scholar Ulrich von Wilamowitz-Moellendorff illustrates the depth of
the feeling at the time. He noted, "I once heard a well-known
scholar complain that these papyri were found because they
deprived antiquity of the noble splendor of classicism."[9] Since
the Papyri were located in Europe, World War II also inter-
fered considerably with the process of translating and publishing them. In fact, the galley proofs for the book that was to be
published were almost destroyed during the bombing of
Leipzig. Fortunately, they did survive and with the end of the
war, as well as increasing interest in the study of world religions, the Magical Papyri were finally published.[10]

In addition to the workings recorded in the Papyri, we
also have some other clues as to the way in which magical and
divinatory operations were worked in Egypt at the beginning
of the Common Era from amuletic carvings on gemstones and
other materials. Gemstone talismans from this period are particularly numerous.[11] And while the Egyptians had used personal amulets and talismans made of durable materials such
as metals and stones for centuries, this practice was not as
common in the hellenized world until later. The idea of combining text along with amuletic design also had an Egyptian origin.[12] By studying the magical images, the epithets of deities,
and the purposes for which the talismans were designed, we
can gain a greater understanding of the use of magic in people's lives. The gemstone amulets record fragments of religion
that would have otherwise been lost. In addition to the Papyri
and the gemstone amulets, some of this kind of material has
also been preserved for us in Gnostic, Hermetic, Neopytha-
gorean and Neoplatonic texts.

Many of the workings in the Papyri are what we might
consider "low" magic, i.e., workings to bring a lover to one's bed,
to punish a lover who *won't* come to one's bed, to bring wealth, or
luck at the chariot races. A number of them, however, are specifically spiritual workings. The Papyri's famous *Mithras Liturgy*
is an example. In this working the operator is attempting to
enter the company of the God by using a series of invocations,
vocalizations and visualizations. I believe that many modern

9 Urlich von Wilamowitz-Moellendorff, *Redon und Vortrage* (Berlin: Weidmann, 1902), pp. 254-255.
10 Betz, *op. cit.*, p. xlvi.
11 Bonner, Campbell, *Studies in Magical Amulets, Chiefly Graeco-Egyptian* (Ann Arbor: The University of Michigan Press, London: Geoffrey Cumberlege, Oxford University Press, 1950), p.3.
12 *Ibid.*, p.8.

magicians who read this Liturgy would not only understand it but would even feel at home with much of the ritual.

There are other workings in the Papyri which seem strangely mixed, as if part of the working was originally a spiritual working (there actually are some quite powerful invocations in the Papyri)—and then someone tacked a practical magic ending on it. In fact, this may be exactly what happened.

At the beginning of the Common Era, as Christianity became more and more dominant, many of the Pagan temples were closed down and the priests (primarily, but priestesses, too), would have been out of work. It seems likely that some of them would have become freelancers, perhaps selling their knowledge of temple rituals, divinations, and talismans as they traveled through villages, towns and cities. This could explain the strange mixture. Even if these workings were not originally intended for practical magic use, once in the hands of non-clergy, they would naturally be turned to use for personal concerns: love, money, personal power—issues that have been and always will be of deep concern to human beings in all social strata.

As noted earlier, the Papyri are recorded in Greek and Demotic Egyptian, a late form of the hieroglyphs. It is an interesting comment on the degree to which the Greek and Egyptian cultures mixed, at least in the magical communities, that some of the papyri are recorded bilingually—within the same working. The deities invoked are from an international group of Pantheons, too, (mostly Greek, Egyptian and Hebrew, with some Babylonian, Zoroastrian, Scythian and Thracian thrown in for good measure). Hekate, in her underworld aspect, is one of the most often-invoked deities of the Papyri. Apollo and Selene as Sun and Moon also have many invocations addressed to them. Hermes Trismegistos and Thoth are invoked, but not as often as one might think given Thoth's reputation as a magician. Isis is invoked often, not only in Her magician aspect, but just about every other aspect as well, as are Osiris, Anubis, and other popular Egyptian Gods. In relation to divination and prophecy, again, Apollo appears quite often. Interestingly, IAO is *the* most often-named Deity in the Papyri.[13]

Another fascinating feature of the Græco-Egyptian Magical Papyri is the use of what the *Chaldean Oracles* refer

---

[13] Betz, *op. cit.*, p. xlvii.

to as "the barbarous names of evocation" which the reader is adjured to "change not." These are holy and magical names, words, and in some cases, series of unintelligible sounds, that the operator uses in invocation or as text for marking talismans or other implements used in the rite. In examining these 'barbarous' names (in this case, *barbarous* simply means "foreign" – Greeks called all foreigners barbarians), one can see traces of the origin of at least some of them in the names and epithets of 'foreign' Goddesses and Gods. For example, this partial invocation from the Papyri's *Eighth Hidden Book of Moses:*

ORTHO BAUBO NEORADER SOIRE SOIRE SANKANTHARA ERESCHIGAL APARA KEOPH IAO SABAOTH ABRATIAOTH ADONAI ZAGOURE...

We can recognize easily the names of the Greek Goddess Baubo and the Sumerian Queen of the Underworld, Ereshkigal, as well as IAO, the Greek version of Yahweh, and the Hebrew Godnames Tzabaoth and Adonai in this text. How many of the others are actually Deity names or epithets that were corrupted through scribal error or misunderstanding?

The Papyri also contain a number of palindromes (words spelled the same forwards and backwards), such as the famous ABLANATHANALBA—probably the source of the stage magician's exclamation "abracadabra!" These are often used to create new sacred words by dropping one letter each time the word is spoken. The Papyri also show these palindromes used as amuletic text written in a triangular formation known as "the wing," again dropping one letter each time as the word is written from bottom to top or top to bottom.

The practice of what the Golden Dawn knows as 'the assumption of Godforms,' in which the operator declares that she or he is this or that particular Deity and, for a brief time while in contact with the energy of the Deity, acts as the Deity, is another prominent feature of the Papyri. Also prevalent is the Egyptian practice of 'threatening the gods.' This is a magical technique, often used in conjunction with the assumption of Godforms, in which the operator demands that the god/spirit/elemental obey her or his commands either because of the magician's own magical power or by virtue of the power of the Deity which the magician wields. Both these techniques were quite foreign to the Greeks and were even aspects of the Papyri magic which were likely to have been uncomfortable for them. Many Greeks would have considered these practices hubristic and thus dangerous.[14] On the other hand, the titillation of dangerous magic, along with the powerful, even legendary, Egyptian reputation for magical knowledge could have added to Greek attraction to Egyptian methods.

Since so many of the methods of working shown in the Papyri are Egyptian, it is worthwhile noting the esteem in which the Egyptian clergy, who were almost without doubt the original creators of the Papyri workings, held magic. John Baines, professor of Egyptology at Oxford University, says that to the Egyptians magic was "a realm of legitimate action and a mode of understanding which, like conceptions of the cosmos, involved all of creation from the highest to the lowest."[15]

The Egyptians considered the God Magic (Heka) as a per-sonified primordial force that existed from the beginning and was essential to Creation.[16] Many, perhaps even most, Egyptians used magic every day in simple ways such as wear-ing amulets or carrying talismans. From Pharaoh to peasant, people commonly used simple yes-or-no divinations to either confirm or help them make decisions.[17] Dreams were another way of obtaining oracles. To help in interpreting their dreams, people would turn to a priest with a dream book or perhaps to the local psychic, "the wise woman," as several New Kingdom texts from Deir el-Medina call her.[18] She would supply advice and consult over the meaning of an oracle. In the *Instruction to Merikare*, magic was given to humanity to avert "what may happen." Magic, then, was a way of overcoming Fate.

During the period of the composition of the Magical Papyri—the centuries surrounding the beginning of the Common Era—there was considerable belief in predestination, in the rule of Fate. Initiation into the Mysteries was one method of overcoming one's Fate. The Grace of a particular Goddess or God was another. A number of the most popular deities of the time, such as Isis, Sarapis, Persephone and increasingly, Jesus, were considered Saviors and Rulers of

---

[14] Bonner, *op. cit.*, p. 23.
[15] Shafer, *op. cit.*, p. 165.
[16] *Ibid.*
[17] *Ibid.*, p. 170.
[18] *Ibid.*, p. 171.

Fate. Combining the power of Deity with magical working was yet another method of freeing oneself from the bonds of Fate.[19]

Of course, to be able to free oneself from Fate, one had to know what that Fate was. Enter divination. The Magical Papyri show us a number of the methods of divination which were in use at the time, including scrying and a kind of geomantic divination with leaves. A compilation of a number of the methods in general use (at least in Rome) at the time of the Papyri was made by the scholar Marcus Terentius Varro (116-27 BCE) in his work entitled *The History of Rome and its Religions*, a work which is now, unfortunately, mostly lost.[20] Varro broadly categorizes types of divination by Element: geomancy, aeromancy, hydromancy and pyromancy. Then there are various "sub divinations" in each category. For example, under the category of hydromancy, we might also find scrying in any reflective surface, such as a polished soldier's shield (*catoptromancy*), scrying in a glass bowl (*lecanomancy*), or even "divination by the belly" (*gastromancy*) which actually referred to a belly-shaped vessel filled with water.[21]

The Magical Papyri that we have left to us demonstrate a number of these methods, however the Papyri's most popular methods of divination by far are direct revelation from the Deity and dream oracle. Direct revelation might be by Divine communication with the operator herself or himself or by use of a 'channel,' usually a virgin boy. Those desiring information could seek visions in lamps or bowls. One of the texts for a bowl divination states that it was "the divination of Isis when She was searching for Osiris." For dream communication, the operator would follow the ritual requirements and go to sleep, sometimes taking a symbol of the working to bed with her or him. By morning, the dreamer would have their answer. Divination by omen is also found in the Papyri; these are usually ritual workings followed by a period of waiting to observe the hoped-for omen. There are also a number of workings to divine the identity of a thief, including one in which the operator uses the head of a drowned man to reveal the thief.

19 For more on the idea of Fate and Predestination (*Heimarmene* and *Ananke*) during this time period, see Walter Scott, *Hermetica: the Ancient Greek and Latin Writings Which Contain Religious or Philosophic Teachings Ascribed to Hermes Trismegistus* (Boulder, CO: Hermes House, 1982).
20 Luck, Georg, *Arcana Mundi, Magic and the Occult in the Greek and Roman Worlds* (Baltimore & London: The John Hopkins Unversity Press, 1985), p. 253.
21 *Ibid.*, p. 255.

Simple yes-or-no type divinations do not appear commonly in the Papyri.

The Græco-Egyptian Magical Papyri are documentary evidence of our human magical heritage. They provide the modern magic worker not only with fascinating reading but with an opportunity to touch and experience that heritage in a way which our purely scholarly sisters and brothers cannot. As people who *do* magic as well as study it, we have a better chance of understanding what the magicians of the Papyri intended, what they hoped to accomplish. Many scholars, for example, would dismiss the idea that magic actually works out of hand. As magicians ourselves, we would not. Nor would we be likely to consider belief in Apollo as a sign of an undeveloped spirituality. We might even have a better understanding of why a particular ritual action was called for because we have taken that same ritual action and can appreciate its effectiveness.

On the other hand, we would also find much that we might consider either silly or objectionable in the rituals of the Papyri. In fact, almost none of the rites are relevant for magicians today without adaptation. The Papyri are thousands of years old; the human race has changed during that time and our rituals *must* change with us. Unless our rites make psychological, magical, and ethical sense to us today, either they simply will not work or they could have serious psychological consequences for us. Many of the Papyri rites, for example, involve animal sacrifice, a common and pious act when they were written, but hardly acceptable to the Western magician working today. Nonetheless, I am convinced of the power which these ancient workings have to act as roots from which to grow new rites—rites that *will* be relevant and workable for modern magicians.

About the Rite

The ritual that follows is a new lamp divination which employs the form of the rituals in the Græco-Egyptian Magical Papyri. *The Divination of the Lady of the Lamp* is my attempt to grow a new rite from some of those ancient roots. Partly because I wanted to provide readers who have not yet had the opportunity to examine the rituals of the Magical Papyri with a taste of the 'flavor' of the Papyri rites, and partly because I found the style charming, I have attempted to mimic the style of writing in the Magical Papyri. The language is deliberately archaic and I have used bits and pieces from a number of the magical workings to create the invocations of my rite. The manner of using the Lamp for vision is also authentic to the Papyri. The hieroglyphic attributions are new, however, and notes on these attributions follows the ritual script.

As part of this introduction to the rite, I will quote from the Golden Dawn's teachings regarding divination: "The more rigidly correct and in harmony with the scheme of the Universe is any form of divination, so much the more is it likely to yield a correct and reliable answer to the enquirer [sic]."[22] Since this divination ritual asks the inquirer to place the nature of her or his question in correspondence with the Elements, the Planets and the powers of the Zodiac, it is well in harmony with the nature of the Universe and should yield the seeker a profitable answer. It may be used with any type of question, but since it is a form of divination which gives the operator a revelation by direct vision, a question that goes beyond yes-or-no would probably be best. Besides, undertaking this rite is quite a lot of effort for a simple aye-or-nay.

For the magician wishing to work this rite, I can also recommend other Golden Dawn advice on seeking oracles: that one should enter into divination with a clear and unprejudiced mind; that one should be neither angry, fearful, nor prejudiced by love at the time; and furthermore, that one should have a sound knowledge of the correspondences in mind. The system also advises not to divine repeatedly on the same matter, to do the divination in a ritual setting for greater concentration, to purify and consecrate all implements used, and to always invoke the Higher first.[23]

---

22 Regardie, Israel, *The Golden Dawn* (St. Paul, Minnesota: Llewellyn Publications, 1971) Vol. IV, pg. 177.
23 *Ibid.*

Book of Thoth ✳ Table of Hieroglyphs

No.	Egyptian Hieroglyph	Yeztziratic Correspondence		Hebrew Equivalent		Approximate Pronunciation
01		△	Air	א	Aleph	A as in father
02		☿	Mercury	ב	Beth	B
03		☽	Luna	ג	Gimel	G as in gimel
04		♀	Venus	ד	Daleth	D
05		♈	Aries	ה	Heh	H as in hat
06		♉	Taurus	ו	Vav	U/V
07		♊	Gemini	ז	Zayin	Z
08		♋	Cancer	ח	Cheth	Ch as in loch
09		♌	Leo	ט	Teth	T
10		♍	Virgo	י	Yod	Y, or I as in fill
11		♃	Jupiter	כ	Kaph	K
12		♎	Libra	ל	Lamed	L
13		▽	Water	מ	Mem	M
14		♏	Scorpio	נ	Nun	N
15		♐	Sagittarius	ס	Samekh	S
16		♑	Capricorn	ע	Ayin	O as in core
17		♂	Mars	פ	Peh	P
18		♒	Aquarius	צ	Tzaddi	Dj as in adjust
19		♓	Pisces	ק	Qoph	Q
20		☉	Sol	ר	Resh	R
21		△	Fire	ש	Shin	Sh
22		♄	Saturn	ת	Tav	T
23		▽	Earth	ת	Tav	T
24		⊕	Spirit	n/a		H as in ha!
25		♅	Uranus	n/a		I as in ravine
26		♆	Neptune	n/a		Ch as in loch
27		♇	Pluto	n/a		F

THE DIVINATION
OF THE LADY OF THE LAMP

*A lamp divination in the style of the workings recorded
in the Græco-Egyptian Magical Papyri*

*(This was given to Isidora by Thoth, Chief among Magicians,
Great, Great, Great, discoverer and founder of the Sacred
Letters which He wrote with His own fingers. It is most effective. See that you do not perform it frequently or lightly. This
rite is Divine and if you perform it devoutly, you will be successful. It is very powerful and unsurpassable.)*

These are the correspondences of the Sacred Writing
given by Hermes, called Thoth, in his Sacred Book. (See chart.)

From these Sacred Letters, you are to formulate the holy
and secret name of the Divine Goddess, the Lady of the Lamp,
a most-wise Daimon[24] Who will give truthful answer to that
which you desire to know.

This is how you do it: Keeping in your mind the question, assign its Nature to one or more of the five Elements of
the Greeks: Earth, Air, Water, Fire or Spirit. Choose as many
as you wish, or choose none. Write both the Sacred Letter of
Thoth and the English letter to which the Element corresponds
in black ink on pure paper (or papyrus if you can get it).

Next, assign the nature of the question to the ten
Wandering Stars.[25] Again, choose as many as you wish or
choose none. Write the Sacred Letter and the English letter on
the pure paper.

Then assign the nature of the question to the Zodiacal
signs. Choose as many as you wish or choose none. Write the
Sacred Letter and the English letter on the pure paper.

These are the letters of the Sacred Name of the Lady of
the Lamp, the Wise Daimon. You are to write the Sacred
Letters of Her name in a pleasing arrangement and place them
within a cartouche.[26] To discover Her name, you are to arrange
the letters in any order you wish, placing the English vowel 'e'
wherever you need it in order to be able to pronounce the
name. See that you formulate a pleasing name for the Lady.

---

24 A Daimon is a divine spirit, not to be confused with 'demon'.
25 That is, the ten modern planets.
26 A cartouche is the Egyptian symbol for Eternity often seen surrounding the names of Pharoahs.

Once you have done this, you are to consecrate the Lamp with Her name. Take a purified oil Lamp, not colored red[27], and write upon it the name of the Lady. Write it in the Sacred Letters and in English. If you are using a candle, also not colored red, you should carve the name into the wax or wrap the candle in the pure paper upon which you have written Her name. See that you do not use too much paper as you will burn the candle completely. Put the Lamp upon your Altar until the day you will perform the rite. Or you may proceed with the rite now.

You may perform your rite according to the nature of the quality to which it corresponds. If of the nature of Increase, perform when Selene[28] is waxing. If of Decrease, when the Goddess is waning. If of Balance, perform when She shows Her full face.

On the day you wish to perform the rite, bathe yourself well and put on pure garments made of linen. In any case, see that you wear not wool. Then, in a room you have set aside for the purpose, place an Altar in its center and cover the Altar in white linen. Place upon it your Lamp, pure water (Nile water if you can get it) in a shell, and white wine or milk with white flowers of the season as an offering to the Lady. Have also a means to light the fire of Her Lamp.

Here is how you invoke the Lady: Approach the Altar, lift up your hands and say,

"I call upon the Most High One to attend my rite!"

"NAIENCHRE. (pronounced: Nigh-en-kray) NAIEN-CHRE, Mother of Fire and Water. NAIENCHRE. NAIENCHRE, Mother of Air and Earth. Elements, be still and be no hindrance to my divination! But open my senses that I may know the presence of the Lady of the Lamp, the Lady of Flame, the Lady of Wisdom."

Light the Lamp chanting the name of the Lady which you have formulated previously as you do it. Next take up the Lamp and bring it to the East of the room. Show it forth to the East and say,

"Great is my Lady (*NAME*) for She causeth me to know."

---

[27] Red is the color of Set, enemy of Isis, Osiris and Horus, and according to Egyptian tradition would not be appropriate for beneficial magic.

[28] The Goddess of the Moon and the moon itself.

Do this also in the South, West, and North. Return to the Altar and hold the Lamp on high and say,

"Great is my Ethereal Lady (*NAME*) for She causeth me to know."

Hold the Lamp to Ge[29] and say,

"Great is my Chthonic Lady (*NAME*) for She causeth me to know."

Now, this is the powerful invocation. You speak this to the Lady and She will come and reveal to you concerning the thing you wish.

Seat yourself before the Lamp and look into its flame as you speak.

"I call upon Thee, Lady (*NAME*), Living Lady of the Lamp. I conjure Thee Holy Light, Holy Brightness by Thy Holy Name (*NAME*). Invisible Mother of Light, give Thy strength. Give Thy Divine Spirit. Let there be opened for me the House of the Lady (*NAME*) Who Knoweth All Things. Let there be Light, Breadth, Depth, Length, Height and Brightness. Enter in and show me that which I desire to know. Answer me with Thy holy voice so that I may understand Thee clearly. Leave the sweet Light and render me this service. Reveal to me concerning my question."

"Open to me O Flame of Prophecy! O Holy Light! O Holy Brightness! ABRAAL. BAIBEIZOTH EBAI BEBOTH. ENOSADE. THIAOTH IOVEL. MANE OUSEIRI MANE ISI MANE THIOTHI. AZARACHTHARAZA IO SANKANTHARA." (Pronounced: Ah-bra-al. Bye-bay-zoth Eh-bye Bay-both. En-oh-sah-day. Thee-ah-oth Yo-vel. Mah-ney Oo-say-ree Mah-ney Ee-see Mah-ney Thee-oh-thee. Ah-zah-rock-thah-rah-zah Ee-oh Sahn-khan-thah-rah.)

"O Thou Lady (*NAME*), open to me! Hither come hither come hither Lady. By Thy name I conjure Thee, by the Sacred Letters of THIOTHI, I conjure Thee, by ABLANATHANALBA, (Pronounced: Ah-blah-nah-thah-nahl-bah.) **I conjure Thee. Holy Lady, come!"**

After saying the Light-bringing spell, you will perceive Her presence. If you do not yet perceive Her presence, repeat the Light-bringing spell once, twice. Then close your eyes and

---

29 The Goddess of the Earth and the earth itself.

anoint them with the pure water from the shell upon the Altar. Keeping them closed, say,

"AHH. EEE. EHH. III. OOO. YYY. OHH."[30]

Repeat this two more times with your eyes closed. Then with eyes open, see the bright light of the Lamp. It is very bright and soon you will see the Lamp fire becoming like a great vault surrounding you. And there, within the Light, you will see the Goddess. When She comes, say,

"Welcome, Lady (*NAME*)."

Ask Her your question. She will give swift and truthful answer to all that you ask. When you have received your answer, thank the Lady, and so that the Light Magic may remain with you, pass your hands over Her flame three times, saying Her name. To dismiss Her, say;

"I thank Thee, Wise Daimon, Lady of the Lamp Who hath given truthful answer. This wine for Thee."

Pass the cup of wine over Her flame.

"These flowers for Thee."

Pass the flowers over Her flame.

"My thanks for Thee."

Kiss your hand and pass it over Her flame.

"Thou hast brought Light, Breadth, Depth, Length, Height and Brightness. O holy Lady, leave me now with Thy blessings."

Leave the offerings for Her upon the Altar. Allow the Lamp to burn out completely. *This is the end of the divination.*

Notes on the Method of Attribution of the Hieroglyphs:

My aim in making these attributions was to be able to use the Egyptian Sacred Writing with the Golden Dawn/Yetziratic system of correspondences. I wished to include attributions for the 12 signs of the Zodiac, the 10 modern Planets and the five Elements (with Spirit) for a total of 27. An obvious place to start looking for these correspondences was with the monoliteral (single sound or phonetic) hieroglyphs since a number of these already correspond to some of the Hebrew letters.

There is not always complete agreement among scholars as to which of the hieroglyphs should be included in the list of

---

[30] These sounds represent the seven Greek vowels and correspond to the seven ancient planets.

monoliterals. I used Barbara Watterson's book, *Introducing Egyptian Hieroglyphics* as the source for my list of monoliterals (which I believe is in agreement with most modern scholarly opinion); this list totals 25. I added two additional hieroglyphs to complete the list, choosing the Egyptian word for Earth (*Ta*) as the correspondence for Elemental Earth and Tav, and the glyph LION which sometimes represents the sound 'R' and sometimes 'L', for Libra and Lamed. (As is found in many Oriental languages, the Egyptian language sometimes confused the sounds 'R' and 'L'. One finds translations where both the glyphs MOUTH and LION are sometimes translated as 'R' and sometimes as 'L'. I chose to assign MOUTH to the Sun and Resh and LION to Libra and Lamed.)

Whenever possible, I matched the hieroglyph with the Hebrew letter to which its sound corresponds. In cases where this was not possible, either because several letters had a similar sound or because I wished to assign separate hieroglyphs to each Elemental, Planetary or Zodiacal power, I did try to make the assignation with a reason in mind, rather than just making a random assignment. I would like to make note of those reasons here:

For Spirit, I chose the glyph TWISTED ROPE or WICK. The sound of this letter is a breathy 'H' sound. In a number of languages "Breath" and "Spirit" are the same word (e.g., Greek *pneuma*; Latin *spiritus*; Hebrew *ruach* and *neshamah*); in Golden Dawn ritual, "Breath is the evidence of Life" and 'H' is "our mode of representing the ancient Greek aspirate, or initial breath and breath is the evidence of Life." If the glyph represents a Wick, as some scholars think, then the Fire of Spirit could also be represented here. For Neptune, I chose the SHADED CIRCLE glyph. Some scholars theorize that this represents the placenta. If so, the waters of the womb and the deep watery unconscious of Neptune are aptly represented by this glyph. For Uranus, I chose the glyph TWO FEATHERS. These are the feathers of Shu, Lord of the Air and a correspondence for Uranus' airy attributes. For Pluto, I chose the HORNED VIPER whose dangerous power corresponds to the sometime life-shaking transformations of Pluto. The serpent, like the Planet Pluto, is often a symbol of transformation and regeneration. In addition, the sound of the hieroglyph, 'F', is similar in sound to the hiss of a snake.

An example of the creation of the Name of the Lady of the Lamp:

As an example, we will use the question, *"What changes must I make in my life in order to enhance my spiritual growth?"*

The Elemental correspondence is obviously Spirit (the glyph TWISTED ROPE and the sound breathy 'h'). You could also consider adding the correspondences for Elemental Fire, as your intuition guides you. For the Planetary attributions, again be guided by your intuition and your knowledge of the correspondences. For the concept of change, you could choose Uranus or the Moon; the Moon might also serve to represent growth. Or you could choose the Sun to correspond to the Adept's Tipharetic spiritual work. In this case, I'll choose Uranus (the glyph TWO FEATHERS and the sound 'i' as in ravine) and the Sun (the glyph MOUTH and the sound 'r'). For Zodiacal correspondences, I'll choose Aries (the glyph SQUARE SPIRAL and the sound 'h') since I am a sun-sign Aries and it is myself I wish to change. I will also choose Libra (the glyph LION and the sound 'l') since I suspect there is something I need to balance in order to make change.

To make the symbol of the Lady's Name, arrange the hieroglyphs TWISTED ROPE, TWO FEATHERS, MOUTH, SQUARE SPIRAL and LION and enclose them in a cartouche. To pronounce the Lady's name, use the sounds: breathy 'h', 'i', 'r', 'h', and 'l', and add the "helping letter 'e'" (as Budge calls it) between the consonants to create the Lady's Name. In this case, the Name would be Hirehel. You may also choose to rearrange the letters: Irhehel, Hileher, or Rileheh. This may be done by intuition, aesthetic choice, or for a magical reason. For example, if I wished to have the Name begin with the Solar correspondence, I could choose to use the Name Rileheh.

ABOUT THE AUTHOR

Morgan Isidora Forrest has been a practitioner of the Golden Dawn system of Magic for more than ten years. She is an accomplished ritualist who, with her personal and magical partner, Adam Forrest, teaches The Art of Ritual, a workshop series which helps participants enhance their ritual abilities. In addition to her Golden Dawn and Hermetic work, Isidora is a leader in the Portland, Oregon Neo-Pagan community. She has served the Goddess Isis as Her Priestess for more than seven years. She also serves Phoebus Apollo as His Pythia at 'new Delphi'. Isidora has authored many dozens of Neo-Pagan, Hermetic, and Isiac rituals, has contributed material to Chic and Tabatha Cicero's *Secrets of a Golden Dawn Temple*, and is currently writing her first book, *The Book of Isis*. In non-magical life, Isidora is a freelance commercial writer and an artist.

The Gypsy Runes*

Dolores Ashcroft-Nowicki

During the war I was evacuated from the Islands with my parents and we went up north, both my father and my mother being of northern stock. We settled in The Wirral, a place where the veil between the dense and the astral worlds is very thin indeed. The Wirral has very strange vibrations and one can penetrate that veil very easily.

There I attended a school consisting mainly of other Channel Island children, who were also far from home. This school was some two and a half miles from where I lived and if you were unlucky enough to be kept in after school (a frequent state of affairs with me), then it was a case of walking home. At that time it was all open country and the walk was an eerie one, especially on misty Autumn days when the days drew in. On one side of the road, about halfway between the villages, was an open moor and here, twice a year, a family of Gypsies used to make a wayside camp.

There is a tradition in my family that on my father's side, we have a strain of Gypsy blood. Be that as it may, we never turn any of the traveling folk away from our doors. It was, therefore, only a matter of time before I was a frequent caller at the camp fire. On my first approach, I was taught my manners in no uncertain way and afterwards treated the fire with the respect due it. I learnt never to pass between a man and the fire, and NEVER to approach any fire for the first time without asking permission. All this I learnt from Vashti, an incredibly ancient (to me at that time) grandmother. I never dared tell my parents where I spent my time—gypsies were supposed to steal children—and gypsy blood notwithstanding —I knew they would have worried. After many weeks the fami-

---

* First published in *Quadriga* 1977

ly left to go south and I felt the loss of my friends keenly, especially the grandmother.

When they returned in the Spring, I renewed my visits and this time I made no bones about preferring the company of the old lady to that of the children. I learnt a little of the Romani language and could make an attempt to "rakker romani" with the other members of the group. But to me, the most important lessons were those in palmistry and the art of "dukkerin," or fortune telling. I could listen for as long as she would talk and never tire.

Once, however, old Vashti said to me, *"Thisna tha way fur 'un, youm be of the sea folk and should use t' Sea Stones."* This was something new and I gave her no peace until she settled down to tell me of the *Stones o 'Leary*. Many years later, when I was more knowledgeable in the old lore, I realized that this name was what common usage had made of the Stones of Llyr, the ancient Celtic Sea God.

Vashti told me the story that long ago, Llyr (she called him Leary) had given ten stones of the sea to a woman who had hidden him from a hunter while he was in his seal shape. He taught her how to gather them and mark them and told her that they would tell her the future. He also told her the rhyme without which the stones would not speak.

The old woman told me that one of the ten had been lost and since then, although the stones would still speak, they would never tell the whole of the picture. She also told me of other kinds of "Telling Stones." Some were Earth Stones, some were made of slips of wood (Athene Williams has written of these in *Prediction*.) Still others were of jewels, though these were a special kind—each jewel had to be different and had to be received as a gift; each one from a different person—male if the recipient was a woman, female if it was a man. It seems to me now that this kind of "Speaking Stone" may well be related to the Urim and Thummin of the High Priest in ancient days.

I asked her if she had any of these stones and she told me *"no,"* she used the hand and the water bowl and *"Nowt else."* But her grandfather had two wives and the second had come from a family who *"traveled agin the waves."* This meant that she came from a family whose traveling route took them along the coast roads. Every family has a route and they stick to it, rarely straying from it unless to attend one of the big fairs or, more rare still, a *Talking Fire* or gathering of several families usually to arrange a marriage.

It was from her grandmother that Vashti had learnt of the Stones; the different kinds and the making and using of them. An Earth person used Kerry Stones (stones of Ceridwen, the Earth Goddess). These must be searched for at a time of day which is neither light nor dark, and should be taken from just below the surface of the Earth. Only an Earth person could use Earth Stones, just as only a Sea person could use the Sea Stones. All this old knowledge was given to me freely from the store of folk memory of an old Romani woman.

Green as I was, I knew enough to ask about the other two Elements. "Are there stones for Fire and Air as well?" *"No"* She told me, *"for Air you used feathers, one from each of nine different birds—the tenth as with the others had been lost."* The name of these she gave me as *Foweys Feathers*—a term that puzzled me for years until I came across a reference to Fohla; though I do not claim it to be the right one, it has a certain kinship to the name used by the old woman. I asked about Fire and was told that Fire was the King of all. It has to be used in a different way, with special berries and woods, dried and cast on the flames—the smoke was then used to tell the future.

It took many visits to wheedle all the details from Vashti but I soaked it all up like a sponge. All through the weeks of their stay I learnt about the "Talking Stones" and a lot more besides. When they started packing up to leave my old teacher took me aside: *"There be summat to tell 'Um, some byes the top 'arf of un fergits things, but th' belly part, that niver fergits, when t'time be reet, all I've taught 'unll coom bak, and likey a bit more besides if'n you'll list to th' belly. Yer not a Romani chil, and yer'll coom late ter yer dukkering, but coomt' will. Yer'll have no need o' hokkibens (lies) yer'll see clear enuff. Kusto bok now.'*

I never saw her again. She died down south and was burnt along with her old Vardo in clothes that had been turned inside out as was the custom in her family. I left school and went to work, and the "top arf" forgot a lot of things until many years later when the study of hidden lore had become my life's work. A friend showed me a small leather bag of stones that he had bought from a sea captain. There were nine round stones, each with a painted symbol on it, and suddenly I was back by a smoky fire listening to old Vashti saying *"Twill all coom back*

and a bit more besides if'n yer listen t' th' belly." Holding them
in my hand I murmured the rhyme that I had learnt so long
ago, and threw them, forming my question as I did so. They
answered after a fashion and I had a curious feeling that the
old lady was there watching me. We "dukkered" with them for
most of the evening, but the answers were never clear cut and
eventually we put them away.

Events changed and my friend moved away. Again the
stones faded from memory until one summer day, walking by
the sea and throwing stones into the wave, I picked up one
with a pattern on it—it awakened a memory and the old symbols flooded back. I looked down and found another but with a
different pattern on it—and there, with the Element of Llyr
washing around my feet, the tenth symbol fell into place.
There had to be an EYE Stone, a Stone that symbolized the "I"
of the Querent—which gave the others something to react to. I
started looking around me, all the old instructions coming
back. *"It mun be on t' ebb just, tha's when the land and the sea
be together like...tis neither one thing nor t'other. Round enuff
ter rool, flat enuff ter fall steady, tek your time chil."* It was as
if she was beside me again.

I took my sea booty home and painted them, waiting impa-
tiently for them to dry. Placing the Eye Stone some way away, I
cupped the others in my hands and whispered the old rhyme:

> *Stones o' Leary,*
> *Stones o' Leary,*
> *tell me truly,*
> *tell me clearly,*
> *give to me an answer true,*
> *show me what I am to do.*
> *Let my EYE see clear and bright*
> *that I may keep my future right.*

The stones rolled toward the Eye stone and came to rest.
As I had been taught, I took away all those that were upside
down with no symbol showing—the Birds of Good News flew
near the Eye Stone, and close by the Waves of the Sea. Below
them rested the Ear of Wheat and the Sun Stone, the most
powerful of all. My good news had come to me across a distance
of time—the harvest of the old knowledge was sun-ripened and
ready to be gathered.

I tried many questions that night and every time the Stones answered truly. At last I threw them and every one lay turned over. I took the hint and placed them in their leather bag and put them away for the night.

Old knowledge, if it be true knowledge, is never lost. This I have proved to my own satisfaction. Anyone can make and use the Rune Stones, the most difficult part is just finding out if one is better working with Earth or Sea. I have found that nearly everyone falls into one or the other of the two. I have never tried to use the feathers—apart from the difficulty of getting ten different ones, I find the other two suffice.

Sea Stones must be gathered in the moment of the Ebb tide. I have found that stones gathered at the Spring tides or Autumn storm seas are more vital than those gathered in the calmer Summer seas or cold Winter ones. They should be well shaped and of a color that will take the clear painting of the symbols. Earth Stones are gathered at dusk and from just below the surface. The same guides in shape and color apply to them. The same rhyme is used but the name of Kerry is substituted for Leary. The Eye Stone is best when approximate to an eye shape. It can be painted in a very lifelike manner. Size is up to you but common sense tells you not to collect small "boulders."

The symbols are simple and no skill with painting is required. In fact, the cruder the better for reasons that I think are because they are more like those of early times and so draw on that part of the race memory.

The *Sun Stone* stands for all the good things in life— Health, Wealth and Happiness. It can also mean (when combined with the *Wheat Stone*), a coming to fruition, i.e., birth or reward. The *Moon Stone* stands for another woman, a period of time, a clouded vision. It pertains to the personality of the Querent as well. The *Rings* can mean marriage or a tie of some kind. In any case it joins things. The *Birds* bring news or they can mean children, or letters, or even ideas. *Waves* speak for themselves—journeys, space to be crossed, inspiration or parting. *Wheat* is always the culmination of something—a harvest to be enjoyed, or if not well earned, then a counting of the cost. The *Crossed Spears* tell of parting and angry words, quarrels, etc. The *Sickle* is death, a cutting off or cutting down; an ending. The *Star* is a hope, a wish, a dream, a goal.

Remember that all the Stones have many combinations according to where they fall in relation to the Eye Stone and

The Gypsy Runes

Eye Stone

Sun

Wheat Sheaf

Three Rings

Birds

Waves

Crossed
Spears

Moon

Saturn
or

Star

Sickle

each other. It takes a long time to learn the subtle nuances of the Stones' speech. It cannot be taught entirely from words—they must be thrown again and again until the meaning becomes apparent in the mind.

Place the Eye Stone about three feet away and form your question clearly in the mind. When you are sure of it, repeat the rhyme—this serves to link the subconscious mind (which is really doing all the work) with the racial memory and group soul. It is from this source that the answer will come, using the mind of the questioner as a channel. The Stones, influenced by the mind power or *Pk*, will then fall in the pattern to make things clear to you. Always keep them in a bag when they are not being used. I made my bag out of a piece of chamois leather. The Stones can be "cleaned" easily by holding them under running water for a few minutes, (although I take mine to the sea and let the waves flow over them).

When you have thrown the stones toward the Eye stone, take away all those that have fallen with the symbol turned face down. These are "dumb" and say nothing. Make your judgment by the others and their nearness to both the Eye Stone and to each other. The nearer the Eye Stone, the more and quicker it will affect you; the nearness to the other stones will strengthen or lessen the effect. In fact, they act in a similar way to the aspects of conjunction or opposition in a horoscope.

As you throw them keep a notebook handy, and put down the many meanings as you come to them. This is the best way to learn. Gradually you will build up a whole series of meanings that are special to you alone. Take your time in looking at the way they have fallen. Don't jump to conclusions quickly, for the Stones have a sense of humor—they can joke with you, and I assure you this is true. Attempt to use them to gain information with which to harm another and you will regret it. Do it too often and you will find, as did someone who fell into this trap, that the Stones will play you false and eventually refuse to talk to you. Stones have always had a peculiar affinity with man, there are many stories of "Living Stones"—the Rune Stones are no exception—one set will last you a lifetime, and if you make them yourself they will be more effective. Place them where they will take heat from your body a short while before you use them and they will work even better. Just as a Flamenco dancer will tuck her castanets inside her bodice for a half hour before she uses them to "draw the spirit from the heart," so the Stones will grow closer to you and a link will be formed that will serve you well. Try it and I wish you *Kushto Bok* with them.

ABOUT THE AUTHOR

Dolores Ashcroft-Nowicki has worked with magic since childhood. She was born and raised in the Channel Island of Jersey, (UK) where she still lives with her husband. She is the Director of Studies for The Servants of the Light School of Occult Science. This was founded by the Rev. W.E. Butler who was in the twenties a founding member of Dion Fortune's school, The Society of the Inner Light. A highly trained and gifted Cosmic Meditator and a third generation psychic sensitive, Dolores has been writing text books on the occult for over ten years. Her books include: *First Steps in Ritual, The Shining Paths, The Ritual Magic Workbook, Highways of the Mind, Inner Landscapes*, and *The Tree of Ecstacy*.

Ceremonial
Archangelic Divination
Oz

ivination is often thought of as a symbolic system that is used to answer questions. Either one person reads for another, or a person reads for her/him-self. This is the most common use of a science that employs archetypal symbols to access deep subconscious and intuitive realms, as well as higher realms and all consciousness that lies beyond our individual selves. Direct access to archetypal beings is of a somewhat unique nature as a divinatory form, although this may be used quite effectively to obtain such information. Many similar varieties of workings fall under the great category of communications currently labeled as "channeling". Actual divination with and by the Archangelic forces is a combination of the use of divinatory skills and direct information access. Unlike "channeling", the information comes through interpretive contacts rather than using individuals to speak for particular entities. As such, it may be used to obtain a balanced and often more unbiased type of information than is available through the use of a "channel". As we constantly evolve our own skills as magickal people, the ways that we obtain information not readily available to our everyday senses and individual logical processes are becoming more and more creative. "Divination by Archangels" may not fit the classical idea of using a set of pictures or objects or a mathematical system to read the Universe. In this case, the archetypes themselves—The Archetypes of the Universe—present the symbols directly. The result is a variety of information that is both precise and broad. As in all forms of divination, of course, the real value of the outcome lies in the abilities of the readers to interpret the information that is gathered.

This is a divinatory form that works best with and for a group. Four or five people are the preferred number to perform the actual divination, although the interpretation may take place in a group of any size. Ideally, four persons should take on the jobs of being a contact for each Archangel, and one other person should be available to facilitate, ask questions, and record responses. If a fifth person is not available, questions can be determined prior to the working and the session can be recorded. In certain cases, two people could each take on two of the Archangels, but it is difficult to get the objectivity and balance that this form provides unless you are both highly practiced Adepts. In no case would I recommend any single person attempting this divinatory form with all four Archangels simultaneously. The result could affect the balance within the individual in a negative way by splitting the psychic attention too broadly, resulting in a certain form of temporary psychic schizophrenia. A single person speaking for all four Archangels also will bring a personal interpretive bias to all the information, which is the same effect that operates when using any single channeler or medium. No one is able to completely turn off the inner "filtering" process which adds personal bias to what is psychically seen and heard through their own personality. The use of a balanced quadrant of four beings and four voices offers an effective way to minimize the often misleading effects of human deciphering of divine guidance.

Preparation:

The first and most important aspect of this process is to determine the question(s). Often, the nature of any particular divinatory form is better suited to a specific type or nature of question. Any matter that concerns the consultation of the Archangels should be a matter of significant magickal importance. Personal problems, daily consultations, health and business questions, relationship matters, etc., are most adequately addressed through the more traditional Tarot, Geomancy and Astrology.

The consultation of Archangels is best undertaken when the matter concerns high magick. In the performance of ceremonial magick, we are often faced with the important question of whether a magickal operation is appropriate to perform, and whether the ultimate effects of such a change in consciousness will be desirable or beneficial to a greater sphere of influence than just the personal. Situations involving a magickal group, an order, a lodge, or any other tradition might be fruitfully addressed by consulting Archangelic forces. Magickal operations or magick-related actions that may have a profound effect upon the world outside one's personal sphere are also suitable for this type of divination. Examples of activities and situations where Archangelic consultation could prove helpful are: in the design of curriculum for a training lodge; in karmic situations between magickal groups; in determining directions of designated healing projects; in ceremonial operations affecting the natural environment (i.e., weather, rain forests, pollution, location of temples). These all are likely scenarios for divinatory comment by Archangels.

When a group has determined that a matter warrants this divinatory form, those participants involved should first gather to clarify the question. Spirits of all kinds are noted for their literal interpretation of answers to questions. Although Archangels may communicate with great clarity, it is still the clarity of the question that best guarantees satisfying responses. If your question is specific, you must be sure to discuss such aspects as when, where, if and how. For example, don't ask, "Will this work?". Your answer may be yes, meaning that it will work after a wait of two thousand years. Don't ask if something is possible, because the answer may be again yes, but meaning only with great divine intervention. Make a list, at least mentally, of different angles and aspects of your questions to address. Refine and restate them until you feel you are asking questions that cannot be answered in any way that might be misleading. If you will have a facilitator, be sure that s/he has a written list of questions that everyone agrees will be most helpful. Changes can be made during the session, but a good preparation will increase the overall effectiveness.

Each of the four "contact" persons should choose one particular angel to associate with and represent during the divination. This may be done by any means that is comfortable for everyone.

For symbolic reference, these are some of the traditional associations of the four Archangels:

RAPHAEL	MICHAEL	GABRIEL	AURIEL
East	South	West	North
Air	Fire	Water	Earth
Swords	Wands	Cups	Pentacles
(or Wands)	(or Swords)		
Mind	Energy	Heart	Body
Thinking	Intuiting	Feeling	Sensing
Tiphareth[1]	Hod	Yesod	--
Yellow	Red	Blue	Either green; earth tones; or olive, russet, citrine and black.

It is helpful to have fairly clear visualizations of these beings in mind prior to the working. Archangels are often imaged as being human-like, but much larger in size. Some traditional images hold these beings as somewhat ethereal, or even semi-transparent, each with great wings and often standing upon clouds. The Archangels may be visualized as of neuter gender. Some prefer to see Raphael & Michael as male (Air & Fire being active), and Gabriel & Auriel as female (Water & Earth being passive). Raphael may be envisioned as wearing diaphanous yellow robes blowing in the wind, carrying a bow and arrows. Michael is often seen as clothed in red and flames, bearing a flaming sword, or stepping through a gateway of fire. Gabriel is wearing blue, and may be carrying a cup from which pours an endless stream of crystal clear water. The blue robes may be covered in diadems of dew. Auriel is perhaps standing in a field of grain, or bearing sheaths of cut grain, or a cornucopia of harvest fruits. This Archangel may be wearing a combination of earth tones or the four colors of Malkuth (as listed in the correspondences above). Alternately, some see the Archangels as pillars of brilliant light or columns of radiant color. Choose the specific images of the Archangels on the basis of whatever brings the strongest "feel", whether they are traditional or not.

---

[1] In some traditions other than the Golden Dawn, Raphael is attributed to Hod, while Michael is assigned to Tiphareth.

MICHAEL

GABRIEL

244

RAPHAEL

245

AURIEL

246

OPENING CEREMONY:

At the beginning of the working, the four contacts should sit upon chairs in a circle facing inwards. Chairs around a comfortable table are suitable, as are chairs around the altar in a temple. The contact for Raphael sits in the East, for Michael in the South, for Gabriel in the West, and for Auriel in the North. Each contact should have writing paper and pen close at hand, either upon the table or near enough so that it may be comfortably used on the lap. The facilitator may sit anywhere, preferably within the same circle as the contacts, and should also have pen and paper at hand. A tape recorder may also be used, but notes taken are usually of much more value than taped recordings. If others are present, they should sit outside the inner circle, ideally in a surrounding circle.

Begin the divination with the Lesser Banishing Ritual of the Pentagram. (The standard form of this rite can be found in many sources, including *The Golden Dawn* by Regardie, *Secrets of A Golden Dawn Temple* by Chic & Sandra Tabatha Cicero, or Don Kraig's *Modern Magick.*) This serves both to cleanse and prepare the space as well as to begin to attune the contacts.

All who are attending the divination should stand, and may participate in the vibrations of the LBRP. All participants face East. The facilitator moves around the circle and stands to the East of the group, beginning with the Qabalistic Cross. The facilitator then draws a pentagram in the East and all vibrate **"YHVH"**. The person who will be the contact for Raphael should at this time close the eyes and visualize the corresponding letters (preferably in Hebrew) within the pentagram, in radiant astral blue light. Following the same procedure in the South: the facilitator moves along the outside of the circle and draws the pentagram. All participants vibrate the appropriate name, while the contact for Michael should close eyes and visualize **"ADONAI"**. In the West, the contact for Gabriel visualizes **"EHEIEH"** as the pentagram is drawn and charged. In the North, the Auriel contact visualizes **"AGLA"** in the pentagram.

The facilitator returns to the East, and says **"IN THE EAST...,"** and all vibrate the name **"RAPHAEL"**. The Raphael contact turns to face the inside of the circle. The image of Raphael may be visualized as hovering just above the contact person, or alternately standing just behind her/him.

In the South, the facilitator says **"IN THE SOUTH..."**. All vibrate **"MICHAEL"** as the contact person faces inward and the Archangel is imaged by all.

In the West, the facilitator says **"IN THE WEST..."**. All vibrate **"GABRIEL"** as the contact person faces inward and the Archangel is imaged by all.

In the North, the facilitator says **"IN THE NORTH..."**. All vibrate **"AURIEL"** as the contact person faces inward and the Archangel is imaged by all.

The facilitator returns to the East and leads all in the rest of the LBRP. The facilitator then takes a seat and opens the divination with this prayer of invocation:

"O mighty Beings of the East, South, West, and North, we entreat you to appear and guide us in our search for Understanding. We call upon you with the blessings of the Powers which we adore, and by that great source which is the One Source of all Light. Bring the Wisdom of the four Elements into those present, and allow the images here received to be bright, clear, radiant and right, as are you yourselves, in reflection of the one Light. Hear and answer our questions straightforward, and grant that we may by your Wisdom receive of you those symbols and images which will lead us to Knowledge. For by symbols and images are all Powers awakened and reawakened. So mote it be."

Meditation:

The facilitator then leads the group in a brief meditation: **"Close your eyes. Breathe deeply. Inhale very very fully. Exhale very very thoroughly (Pause.) Inhale to the count of four...one, two, three, four. Hold your breath in for four...two, three, four. Exhale to the count of four...two, three, four. Hold your breath out...two, three, four. Breathe in, two, three, four. Hold in, two, three, four. Breathe out, two, three, four. Hold out, two, three, four."** (Repeat this sequence several times or as long as needed to feel a full sense of relaxation.)

"Let us together image the great Archangel Raphael, standing in the East just within our circle." (Pause.) **"RAPHAEL."**

(All visualize the Archangel standing just behind or floating above the contact who sits in the East. The specific image to be visualized will have been agreed upon prior to the working.)

"Let us together image the great Archangel Michael, standing in the South just within our circle." (Pause.) **"MICHAEL."** (All visualize as before.)

"Let us together image the great Archangel Gabriel, standing in the West just within our circle." (Pause.) **"GABRIEL."** (All visualize as before.)

"Let us together image the great Archangel Auriel, standing in the North just within our circle." (Pause.) **"AURIEL."** (All visualize as before.)

"Let us take a moment to be aware of the presence of these great Beings, to honor and acknowledge each. Allow yourself to ask, within, whether we may ask and receive answers to our questions, respectfully, at this time."

After a moment's pause for the internal verification to take place, the facilitator may continue ONLY WHEN s/he feels sure that the situation is proceeding smoothly. If anyone feels that there is resistance at this point, the divination must be discontinued and attempted at another time. In this case, perform the LBRP and close the circle immediately.

The Divination:

With everyone relaxed and seated comfortably, the actual divination may proceed through the process of asking questions. There is no need to assume a stiff and formal quietude during this time. The contact persons are available for the symbols to flow through, but should NOT act as direct mediums. This means that they are not in trance, nor in any other particularly altered state of consciousness. They should simply remain relaxed and receptive. It is often in seemingly casual conversation that the most profound symbols may arrive. Those observing the divination should remain quiet, however, and allow all conversation to take place between the facilitator and the contacts.

The facilitator begins by stating the question, or the first question (if there are more than one) out loud. Any of the contacts may respond to the question verbally. Those acting as contacts should say anything that comes to mind, in a rather stream-of-consciousness manner. Images, ideas, colors, emotions, and thoughts, whether apparently connected or not, should be verbalized. It is the job of the facilitator to record in written notes, as much as possible, both the responses and which contact made the comment. It is important for later interpretation to keep a record of which Archangelic contact originally gave an image or idea. The contact persons may also use their own writing paper to record thoughts and reactions as well as symbolic images, pictures, designs, and all visual and intuitive impressions.

This process should be continued for as long as there seem to be active responses. Multiple questions should be addressed one at a time, with a clear break and breather time between. If responses seem dull, slow, or are quite long in coming, it is probably better to try again at another time.

The most powerful results will be obtained with a group that maintains a wide-open attitude into which raw informational energy may flow. Imagine that you are gathered in the presence of some very dear friends for an animated talk session. Do not let self-consciousness or a false belief that you must have "correct" or earth-shattering words keep you from allowing a free flow of images to present itself. If a sense of stifling or tension becomes apparent, a little humor may loosen things up. Archangels seem appreciative of a good human ability to make fun of themselves, and this may actually increase the accuracy of the working significantly.

Closing:

When the facilitator determines it's time to close, thanks must be given to the Archangels:

"Great Beings of the East, South, West and North, we thank you for your presence and your guidance in this our rite of divination. Be released from our presence with our most sincere gratitude, and go with the blessings of the One Source of all Light. YEHESHUAH YEHOVASHAH."

The standard LBRP is then performed as a final closing and clearing.

Interpretation:

As stated before, the most useful piece of any divination is the interpretation of the symbols, images, and in this case words and phrases. Interpretation of the Archangelic divinations may take place in an informal, kibitz-like atmosphere. The facilitator and contacts may choose to work on the divination alone, or may profit considerably by the additional input of other interested persons.

Whatever information came as an answer to a single question should be considered first as a whole. Take a general look at all responses received—statements, images, drawings, and even any significant body language. Patterns, repetitions, and connected ideas should be examined. Any words, ideas or images that came up more than once, and especially if stated by more than one contact person, are of special significance.

To interpret individual words and images, bear in mind the source of the information. Which contact person delivered the concept, representing which Archangel? This may tell something about the application of the meaning of the information. Words from Raphael will deal more with the intellectual or mental aspect of the question. Michael's responses may represent the intuitive angle on the situation, or may have to do with transformations that are called for. The emotional side will be addressed by Gabriel, so you can expect these images to represent the heart of the matter, both literally and figuratively. The physical nature and the practical advice will most likely come from Auriel. All these factors should be taken into consideration as the information is discussed and interpreted.

To interpret particular images and concepts, all other divinatory symbologies may be drawn upon. The Qabalistic and gematriatic meanings of numbers should be considered. Sephirotic attributions of colors, animals, plants and other magickal correspondences may have bearing on the translation of the information. (Crowley's *777* is an acceptable source for guidance in this, although many other attributions may be considered and may be more accurate.) Traditional Tarot archetypes should be taken into consideration. Any connections to Elemental and Astrological correspondences may also be drawn upon for elucidation.

As in the performance of the divination itself, the conversation that unfolds in the interpreting process will often lead down interesting side lanes that may ultimately present more information. In general, the interpreting group should look for consistency in impressions and ideas. Consensus of opinion is certainly not necessary, but general agreement is undoubtedly indicative of a sound interpretation. It is most wise to keep an open mind when interpreting the images presented by Archangelic beings, since they exist on a much higher plane than is usually contacted in divinatory practices. Just as in dream interpretation, literal interpretation of these symbols may not be as valuable as looking for puns, double meanings, and metaphors. Thus the interpretation can itself be a powerful exercise in magickal exploration.

Some generally agreed upon synopsis should be written down at the end of the interpretation for each question. Seemingly stray images that do not at first seem to fit into the integrated interpretation should also be recorded. Sometimes the written interpretation reviewed months or even years later may reveal astounding correlations, especially of those details that are not originally understood.

In the case where the divination was recorded only on tape, it is usually wise to listen to the tape in sections, one question at a time. Reviewing the tape to take notes is the best way to make the information more available for interpretation, but is very time consuming.

Divination by Archangels is a rather new concept within the traditional framework of modern Golden Dawn practices. Those who work with this form are encouraged to record their experiences and send them to the author, in care of this publisher. All responses will be used to help develop these and similar lines of ongoing magickal work and theory. As we develop stronger practices it is important to keep the lines of communication open, both between the worlds and between our minds and our circles.

ABOUT THE AUTHOR

Oz is a Wiccan Elder, a Priestess of Hekate, an active practitioner of Hermetic Golden Dawn Magick, and a member of the Servants of the Light. She resides in her native New Mexico where she weaves the Native spirit with her variety of other magickal interests. Her home is a spiritual sanctuary dedicated to the Goddess, and primarily to Hekate. She is also cofounder of the La Caldera Foundation, dedicated to working the mysteries to assist in the process of death and dying. In her third decade of magickal training and teaching, she finds herself still treasuring mostly the simple howling at the moon and dancing and drumming into the night.

What to Do
for an Oracle Addiction
Madonna Compton

hat relationship should divination have in the life of the budding magician? In the Golden Dawn and its offshoots, we frequently see that divination, especially using the Tarot, Astrology and Geomancy, is an important part of the tradition. Yet certain teachers that work with the Tarot and the Tree of Life, including myself (following the tradition of Paul Foster case, whose teachings I primarily focus on in my Tarot classes), suggest great caution in this area. Why?

Most all of the *greats* in the Golden Dawn tradition, whether they advise using divination or not, emphasize that the most important faculty which the occultist needs to develop —if necessary, to the *exclusion* of all others—is strengthening of the *Will*. Frequently what I notice, especially in young (not necessarily chronologically) students, is a great fascination with divination, channeling, and other forms of contacting an external locus of control for guidance. Some are even immobilized in term of making important life decisions without running to consult an oracle, astrologer or psychic for answers (many of which may conflict with one another). I question the efficacy and validity of this kind of frenetic activity which is increasingly prolific among those with an interest in magic and occultism. For one thing, it often presupposes that some spirit entity (behind the oracle or channeler) not only knows a lot more about the present situation of the oracle seeker (as the old adage goes, why should one's knowledge or insight be superior simply because one is dead?), but actually has the seeker's best intentions in mind when giving information.

One thing an accomplished occultist discovers after a certain amount of experimentation is that there is a 'trickster' element involved in many aspects of psychic work, i.e., oracles are sometimes (I dare say oftentimes) *wrong*, (especially at your local psychic fair). Whether one views this as an inability to correctly "read the signs" (assuming that the information comes from the subconscious or unconscious) or whether one is actually "teased" or "tricked" by the entity that is connected to the oracle matters not: the principle point here is that one is undermining the development of concentration and strengthening the Will—so important in Qabalistic work—in seeking answers outside him or herself, especially when making critical choices. The opportunity for choice is precisely the place where the magician's Will is most challenged and therefore can be weakened or fortified. One can contact one's intuitive powers directly, according to Dr. Case, that is, without the use of oracles. This is, in fact, the inner meaning of the Hierophant, who is the Inner Teacher, also called 'Magus of the Eternal.' "Hierophant" is from the root of our word *revelation* —'hier-phaine' means "to reveal," and to the Hierophant is attributed the function of hearing (implying the development of clairaudiance).

However, Case once said that if you hear 'voices' or spirit guides *telling you what to do*, it is not the true Inner Teacher, who may suggest, (that is, give intuitive 'tips' about a situation) but who never interferes with the aspirant's Will. If one does hear an actual 'voice,' it should be tested; that is, the aspirant should know that the Inner Teacher does not do certain things: it does not demand obedience, it does not flatter, it does not promise anything (wealth, power, love). It may, however, instruct, generally using "eternal principles." The primary purpose of working with the Hierophant is to tune into "interior hearing," which, in Case's interpretation, is understood to be a *direct perception* of timeless principles which, nonetheless, can be applied to solving human problems, as well as learning better control over one's environment.

The Magician Key, in Case's interpretation, represents perfected attention and concentration, brought about by the development of Will-power. It is for this reason that the elements (suggested by the Magician's tool on the table) are at his command—because his Will is at one with the Will which has control of all elemental forces. Therefore, he is identified with the Intelligence of Transparency. So, in order to apply the Will-power of the Magician, it is most important to use the

directing forces which issue from concentration and meditation, which come from within, rather than weakening the Will
by habitual use of oracle-consultation. Although Case gave an
exercise for reading Tarot cards in the back of his book *The
Tarot*, which was available to the public (and served somewhat
as a veil for deeper Tarot study), in his private lessons to
students, he only treats of the subject of divination after 6
years of Tarot and Tree of Life study.

What's more, Case stresses that Tarot divination is not
fortune telling. Where fortune telling is predicated upon the
belief that human life is governed by fate, (or powers external
to the control of the Will), true divination rests on the occult
truth that the real causes of life's events are internal, and
these are the factors that need to be examined when dealing
with critical life choices.

Tarot can be an expert tool whereby Superconscious
knowledge may be contacted to gain insights into the *principles* behind specific problems which confront us at the level of
self-conscious waking existence. It is this primary idea we need
to bear in mind in Tarot divination. Case felt that to deal
lightly with this issue is to profane the most sacred of the
mysteries and that one who debases the Tarot for mere fortune-telling (especially in exercising power or control over
another person), even out of idle curiosity, will rob him or herself of whatever insights he or she may be developing, as well
as open the door to dangerous obsessions (one of the dangers of
an undeveloped Will).

In the *True and Invisible Rosicrucian Order*, Dr. Case says:

> *A Master of the Temple realizes to the full meaning of
> the statement, 'Filled with understanding of its per-
> fect law, I am guided, moment by moment, along the
> path of liberation.' He feels within him the urge of
> that resistless Will that others, of less understanding,
> mistake for something of their own. He makes no
> plans, but carefully follows the Great Plan, step by
> step, as it is unfolded to him. (p.274)*

This is why meditation and pathworking are of the
utmost importance in doing Tree of Life work. In pathwork,
one uses the Tarot images as a jumping off place for inner journeys, which frequently also offer surprisingly correct informa-

tion about the aspirant's present condition—whether s/he brought that as an intention to the pathworking session or not. That is, it reveals what the aspirant *needs to know*. This is quite different from pulling random cards out of the Tarot deck and then attempting to interpret (or have someone else interpret) what they mean for a specific situation.

On very rare occasions I do a Tarot reading (never for someone else) to glean insights for a particular situation. However, my suggestion is that the more 'needy' you feel about an oracle's advice, the more it tends to control you, and therefore the less you look to it for answers, the better. One way, however, you can strengthen your Will in regard to divination is to *challenge it*. I did this a number of years ago when I consulted an oracle about a geographic move, which the reading did not advise. After pondering the repercussions of this (and ending up feeling rather like an idiot because I was letting *it* instead of *me* make this decision), I spoke directly to the oracle, saying, in effect: "OK, so maybe, like an overly concerned parent, you advise me to stay in my contented little nest instead of venturing out into the scary unknown. Thanks for the help, but I'm going anyway." The move turned out to be an extremely exciting growth-filled adventure, and I have never regretted it. What would have happened if I would have heeded the oracle's advice and not made the major transition I was planning at that time in my life? I probably would have had a different destiny. As it turned out, I am quite satisfied with the one I presently have and am empowered because I *chose* it.

Why do oracles sometimes seem to give untrue, confusing, conflicting or misleading information? (Aside from the most obvious reasons of an inept reader, misinterpreted symbols, etc.) I think one reason is to test us. There seem to be critical places in the life of every serious aspirant where he or she has the choice of making a real commitment to a certain issue which manifests in his or her spiritual path. And frequently, it seems as everything in the knowable and unknowable universe then suddenly appears to thwart that decision. It is at this time that one can be most vulnerable to psychic influences, which can often be misleading. And it is precisely here, at such a critical junction, that one needs to deepen one's consciousness and Will.

What can you do if you feel like you are turning into an "oracle-junkie" and can't make decisions on your own without heading to your favorite Tarot deck, rune set or local psychic? I suggest first working with the Hermit Key, which (in the traditional Golden Dawn interpretation) represents the *Intelligence of Will*, or one of the other two Keys mentioned earlier. The best way is to do some inner journey-work (pathwork) and engage the archetypal figure in the Key directly. Ask what it wants from you and what service you, in turn, can offer the archetype (which may look quite different in your visualization from the Hermit, Magician, or Hierophant in your Tarot deck).

To be most effective, pathwork should take a considerable amount of time and include working with the correspondences of that path in as much detail as possible. I set aside at least a two hour period for a pathworking session with my students. This includes doing some kind of work with imagery at the external level first, i.e., either painting an image which resembles the Key one is consciously working with, the Hebrew Letter or Tattwa which corresponds to it, etc. Or some other form of external contact may be useful: an image in clay or writing a poem, or reading about the myths that are connected with the archetype, for example. This is followed by a period of meditation, which could be silent or include chanting, music, etc., in the background, and is accompanied by some kind of breathing exercise. I find 20 minutes of rebirthing or holotropic breathwork to be extremely useful. Then immediately go into the pathwork, which yields the best results if prepared ahead of time: i.e., either you are familiar enough with the landscape which corresponds to that path through your own prior research, or else some other person (a pre-recorded tape is fine) reads the guided visualization to you. When you have contacted the archetype, *dialogue with it*. The two questions mentioned above are from Edwin Steinbrecher's *Inner Guide Meditation* (highly recommended by Gareth Knight) and can provide excellent results. Then record your immediate impressions (which may not even seem to make sense at the time). This is important, because you will forget, and your own intuition may provide valuable clues that emerge from the pathworking session but may not "fall into place" till later.

Another powerful archetypal energy to work with if you are in a "divination dilemma" is the 2nd Sephirah, Chokmah, on the Tree of Life. Sometimes contacting Sphere energy directly through pathwork is for the more advanced student, so if it fails to be meaningful, continue with the Tarot images themselves; the Sphere energy will be balanced naturally when doing pathwork with the Tarot landscape. The aware student will know which is the appropriate path to tread when contacting this Sphere. Chokmah is a very numinous archetype (rather, it is only an *attribute* of the archetype, which is too amorphous to apprehend directly) and it's meaning is Wisdom. Proverbs says: "Wisdom is the principle thing; therefore get Wisdom" (4:7). It may be that wisdom, not knowledge of the future, can best guide our actions when we need to glean insights into our motives, responses, and the consequences of our actions.

Interestingly, to Chokmah is attributed the Sphere of the entire Zodiac, which are frequently said to be the planetary influences which "govern" our lives. Chokmah is also said to correspond to Yod, the first letter of the Tetragrammaton and also the Hebrew letter attributed to the intelligence of Will.

There are two other Tarot Keys which I think would be helpful to work with in order to better understand one's behavior and environmental circumstances (instead of resorting to consulting oracles). They are the Chariot and the Star. To the Chariot are attributed the qualities of Will and receptivity, in addition to the Intelligence of the *House of Influence*. Working consistently with this Key will develop mastery, intuition, (its planetary influence is Cancer, ruled by the Moon) as well as *equilibrium*. When used as a path, its destination is Binah, Understanding.

Finally, I would like to conclude with some comments on Tzaddi, the Star, which in the Case interpretation, is associated with the function of meditation and revelation. The idea of meditation is often a process of "unveiling," which is why the figure in the Key is nude—she is the Mother revealed or Isis Unveiled. The Mother is frequently associated in Qabalistic and Jungian thought with the unconscious, the reservoir of all psychic impressions, including memory, myth and archetype, and of course, all sensory impressions which have become imbedded in the body. Case tells us that the reason we can sometimes receive psychic impressions about the future is because this faculty of the collective or personal unconscious has no sense of time. It is also *superstitious*, meaning it believes one statement made to it by consciousness (e.g., I am going to get this job) as well as another (e.g., I should have my head examined). It has no value judgment or sense of discrimination, believing whatever consciousness tells it, and then tries to go to work for us to validate that statement.

Therefore, through careful choice of affirmations (the things one says daily to oneself), conscious use of concentration and meditation, and ever-vigilant use of will-power, one gradually comes into a harmonious relationship with the subconscious, so that it works better for us (in terms of giving us reliable information) since we are *consistent* about the suggestions we give to it. Then when we go fishing (Tzaddi means fishhook) in the waters of the unconscious—which is the Qabalistic form of meditation—we can gather intuitions that are often quite reliable and valuable. This, however, takes practice—it is not as simple as throwing I-Ching coins or pulling some runes out of a bag.

Case tells us that the fishhook is a symbol of *mental angling*, a way of investigating the unknown that can only be perfected through repetition, persistent effort and much experimentation. Therefore, the metaphor of the fish-hook becomes clear: this is why meditation, in the western tradition, was said to take the form of a fishing expedition: it should never be purely passive, but should always have as its function a sense of *quest and experimentation*, that is, of seeking knowledge or information (not necessarily personal). Case believed that in this kind of meditation, we gather impression after impression from our particular object of concentration, eventually becoming aware of its inner *nature* (Tzaddi is called the Natural Intelligence.)

So I would like to conclude with quite a simple little exercise, not nearly as complicated or time-consuming as pathwork, but which is extremely effective in developing the qualities so important in the life of a true occultist, as well as procuring information from the unconscious which can lead to fascinating and insightful discoveries. A shortened version is found in my book, *Archetypes on the Tree of Life*:

Contemplate the Star Key when you are seeking an answer to something. Bait the hook of your concentration and cast it into the still, deep waters and be attentive with it there. Do not simply let your mind go blank, or wander into some nowhere land. Bring your attention back to your question, if necessary, by staring at the Key, or devise a similar star sym-

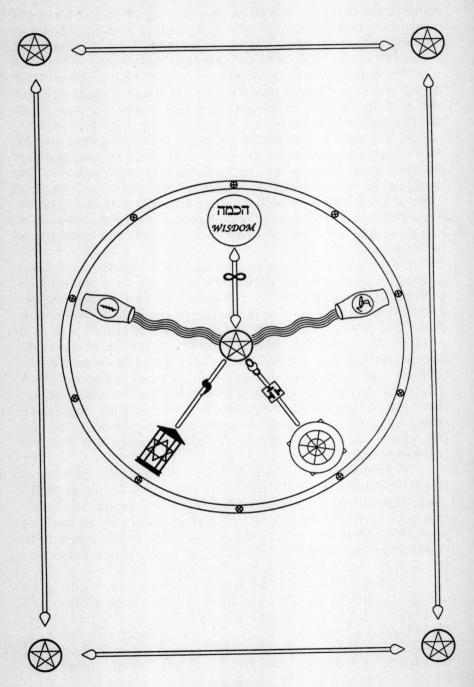

bol in your room to represent the *fixing of your attention* and concentrate on that. When one is fishing, one must angle for the fish. To angle correctly is an artful means of obtaining an objective. To be most effective, one should spend 5 minutes of unbroken eye contact with the image of the Star, then close your eyes, bathe yourself in the color *violet* and imagine yourself casting your question or need into the pool in front of you (pictured in the Tarot Key).

Sit attentively with the fishhook you have cast. Repeat your need to your subconscious in the form of some kind of prayer or affirmation, and as you do, imagine Isis behind you, pouring her vase of water from the pool over your head to merge with your subconscious response. Then imagine her pouring the other vase over your head to represent the answer on the conscious, physical level. Feel the water pour *through* as well as over you. Bathe yourself with violet again and release your thoughts as you give thanks to the universe that has a revelation for you concerning the object of your meditation. Don't expect an answer right away. Keep paper and pen close to your bed, as insights will frequently come after sleep or dreaming.

Dr. Case felt that when we use occult methods for controlling what Eliphas Levi frequently referred to as the 'astral light' (such as working with sound, color, imagery, pathwork, etc.), activities are set into motion which eventually result in drawing to us whatever we need for our spiritual unfoldment, even including changes at the cellular level. I have seen this borne out numerous times both in myself and in friends who consistently apply the spiritual methods advised by him and other Golden Dawn adepts. There is a great sense of freedom in learning to trust the universe, but this sometimes comes only at the cost of releasing our need to *know* what future it holds for us. I would like to close with a quotation by author and transpersonal therapist, Jean Houston: "The best way to predict the future is to invent it."

ABOUT THE AUTHOR

Madonna Compton, author of *Archetypes on the Tree of Life*, has studied Tarot and Qabalah for 20 years. She has a Masters in Religious Studies and is currently working on a Ph.D. in Philosophy and Religion. She has written numerous articles on theology, mysticism and the paranormal. Her current research focuses on the ongoing Marian apparitions around the planet and related miracles, as well as the translation and interpretation of the Renaissance Qabalistic platonists, principally Pico Mirandola and Christian Knorr Rosenroth. She teaches in the department for the Study of Human Consciousness at John F Kennedy University in Orinda, CA., and through a small lodge in the Western esoteric tradition in Berkeley.

Towards a General
Theory of Divination
Sam Webster

ivination has often been vilified as mere fortune telling. Its preoccupation with the future has made divination the object of ridicule. A common view is that either the future is undetermined and cannot be predicted, or it is predestined and so we have no free will and no amount of prediction will change our fate. Both of these views are unnecessarily extreme, however. By knowing about the present we have some knowledge of the future but not a complete knowledge. And since not all of the decisions about the future have yet been made those future decisions will yet effect future events. Thus we can say that the future is conditioned by the present but not wholly determined by it.

In any decision making it is to our advantage to learn what we can of the present so that our decision may be well informed. Divination has long been used in this manner. Now is an opportune moment in which to examine how divination works. New philosophical and analytical tools have been developed that can interpret the process of divination as something intelligible and not wholly ineffable. For this study we will apply the philosophy of organism developed by Alfred North Whitehead also called *process thought*, general systems developed by Ervin Laszlo, and cybernetics as presented by Gregory Bateson. Besides understanding the issue better, the value of a theory is that we can generalize from one application to others. We who practice magick are aware of the reality of our work. It is time to explain ourselves so that we may better understand ourselves and so that we may be intelligible to those who would seek to understand us.

Two questions emerge when we attempt to form a general theory of divination. First, how can the World in which the diviner operates effect the divinatory system or technique, and second, how can the divinatory system adequately express the real condition of that World?

To describe the link between a divinatory system, the diviner, and their World, many would use the Hermetic aphorism, "As above, so below." But, since our planet is whirling around its star through space which has no up or down, some interpretation of this metaphor is necessary to apply it.

In the first place, the diviner, or querent, is coterminous with his/her World. No real separation can be made, so what is happening in the World is also happening in the subject. In our tradition this is described in those expressions that see the human as a Microcosm of the World as Macrocosm. While this is an apt poetic or metaphorical expression it does not tell us how the process works. To explain it we turn to Whitehead's philosophy of organism.

The relationship between a Macrocosm and the Microcosm arises out of the real and mutually dependent relationship that the World, the entities in it, and the moments of their existence each have in the process of their genesis. Creation is not finished but is a continuous process constituted by the coming into being of each moment of experience. Each moment is a manifestation and a result of the total process of the World and everything in it. A moment comes into being fleetingly, and is the experience of that moment; then time passes on to the next moment. The moment that *was* ends, but in its ending becomes a factor that effects every moment thereafter.

There are several important aspects of this process; the whole World effects every individual moment of existence, each moment of existence embodies the influence of the rest of the entire World, and that moment, after it has ended, will effect all future moments. An important quality of any individual moment is its unity. Any given moment may be constituted by several parts, such as the diviner, the querent and the pack of cards; but the moment of the reading possesses a unity from being a single experience.

Returning to our aphorism, "as above, so below," *above* can now be interpreted as the World that impinges on and determines the *becoming* of each moment. *Below* is then the actual moment that is becoming and which recapitulates that which is *above*. When we apply this to a divinatory reading, all of the past finds expression in the moment in which the reading is made. This includes the diviner, the querent and their intentions as formulated in the question, as well as the World in which the moment of the reading occurs.

Another factor contributing to the unity of the moment of the reading is the effect of feed-forward and feed-back between the reading and the divinatory technique. The discipline that examines this process is called cybernetics. *Cyber* means "pilot" and we will have further use of the piloting metaphor later. However, now we may draw out the unity of the process through this example from Gregory Bateson: The consciousness of a blind man walking down a street, feeling his way by means of his cane. Rather it must be seen as spread throughout the whole loop from brain to hand to cane to foot to ground to ear, etc.,—feeding back perception and feeding forward course corrections. In the same way the consciousness of the reader can be said to be spread through the device as well as through his/her body, the querent, the World, and so on. Thus the reader and the technique all form a unity whose character is determined, as discussed above, by all antecedent influences. Like the blind man's use of the cane, a divinatory system is used to extend the range of the reader's senses.

Since everything within the feed-back/feed-forward loop of the moment of the reading (to combine both approaches) is effected by the influences of the World, an undetermined potential such as the randomness of the cards or coins or taps on sand, will be determined by the influence of the World of the diviner and querent. The mechanism of *chance* is used as a means of harvesting the subtle effects of the World upon the reading. The undetermined arrangement of the symbols through the randomizing of those symbols during, for example, the shuffling of the cards, is made open to determination by those influences that can effect otherwise "random" events. The randomizing lays the symbols open to subtle manipulation. This is because there can be no true randomness in actuality, only in potential. Once the cards are shuffled they must be in some determined order. Traditional cultures had long concluded that the Gods were able to influence the outcome and so used the drawing of lots to determine answers. Hence this discipline is called divination, as it gives the Gods a chance to speak. What *was* the potential of randomness before the reading is *now conditioned* by the presence of the question and the questioner, and presents the influences it is able to express to the reader. What is needed is a way to harvest those influences adequately.

In traditional societies the notion of "omens" and the practice of reading them is common and important. Omens are moments in time where certain phenomena co-occur and are able to be interpreted by someone attentive to the pattern embodied by the phenomena. These classically occur at the moment in which a crucial decision must be made. Then a flight of birds, an over-boiling kettle, or the sudden sighting of a particular meaning-laden number clarifies the choice to be made. In recent days C.G. Jung termed this "acausal co-arisal of events" *synchronicity*. What is happening in an omen and its interpretation is the intuitive apprehension of the general character of a whole series of events (the decision, its antecedents, its consequences and all concerned with them), in a single event (the omen).

The relationship of part to whole determines the adequacy of the divinatory system's expression. In the same way as an event that is part of an entire stream of events shows the character of the entire stream, so can a set of symbols (what we are usually dealing with in divinatory systems) show the character of the entire World for a question. The adequacy of any system of divination directly depends on how well that system models the larger system that is the diviner's or querent's World and life. If it can not represent a particular influence impacting on the individual, it will not be able to indicate that in the reading. In our World, however, there are innumerable influences that impact us. Representing them all with individual symbols in a system of divination would render it huge and unwieldy. Nor would it be able to engage influences that had not previously been catalogued.

There is a principle in the World that will permit us a way through this dilemma. It is the *systems* nature of all experience. The essential nature of a system is that it has an inside and an outside. While this is a spatial metaphor it also applies to temporal phenomena in that every event has both a beginning and an end which *bracket* the temporal *region* in question.

Systems, by the fact that they enclose, have a property of wholeness about them that can be exploited for divination. Any wholly enclosed region comes into contact with the whole of the rest of the World at its boundary. In this way the part of the whole World that is the system under study maps the *space* outside the system onto the *surface* of that system. Transferring this analogy to a semantic system of symbols, the adequacy of a symbol set comes through the degree to which it maps the whole of the World it addresses.

Every divination system (that I have seen) contains a finite number of parts. Through the permutations of those parts it is able to present a description of a situation in the larger World of the diviner. Whether it is doing this through the 78 Tarot cards, the 64 I Ching hexagrams, or the 16 Geomantic symbols, it is doing so by means of the correlation between a whole set of symbols and the ultimate whole that is our World.

Although they do not look alike, a set of images (i.e., Tarot) and the human-experienced environment both have deep structural similarities because they are both closed finite sets. Obviously the 78 cards are finite, but so is every occasion of human experience as it has a beginning and an end, if only birth and death. This finiteness enables each to be compared, even if the finiteness of the one is as a symbolic representation of the Universe, and the other a temporal finiteness of a life.

Two differences between systems of divination are particularly relevant. One is that some have more parts and possess more potential interrelationships among the parts than others. The other is that finite arena of experience the system addresses in its constitution.

Respecting this finitude, Tarot for instance, can be described as focusing on the unfolding of the soul in its initiatory journey while African Geomancy is excellent for matters of business and wealth and for love and simple happiness. This is partly because its power is rooted in the Gnomes, but also because the symbols it employs principally have their associated meanings in those areas. For determining subtle influences respecting spiritual development Tarot is better, and for determining the time of actions, Astrology is better. This guides the choice of system used by the diviner and is a qualitative matter best left to the practitioner.

However, the focus of this point is quantitative. By having more symbols with which to represent the factors impinging upon the querent, a finer degree of resolution about the matter is available to the diviner. One has more detail about the matter at hand. However, too much detailing will muddy the reading. The problem respecting the quantity of detail is evident in the numbers of cards used in a Tarot spread. For some questions a single card or set of three is adequate but usually it does not give enough data. However, a spread that uses most of the deck would overwelm the reader and render the reading worthless. Thus it is common to use but a fraction of the deck. Doing so essentially asks the question: "What of the whole of the Universe am I facing in this question?" The whole of the Universe is represented by the whole deck. The part being faced is represented by the set of cards drawn in the reading.

Now we may return to our cybernetic analogy. Cybernetics is the discipline of choosing between actions towards some goal. It is interactive in that choices have to be made again and again in response to circumstances that change with each choice. With *cyber* meaning *pilot*, the root metaphor of cybernetics is that of a ship being piloted on its course which is constantly modified by the wind and waves and with respect to the shore and undersea terrain. *Feeding back* to the pilot is the perceptual skill of determining location by sighting on the sun and stars and by reading maps, buoys and the effects of wind and wave. *Feeding forward* is the pilot's skill at manipulating the rudder and engines. In combination this brings the ship to its intended harbor.

The use of divination is functionally identical. We learn from the reading about the forces impinging upon us and adjust our actions accordingly. We can make judgments about the future by reading the influences of the moment. However, this metaphor can be expanded still further if we recognize that the *space* we are piloting through divination is a semantic *space* of meanings and values.

In this semantic space we may continue to use the analogy of motion. We are either moving *towards* an influence upon our lives which means that it is increasing in predominance, or we are moving *away* which means that it is decreasing. There are naturally many influences upon us all at the same time. It's the union of them that constitutes the total influence. Each influence is, as it were, a single cord pulling us in its direction; and we are at the confluence of a number of such cords each pulling with a different strength. The result of all those pulls is the *direction* we actually travel.

In divination we are seeking to determine what is pulling on us and with what intensity respecting the other influences. In a divinatory system that models the whole of the World, like Tarot, each of the cards represents one influence. If we were to express this spatially we could arrange the cards about our point of view on the surface of a sphere. Let us imagine each card (though this could work with I Ching hexagrams or geomantic figures as well) as a facet cut in that sphere. In abstraction from any real situation, we could say that all of the cards have an equal influence upon us. Expressed in terms of cords as above, each of the cards' cords would have an equally strong draw. For this reason they are arranged equidistantly from us on the surface of the sphere. This symbolically represents the whole of the Universe in a systematic manner. In a real situation, when we lay out a spread, a portion of that whole becomes visible. We expressed this above as the portion of the Universe being faced by the querent. The cords associated with each of the cards visible in the spread may be said to be stronger than those not visible. Also, their strengths respecting each other will be graded by their placement in the spread and nature of the question. The more important the card, the stronger would be its cord. For example in a question about the past, the "past" card will be most important, while in a question about

spiritual influences the "above" card would be most important
(in, e.g., the Keltic Cross).

While this model is really too simple for the Tarot (that is
cards don't really have all the same weight), it gives us a picture of a spherical arrangement of known influences about the
person of the reader. As Cybernaut or pilot one may perceive
the influences expressed in the cards or other divinatory symbols as a ship's pilot does the stars. In a reading one takes
sightings of the *stars* that give location and direction to one's
travel. This constitutes the feed-back phase of the cybernetic
cycle. However all divinatory symbols can also be used for feed-
forward purposes to make *course corrections*. To do this requires
a symmetric reversal of the process of divinatory reading.

In a reading we use randomization to permit the World
and the Gods to effect the outcome and make their influence
known. In this case the World and Gods provide both
meanings, in terms of the symbols presented, and the relative
values of those meaning-symbols by their relationship to querent and question. To reverse this process we must provide both
the meanings and the values. Meaning is easily provided by
the choice of symbols and their arrangement to the senses of
the practitioner. Value can only be derived by the extent to
which the practitioner feels the influence of the symbols. The
more strongly they are felt the greater the impact they will
have on the life of the practitioner. This process invokes the
principle presented above that every moment effects every subsequent moment. Fortunately the ritual and meditative techniques of magick provide excellent methods for doing this.

To use our cybernetic spatial metaphor, what we are
doing is strengthening the cords associated with the symbols
used in the feed-forward process. This changes the balance of
the influences effecting us and thus changes our *direction of
travel*. We are piloting our lives.

Divination can be seen as a process of harvesting from the
World the subtle influences upon the matter. Those influences
effect the reading in same way as they effect everything else,
through participating in the process of their becoming as elements in their constitutions. Divinatory systems can adequately express the real condition of the World through a
portion of that system. The result of the use of divination is the
ability to choose a course of action in its feed-back mode and to

effect a course adjustment in its feed-forward mode. Divination is a tool for magickal piloting.

ABOUT THE AUTHOR

Sam Webster, M. Div., Mage, is a student of transformative ritual. The Director of Crescent Ritual Works, he writes and gives workshops on ritual and Pagan Culture. He is an initiate of the A∴A∴, the O.T.O., several Wiccan traditions, several Eastern traditions and is an adept of the Golden Dawn.

Editor's Forum

The Editor's Forum is designed to stimulate a creative dialogue amongst all of our authors on a specific topic. It is our hope that the Forum will provide the reader with a wide range of ceremonial expertise and advice from working magicians and authorities in the field. For this first issue of *The Golden Dawn Journal*, the question posed by the editors is:

Can A Divination Always Be Trusted?

Steven Marshall:

The question, "Can a divination always be trusted?" is an important one, since it immediately focuses our attention on the important question of what we expect from a divination and the values of those elements of the psyche that govern the process.

The most common expectation of a divination is to foretell the outcome of a particular course of action. Unfortunately, foretelling the future is also the least reliable purpose of a divination. The subconscious and superconscious elements of the psyche that communicate with the timeless realm of the archetypes often have values that are very different from those of the conscious ego. A divination can only be trusted as additional information to augment, not to replace, the other information-gathering and decision-making functions of the psyche. The information that the subconsciousness and superconsciousness have to reveal may differ significantly from information expected or desired by the ego-consciousness.

As with most questions of an occult nature, the answer to the question of whether a divination can be trusted is "it depends." The accuracy and reliability of a divination depend on the degree of cognizant awareness of the value system of the subconscious and superconscious elements of the psyche, and the degree to which the interpreting ego can lay aside its expectations, fears and one-sidedness regarding the outcome. A divination can generally be trusted to provide an important, neglected view of a situation, but only a partial view. Above, behind, beneath and before every divination or question in our lives there is an overruling "gnosis of the heart" that can be contacted through divination and other means. It is this "gnosis of the heart" that can be trusted for guidance and assurance regarding our personal course in life. The question is "Who you gonna trust?"

Gareth Knight:

Can a divination *always* be trusted? The short answer has to be "No." We do not live in that kind of a world.

However, an accurate divination is always possible. The problem is that we do not know just *when*. In my article I have indicated by reference to the Tree of Life what is needed to make up a successful divination. In plain terms there are three levels of operation.

First are the over-riding spiritual or karmic conditions. It takes a high degree of spiritual perception to work at this level so unless you are privileged to consult a high initiate or holy man then no advice you receive is going to be fool proof. And accurate advice from such a source may not be too comfortable. Most of us are seeking reassurance rather than truth.

Second is discernment of the prevailing astral or psychic conditions. This is the level at which most practical divination works. It does not necessarily reveal the future but helps by giving the underlying tides and hidden factors in the situation. One assumes that the Consultant (if a passive psychic) is not just feeding back the Querent's own hopes and fears. Though even this can have its value.

Third are the mundane conditions that can be observed by a discerning consultant. This is a matter of life experience, counseling skills and common sense, and by no means the least important element in any consultation. Unbelievers think that this is the only level at which divination works. There is obviously more to it than this, but being able to operate well in Malkuth is as important as any skills on the inner levels.

Cris Monnastre:

While divination is a technique, it is additionally always an art. And its greatest use is the development of intuition (along with the expectation of an answer to a specific question). In a conversation with Israel Regardie approximately 10 years ago, he felt that his experiments with Geomancy were 80% accurate. He particularly enjoyed entertaining dinner guests (who had no special interest in magic) with the notion that the accepted time-space continuum could be eclipsed by any variety of divinatory technique. His greater view was to expose people to the cornucopic reality of the Inner Planes through the universal fascination with attempting to foretell the future.

From a psychotherapeutic perspective, the value of divination is the "process," and "content" is ancillary. That is, that the specific question is only a small (but very necessary) step in the unfolding of living the magical life. Every sincere and noble act and attempt in living this life is to be trusted in so far as all expected and hoped for outcomes of divinatory questions are consciously placed in the hands of one's Holy Guardian Angel. Then nothing ultimately fails, and there are no "wrong" divinatory answers. What evolves is an aggregate experience of internal dialogue with the deepest parts of oneself toward true Knowledge and Conversation.

Trusting the divination to the inspiration that the Angel brings sanctifies it as a pure magical act and not parlor game fortune-telling. Trust is the keyword in that all magical process NEVER fails although at times it may escape our very narrow vision of life which tends to be seen through the limitations of the five senses and three dimensionality!

The Angel is always available for the fertile marriage of *Sol et Luna*, the Silver and the Gold, the Wand and the Cup, the "Conjunctio" of the King and the Queen. Divination is another (and important) step along this royal road. To learn its discipline is to take another step in piercing the very heart of Tiphareth!

Mary K. Greer:

Yes, I believe a divination can always be trusted. What one can't always trust is the reader (whether self or another) and his or her interpretation. The message is there, but the receiver may have trouble discerning its meaning correctly. Like using a skein of yarn: if you pull on the right end it can unravel smoothly; if not, you end up with an unusable jumble. According to chaos theory there is an underlying order to what appears to be random, that is most apparent in the state of change.* In the concept of synchronicity, everything that happens at any one moment is connected to everything else that is happening at that moment in a meaningful way. You touch a web and the whole vibrates. I see divination as "discerning the will of the Divine" or "communicating with Spirit." The Divine Spirit is always communicating with us, using the elements and the language of the senses—symbolically. That is, as an outer sign of an inner truth. Because we cannot listen to this constant bombardment of meaning and still go about our lives, we humans have always, and in all cultures, selected particular tools, times, places and people through which we direct our attention to some aspect of our lives (a "happening in the moment"). Then we stop, look and listen to what resonates along the thread of that moment—as it appears in the selected tool. We must *always* test interpretations carefully, learning through instruction and then by trial and error when and how to trust our own faculties. It is not the message, but the one who unravels its meaning who must prove themselves worthy of trust.

Frater P.C.:

Divination is an outer tool for the understanding of an inner reality, or the world based on perception. It is in this sense that we can always trust a divination to *bring us to where we must be*. Even a false divination will be used to direct us to our true karmic reality. Karma will use whatever means necessary, including a bad divination, to help us develop and mature spiritually. I am in no way negating the concept of *free will*. I am attempting to highlight the fact that divination in

---

* See Cynthia Gile's explication in her book *The Tarot: Its History, Mystery and Lore* (Paragon, 1991).

the context of free will and action will inevitably prod us to our karmic truth.

In the Golden Dawn system of magic we adhere to a prime principal of always calling upon the Highest Divine name before any operation, including the act of divination. It is an effort to rise above the confusion of the astral currents upon which so much mundane divination depends. The accuracy of any act that relies upon the lesser Neschamah (Intuition) such as divination depends in part on *opening oneself to the Higher*. It is from this summit that we stand over the valley of confusion able to see clearly the karmic currents interweaving through our lives. Although a false divination may not allow us to see with clarity, we can depend on its accuracy to lead us to valuable karmic lessons.

Donald Michael Kraig:

Give a hammer to a child who has never used one and the child may get hurt. Even after the child is instructed on how to use the tool it is likely that many nails will be bent or wasted. Give a hammer to a skilled carpenter and he or she will drive nails home with three blows. Any tool is only as useful as the person who wields it.

A divination can always be trusted to be exactly what it is: a manifestation of the abilities of the person performing the divination. An inexperienced interpreter may be partially or totally incorrect. A reader with an agenda to push (such as trying to work a con game) is likely to focus on that agenda.

With an expert reader the divination can be highly accurate. However, it has been my experience (and the experience of other Tarot readers I have talked with) that when somebody comes for a divination, the cards not only have messages for the client, but also for the reader. Even the expert must be careful to avoid passing messages meant for him or her on to the client.

The true key to this question is the nature of *divination*. The word means, "to make divine." The art and science of performing divinations (not "fortune telling") has the effect of making the interpreter more spiritual. Therefore, I think people should learn to perform divinations for themselves, rather than relying on the interpretations of others.

Thom Parrott:

Always? Of course not. Divination depends on a great many variables, among them, in no particular order: 1) The technical skill of the practitioner in the specific form of divination used. 2) The intuitive talents and skills of the practitioner. 3) The clarity and coherence of the question put by the Querent. 4) Whether the reader is emotionally involved with the Querent, or with some other participant in the subject under consideration. 5) The reader's emotional state and physical condition. 6) The good will of any Spirits, Angels, Divinities and other entities present. 7) The absence of any hostile or destructive entities. And then, there's the other end of the question: Is the Querent ready, willing and able to hear what the Divine has to tell them? Or are they only looking for a way to avoid taking responsibility for themselves and their actions?

How do you get the Querent to hear? Take him or her seriously, treating their questions with respect. Explain the process. Use language they can understand (those of us into divination have our own jargon which we take for granted—remember when you yourself didn't know Orion from Pisces from Futhark from the Wheel of Fortune, and speak accordingly). And find alternatives when the original message looks bleak—help the Querent find ways to take control of the situation, or at least of the irreaction to it.

We are the healers who help those whom the establishment healers can't, or won't, help. And always remember, divination comes through us from the Divine—"Of myself, I am nothing."

Mitch & Gail Henson:

It depends on how the operative in a divination is defined. If you believe that the process is completely subjective—the answer is no. If you believe the divination is objective—the answer is yes. So are we discussing a psychological state of mind that allows us to enter into a sort of shadow realm where intuitive reflex gives us a key to coming events? Or do we depend wholly on the aid of an outside agency to give us a series of relationships allowing us to form a conclusion? The traditional view makes no allowance for the former. So, that leaves us with the latter view.

That out of the way, the answer is still no. For though guidance is asked and received, human judgment is still a major point to consider.

In a world without bigotry, war, oppression, exploitation and deceit one might take a higher view of human judgment than we do. Human error in spite of the "higher" agency that lends itself to our inquiries is the biggest reason that divinations cannot always be trusted.

Adam Forrest:

I imagine that I will be joining my voice to a fair chorus of "No, of course not." Information reaching the consciousness of the Magician from the spiritual levels of Reality must pass through the psychological (Astral) levels of the Magician's mind, where such revelations are inevitably touched by the illusions of the Astral Plane—i.e., distorted by the Magician's ideal and prejudices, strengths and weaknesses, hopes and fears. The Order techniques (the preliminary invocation of the Divine, the alignment of oneself with the Higher, non-attachment to the result, the use of testing symbols, etc.) can—as can a successful course of psychotherapy—reduce the grosser distortions in the Magician's psychological Skrying Mirror.

It always saddens me to see a Magician become superstitious about divination. Divination is meant to bring freedom into your life, not limitation. It should be a way to gain insight and awareness regarding the forces in play in a situation—conscious and unconscious forces, internal and external forces. It is not meant to be a disempowering excuse, and it is certainly not meant to reveal an inevitable, predestined Fate. Divination abusers remind me of the explanation of the very depressing Achilles Tatius (second century CE), that the Gods generously grant humans the gift of divination to allow us advance notice of impending disasters, thus softening the trauma that can result when tragedy strikes without warning.

The healthiest use of divination, in my opinion, is towards the end recommended by the Axiom displayed at Delphi, the greatest seat of divination in the ancient world: *Gnothi sauton*, "Know thyself."

David Godwin:

Can a divination always be trusted? I would say yes, a *properly performed* divination can always be trusted, but the diviner cannot, necessarily. Even though the cards or Geomantic figures or yarrow stalks may indicate the correct answer, or at least something in the nature of helpful information, an inexperienced reader is perfectly free to misinterpret the data in line with his or her own wishes or prejudices.

Why is it, then, that the cards (for example) cannot fall wrong and indicate an erroneous result? It is because everything in the Universe at any given instant is something related to or in tune with every other thing, and there is a sufficiently wide leeway in most divinatory meanings that the correct result is always there, even if only by hindsight. Sure enough, the battle is a great victory—for the other side.

Of course, it is possible to introduce a large chaos factor by carelessness or slipshod methods. Grabbing a card from a deck without any sort of preparation is likely to give a random result without too much useful meaning. Even then, however, there is a tendency to get a relevant result. How many slap-dash *I Ching* readings have I seen which produce the hexagram that says "the inquirer is a fool," or words to that effect? Novices who see a reader at work and who are familiar with some of the basic divinatory meanings may accuse the diviner of reading the result *into* the divination rather than reading the result *from* the divination. But the trick of correct interpretation is to read the correct result into the cards *before* it becomes manifest.

M. Isidora Forrest:

I suspect that very few magicians would say that divination can *always* be relied upon to give a useful/truthful answer. And I won't disagree. However, if for the sake of argument, I wanted to give an affirmative answer to the question, I might say that divination *itself* can be relied upon, but the *diviner* cannot. Divination depends upon a human being for interpretation. Especially with methods like the Tarot, which are highly subject to interpretation, but even with simple yes-or-no type divinations, all the diviners I trust and respect at least factor their own psychic impressions into the reading.

Divination relies upon interaction and harmony between the Universe (whether Macro- or Microcosmos), the method of divination, and the diviner. The Universe is how it is—that's the subject of the divination. The method of divination may be either appropriate or inappropriate to the type of question, but unless you're missing some cards from your deck or runes from your pouch, there is rarely anything 'wrong' with the method itself. The diviner, on the other hand, is the one factor in this equation most likely to be out of harmony. She or he may be distracted, tired, or just 'not on her/his contacts.' Fortunately, there are methods for increasing harmony. The more the diviner (and the querent, if one is not divining for oneself) prepares for the reading by ritual, meditation, or other focusing technique, the better the chances of getting a useful reading.

Dolores Ashcroft-Nowicki:

I can only give a personal answer and many will disagree with me. (So what's new!) My answer has to be NO! You can't.

Why? Because you can't always trust yourself and that's who is doing the divination. Whatever type of divination you choose, what you are doing is getting in touch with yourself on a level so far above your everyday personality you need to give it another name. (God[dess] will do.) You solve problems by getting that higher self to talk to you. But we have become so skilled at fooling ourselves that if the lower self thinks it will get a wrong answer (...this is all your own fault Bozo, don't blame whoever...) then we are capable of twisting answers.

Can you avoid this? Yes. Don't rush for the cards, coins, or crystal ball, the minute something comes up. No one ever got a right answer if they tried divining when they were in a flap. Calm down, have a cup of tea (not coffee) and put your feet up for 15 minutes. Think calmly about your problem, get the facts straight in your head, and if possible *sleep* on it. THEN do the divination. What you will get is a reasoned answer with less conscious panic and subconscious fears filling in the gaps. Divination is not a cure all, it is a look at the problem from a different, higher point of view.

If you play about with cards, coins, etc. for too long, asking trivial questions, hoping to get an answer you can accept, then your divining tools will play up. Used with discipline, only when really necessary, in a still, centered frame of mind, they can make good advisors. Sometimes it's better to seek out a good "reader" rather than doing it yourself. They are not the one with the problem, so they can see more clearly.

Oz:

Divination answers come from higher-plane consciousness. This may be our own Higher selves, spirit guides, divinatory spirits, or even those from the level of Angel or Archangel. An ideal form of concept is offered by said consciousness to us as an answer, and given in the form of symbol, image, or language. This metaphor is then interpreted by a human brain (or brains), which is itself filled with reactive responses based on its own life experiences. The human brain that interprets a divination may translate the metaphorical information in ways that elucidate the information's original form, yet will do so with a definitive personal bias, easily slanting a reading. This slanting is not a deliberate attempt to mislead, but is a reality of life on the earth plane. The word "perception" is akin to interpretation. Each human perceives the same idea or image in a totally different manner than any other human, hence our individuality. When we perceive the images of a divination, we immediately begin to read into them associations with our own life experiences and other concepts. This is the inherent illusory nature of the earth plane—we can almost never experience anything in its pure essence without the intermediary re-translation. If someone else reads for you, take into consideration their experience, qualifications, and potential for personal bias. If you read for yourself, be aware that you will always be biased about information pertaining to yourself, and the more so according to your degree of emotional involvement in the question. This is why working with groups and using more than one source for verification in important matters is critical in magic.

Madonna Compton:

First, I would ask: Who did the divination come from: yourself or an external source? As far as trusting in one's own powers to prophecy (or interpret a divination, voice, vision), it is probably good not to take oneself *too seriously*. Learning to laugh at oneself—the element of Mirth—is attributed, in Kabbalah, to the Tarot Key sometimes called the great Magical Agent (also known by Eliphas Levi as the Astral Light, source of all visions, dreams and prophecy).

Can a divination always be trusted if from another source? I would divide this question into two. 1) Can a divination always be trusted if one has received a true calling to prophecy, exhibits the classical signs of a real prophet, (see below) and is honestly answering that call—i.e., the "greats" of the Old Testament tradition (Jeremiah, Ezeliel, etc.)? AND: 2) Can a divination always be trusted if you are at your local psychic fair and you just broke up with your girlfriend? The answer, I would reply, is "no" in both cases, but there is a distinctly qualitative difference. The word "no" is directly related to the word "always," however.

In the Jewish Kabbalistic tradition, those who saw visions and helped shape the Israelite nation through their prophecy had a noticeable reluctance to their calling, and were not self-legitimizing. In other words, they were not out to make a fast buck. If I had to use this criteria, and this one only, for having an intuition about trusting someone else's divinatory powers, it would take me a long time.

Other questions I would ask are: Does this person's divination seem to make *connections*? Is its purpose to be efficient and successful? Or is his/her mission to be the empty vessel? Is the divination competitive? Or nurturing and finding points of unity? Finally, is its vision personal or meant for the larger community?

Other than that I would just say: Beware of the trickster element.

Sam Webster:

Divination is a technique for harvesting information about the nature of the world. It can be trusted to the same extent as any other information harvesting system and no more.

In a reading there is always a 'problem situation' which spurs the reading. This may be monumental and explicit or it could be trivial and implicit such as in a daily reading. Regardless, it is the task of the divination, or any other information harvesting technique, to be able to tell us something useful about the situation.

However, there are three general areas in which any technique may fall down. First, the question posed may or may not be relevant to the problem. Skill and experience usually eliminates this problem, but it is often the case that the querent presents a question fairly far afield from the real issue.

Second, the technique may or may not be calibrated to the critical influence respecting the question. One might use Geomancy for a subtle spiritual problem or Tarot for a question respecting physical wealth. Here we come up against the principle limitations of any system. Whole systems design such as we see in the Tarot and discussed in my article handles the problem elegantly.

Third, the diviner may or may not be able to interpret the reading accurately. Here lies the greatest source of error. It does not matter if our technique gives us the correct information if we cannot understand it. Our own emotional static may distort our interpretation. We may be inexperienced with the issue at hand and thus unable to truly comprehend the data.

Or we simply may not have sufficient skill or technique to fully employ the information harvesting tool.

Several problems are special to divination. One may invoke the wrong force to inspire the reading, which is like asking the wrong person for information. Or, if you are really unlucky, an inimical intelligence may interfere and then your skills had best extend beyond divination.

Lastly we must reckon with what we have learned from post-Newtonian physics. Heisenberg demonstrated that any measurement of a system will change that system, and so it is impossible to not change the outcome by the very asking of a divinatory question. This should remind us that we have free will and any reading is subject to a change in decision.

STAY IN TOUCH

On the following pages you will find listed, with their current prices, some of the books now available on related subjects. Your book dealer stocks most of these and will stock new titles in the Llewellyn series as they become available. We urge your patronage.

To obtain our full catalog, to keep informed about new titles as they are released and to benefit from informative articles and helpful news, you are invited to write for our bi-monthly news magazine/catalog, *Llewellyn's New Worlds of Mind and Spirit*. A sample copy is free, and it will continue coming to you at no cost as long as you are an active mail customer. Or you may subscribe for just $10.00 in U.S.A. and Canada ($20.00 overseas, first class mail). Many bookstores also have *New Worlds* available to their customers. Ask for it.

Stay in touch! In *New Worlds'* pages you will find news and features about new books, tapes and services, announcements of meetings and seminars, articles helpful to our readers, news of authors, products and services, special money-making opportunities, and much more.

Llewellyn's New Worlds of Mind and Spirit
P.O. Box 64383-850, St. Paul, MN 55164-0383, U.S.A.

* * *

TO ORDER BOOKS AND TAPES

If your book dealer does not have the books described on the following pages readily available, you may order them direct from the publisher by sending full price in U.S. funds, plus $3.00 for postage and handling for orders *under* $10.00; $4.00 for orders *over* $10.00. There are no postage and handling charges for orders over $50.00. Postage and handling rates are subject to change. UPS Delivery: We ship UPS whenever possible. Delivery guaranteed. Provide your street address as UPS does not deliver to P.O. Boxes. UPS to Canada requires a $50.00 minimum order. Allow 4-6 weeks for delivery. Orders outside the U.S.A. and Canada: Airmail—add retail price of book; add $5.00 for each non-book item (tapes, etc.); add $1.00 per item for surface mail.

FOR GROUP STUDY AND PURCHASE

Because there is a great deal of interest in group discussion and study of the subject matter of this book, we feel that we should encourage the adoption and use of this particular book by such groups by offering a special quantity price to group leaders or agents.

Our Special Quantity Price for a minimum order of five copies of *The Golden Dawn Journal: Book I* is $36.00 cash-with-order. This price includes postage and handling within the United States. Minnesota residents must add 6.5% sales tax. For additional quantities, please order in multiples of five. For Canadian and foreign orders, add postage and handling charges as above. Credit card (VISA, MasterCard, American Express) orders are accepted. Charge card orders only ($15.00 minimum order) may be phoned in free within the U.S.A. or Canada by dialing 1-800-THE-MOON. For customer service, call 1-612-291-1970. Mail orders to:

LLEWELLYN PUBLICATIONS
P.O. Box 64383-850, St. Paul, MN 55164-0383, U.S.A.

SECRETS OF A GOLDEN DAWN TEMPLE
The Alchemy and Crafting of Magickal Implements
by Chic Cicero and Sandra Tabatha Cicero
Foreword by Chris Monnastre
Afterword by Donald Michael Kraig

A Must-Have for Every Student of the Western Magickal Tradition! From its inception 100 years ago, the Hermetic Order of the Golden Dawn continues to be *the* authority on high magick. Yet the books written on the Golden Dawn system have fallen far short in explaining how to construct the tools and implements necessary for ritual. Until now.

Secrets of a Golden Dawn Temple picks up where all the other books leave off. This is the first book to describe *all* Golden Dawn implements and tools in complete detail. Here is a unique compilation of the various tools used, all described in full: wands, ritual clothing, elemental tools, Enochian tablets, altars, temple furniture, banners, lamens, admission badges and much more. This book provides complete step-by-step instructions for the construction of nearly 80 different implements, all displayed in photographs or drawings, along with the exact symbolism behind each and every item. Plus, it gives a ritual or meditation for every magickal instrument presented. It truly is an indispensable guide for any student of Western Magickal Tradition.

0-87542-150-4, 592 pgs., 6 x 9, 16 color plates, softcover $19.95

MODERN MAGICK
Eleven Lessons in the High Magickal Arts
by Donald Michael Kraig

Modern Magick is the most comprehensive step-by-step introduction to the art of ceremonial magic ever offered. The eleven lessons in this book will guide you from the easiest of rituals and the construction of your magickal tools through the highest forms of magick: designing your own rituals and doing pathworking. Along the way you will learn the secrets of the Kabbalah in a clear and easy-to-understand manner. You will discover the true secrets of invocation (channeling) and evocation, and the missing information that will finally make the ancient grimoires, such as the "Keys of Solomon," not only comprehensible, but usable. This book also contains one of the most in-depth chapters on sex magick ever written. *Modern Magick* is designed so anyone can use it, and it is the perfect guidebook for students and classes. It will also help to round out the knowledge of long-time practitioners of the magickal arts.

0-87542-324-8, 592 pgs., 6 x 9, illus., index, softcover $14.95

Prices subject to change without notice.

THE NEW GOLDEN DAWN RITUAL TAROT DECK
by Sandra Tabatha Cicero

The original Tarot deck of the Hermetic Order of the Golden Dawn has been copied and interpreted many times. While each deck has its own special flair, The New Golden Dawn Ritual Tarot Deck may well be the most important new Tarot deck for the 1990s and beyond.

From its inception 100 years ago, the Golden Dawn continues to be the authority on the initiatory and meditative teachings of the Tarot. The Golden Dawn used certain cards in their initiation rituals. Now, for the first time ever, a deck incorporates not only the traditional Tarot images but also all of the temple symbolism needed for use in the Golden Dawn rituals. This is the first deck that is perfect both for divination and for ritual work. Meditation on the Major Arcana cards can lead to a lightning flash of enlightenment and spiritual understanding in the Western magickal tradition. The New Golden Dawn Ritual Tarot Deck was encouraged by the late Israel Regardie, and it is for anyone who wants a reliable Tarot deck that follows the Western magickal tradition.

0-87542-138-5, boxed set: 79-card deck with booklet   **$19.95**

THE NEW GOLDEN DAWN RITUAL TAROT
Keys to the Rituals, Symbolism, Magic & Divination
by Chic Cicero & Sandra Tabatha Cicero

This is the indispensable companion to Llewellyn's New Golden Dawn Ritual Tarot Deck. It provides a card-by-card analysis of the deck's intricate symbolism, an introduction to the Qabalah, and a section on the use of the deck for practical rituals, meditations and divination procedures. The Tarot newcomer as well as the advanced magician will benefit from this groundbreaking work.

The highlight of the book is the section on rituals. Instructions are included for: ritual baths, Lesser Banishing Ritual of the Pentagram, Tarot deck consecration ritual, using the Tarot for talismans, scrying with the Tarot, dream work with the Tarot, the Golden Dawn method of Tarot divination, and much, much more.

The Golden Dawn is experiencing a widespread revival among New Agers, Wiccans, mystics and ceremonial magicians. This book and companion deck are just what people are looking for: traditional Golden Dawn knowledge with new rituals written by authors with "magickal credentials."

0-87542-139-3, 256 pgs., 6 x 9, illus.   **$12.95**

Prices subject to change without notice.

THE GOLDEN DAWN
The Original Account of the Teachings, Rites & Ceremonies of the Hermetic Order
As revealed by Israel Regardie
Index by David Godwin

Complete in one volume with further revision, expansion, and additional notes by Regardie, Cris Monnastre, and others. Expanded with an index of more than 100 pages!

Originally published in four bulky volumes of some 1,200 pages, this 6th Revised and Enlarged Edition has been entirely reset in modern, less space-consuming type, in half the pages (while retaining the original pagination in marginal notation for reference) for greater ease and use.

Corrections of typographical errors perpetuated in the original and subsequent editions have been made, with further revision and additional text and notes by noted scholars and by actual practitioners of the Golden Dawn system of Magick, with an Introduction by the only student ever accepted for personal training by Regardie.

Also included are Initiation Ceremonies, important rituals for consecration and invocation, methods of meditation and magical working based on the Enochian Tablets, studies in the Tarot, and the system of Qabalistic Correspondences that unite the World's religions and magical traditions into a comprehensive and practical whole.

This volume is designed as a study and practice curriculum suited to both group and private practice. Meditation upon, and following with the Active Imagination, the Initiation Ceremonies are fully experiential without need of participation in group or lodge. A very complete reference encyclopedia of Western Magick.

0-87542-663-8, 840 pgs., 6 x 9, illus., softcover   **$19.95**

A GARDEN OF POMEGRANATES
by Israel Regardie

What is the Tree of Life? It's the ground plan of the Qabalistic system—a set of symbols used since ancient times to study the Universe. The Tree of Life is a geometrical arrangement of ten sephiroth, or spheres, each of which is associated with a different archetypal idea, and 22 paths which connect the spheres. This system of primal correspondences has been found the most efficient plan ever devised to classify and organize the characteristics of the self. Israel Regardie has written one of the best and most lucid introductions to the Qabalah. *A Garden of Pomegranates* combines Regardie's own studies with his notes on the works of Aleister Crowley, A. E. Waite, Eliphas Levi and D. H. Lawrence. No longer is the wisdom of the Qabalah to be held secret! The needs of today place the burden of growth upon each and every person . . . each has to undertake the Path as his or her own responsibility, but every help is given in the most ancient and yet most modern teaching here known to humankind.

0-87542-690-5, 160 pgs., 5 1/4 x 8, softcover   **$8.95**

Prices subject to change without notice.

THE MIDDLE PILLAR
by Israel Regardie

Between the two outer pillars of the Qabalistic Tree of Life, the extremes of Mercy and Severity, stands *The Middle Pillar*, signifying one who has achieved equilibrium in his or her own self.

Integration of the human personality is vital to the continuance of creative life. Without it, man lives as an outsider to his own true self. By combining Magic and Psychology in the Middle Pillar Ritual/Exercise (a magical meditation technique), we bring into balance the opposing elements of the psyche while yet holding within their essence and allowing full expression of man's entire being.

In this book, and with this practice, you will learn to: understand the psyche through its correspondences of the Tree of Life; expand self-awareness, thereby intensifying the inner growth process; activate creative and intuitive potentials; understand the individual thought patterns which control every facet of personal behavior; and regain the sense of balance and peace of mind—the equilibrium that everyone needs for phsyical and psychic health.

0-87542-658-1, 176 pgs., 5 1/4 x 8, softcover　　　　　　　　　　**$8.95**

GODWIN'S CABALISTIC ENCYCLOPEDIA
Complete Guidance to Both Practical and Esoteric Applications
Third Edition, Enlarged and Revised
by David Godwin

One of the most valuable books on the Cabala is back, with a new and more usable format. This book is a complete guide to cabalistic magick and gematria in which every demon, angel, power and name of God ... every Sephiroth, Path, and Plane of the Tree of Life ... and each attribute and association is fully described and cross-indexed by the Hebrew, English, and numerical forms.

All entries, which had been scattered throughout the appendices, are now incorporated into one comprehensive dictionary. There are hundreds of new entries and illustrations, making this book even more valuable for Cabalistic pathworking and meditation. It now has many new Hebrew words and names, as well as the terms of Freemasonry, the entities of the Cthulhu mythos, and the Aurum Solis spellings for the names of the demons of the Goetia. It contains authentic Hebrew spellings, and a new introduction that explains the uses of the book for meditation on God names.

The Cabalistic schema is native to the human psyche, and *Godwin's Cabalistic Encyclopedia* will be a valuable reference tool for all Cabalists, magicians, scholars and scientists of all disciplines.

1-56718-324-7, 832 pgs., 6 x 9, softcover　　　　　　　　　　**$24.95**

Prices subject to change without notice.

GOLDEN DAWN ENOCHIAN MAGIC
by Pat Zalewski

Enochian magic is considered by most magicians to be the most powerful system ever created. Aleister Crowley learned this system of magic from the Hermetic Order of the Golden Dawn, which had developed and expanded the concepts and discoveries of Elizabethan magus John Dee. This book picks up where the published versions of the Enochian material of the Golden Dawn leave off.

Based on the research and unpublished papers of MacGregor Mathers, one of the founders of the Golden Dawn, *Golden Dawn Enochian Magic* opens new avenues of use for this system. New insights are given on such topics as the Sigillum Dei Aemeth, the Angels of the Enochian Aires applied to the 12 tribes of Israel and the Kabbalah, the 91 Governors, the Elemental Tablets as applied to the celestial sphere, and more. This book provides a long-sought break from amateurish and inaccurate books on the subject; it is designed to complement such scholarly classics as *Enochian Invocation* and *Heptarchia Mystica*.

0-87542-898-3, 224 pgs., 5 1/4 x 8, illus., softcover   **$12.95**

KABBALAH OF THE GOLDEN DAWN
by Pat Zalewski, edited by Tony Fleming

Of all the material published about the Golden Dawn, one area that has not received the attention it deserves is the Kabbalah—the basis of all Golden Dawn rites. And while the subject of the Kabbalah itself has been well documented from the traditional Hebrew viewpoint, there is less available from the occultist's point of view. Now, *Kabbalah of the Golden Dawn* presents the majority of the Kabbalistic teachings from the Golden Dawn in one unified and fascinating volume. It contains a synthesis of all major Kabbalistic teachings used by the Order, a number of previously unpublished Golden Dawn texts and diagrams, and additional insight into the concepts they contain.

Original Golden Dawn adepts were spoon fed this material over a number of years as they went through the various grade ceremonies. This compact book places all the relevant teachings together for everyone. It does not duplicate already published material on the subject, but adds to and strengthens many areas of previous teachings.

0-87542-873-8, 250 pgs., 6 x 9, softcover   **$12.95**

Prices subject to change without notice.

ARCHETYPES ON THE TREE OF LIFE
The Tarot as Pathwork
by Madonna Compton

The "Tree" is the Kabbalistic Tree of Life, the ageless mystical map to the secrets of the Universe. By working with its 10 circular paths and 22 linear ones, you can find answers to life's most profound questions. By mapping archetypes on the Tree, you can trace mythological and religious themes as well as those symbols that stir the psyche on deep inner levels. It can help you bring out your latent powers and develop your full potential.

Archetypes on the Tree of Life symbolically examines the meanings and uses of the 22 paths based upon their correspondences with the Tarot trumps and Hebrew letters. The first half of the book is a scholarly approach to deciphering the archetypal symbols behind the etiology of the Hebrew letters, names and numbers. The second half is designed to enhance creativity and intuition through meditations and exercises that bring the material alive in the reader's subconscious.

Along the way, you will investigate the mystical and allegorical interpretaions of the Old and New Testaments and compare these and other mythologies worldwide to the Tarot archetypes.

0-87542-104-0, 336 pgs., 6 x 9, illus., softcover   **$12.95**

MAGIC AND THE WESTERN MIND
Ancient Knowledge and the Transformation of Consciousness
by Gareth Knight

Magic and the Western Mind explains why intelligent and responsible people are turning to magic and the occult as a radical and important way to find meaning in modern life, as well as a means of survival for themselves and the planet.

First published in 1978 as *A History of White Magic*, this book illustrates, in a wide historical survey, how the higher imagination has been used to aid the evolution of consciousness—from the ancient mystery religions, through alchemy, Renaissance magic, the Rosicrucian Manifestoes, Freemasonry, 19th-century magic fraternities, up to psychoanalysis and the current occult revival. Plus it offers some surprising insights into the little-known interests of famous people.The Western mind developed magic originally as one of the noblest of arts and sciences. Now, with the help of this book, anyone can defend a belief in magic in convincing terms.

0-87542-374-4, 336 pgs., 6 x 9, illus., softcover   **$12.95**

Prices subject to change without notice.

THE THREE BOOKS OF OCCULT PHILOSOPHY
Completely Annotated, with Modern Commentary—The Foundation Book of Western Occultism
by Henry Cornelius Agrippa, edited and annotated by Donald Tyson

Agrippa's *Three Books of Occult Philosophy* is the single most important text in the history of Western occultism. Occultists have drawn upon it for five centuries, although they rarely give it credit. First published in Latin in 1531 and translated into English in 1651, it has never been reprinted in its entirety since. Photocopies are hard to find and very expensive. Now, for the first time in 500 years, *Three Books of Occult Philosophy* will be presented as Agrippa intended. There were many errors in the original translation, but occult author Donald Tyson has made the corrections and has clarified the more obscure material with copious notes.

This is a necessary reference tool not only for all magicians, but also for scholars of the Renaissance, Neoplatonism, the Western Kabbalah, the history of ideas and sciences and the occult tradition. It is as practical today as it was 500 years ago.

0-87542-832-0, 1,080 pgs., 7 x 10, softcover   **$29.95**

RITUAL MAGIC
What It Is & How To Do It
by Donald Tyson

For thousands of years men and women have practiced it despite the severe repression of sovereigns and priests. Now, *Ritual Magic* takes you into the heart of that entrancing, astonishing and at times mystifying secret garden of *magic*.

What is this ancient power? Where does it come from? How does it work? Is it mere myth and delusion, or can it truly move mountains and make the dead speak. . . bring rains from a clear sky and calm the seas. . . turn the outcome of great battles and call down the Moon from Heaven? Which part of the claims made for magic are true in the most literal sense, and which are poetic exaggerations that must be interpreted symbolically? How can magic be used to improve *your* life?

This book answers these and many other questions in a clear and direct manner. Its purpose is to separate the wheat from the chaff and make sense of the non-sense. It explains what the occult revival is all about, reveals the foundations of practical ritual magic, showing how modern occultism grew from a single root into a number of clearly defined esoteric schools and pagan sects.

0-87542-835-5, 288 pgs., 6 x 9, illus., index, softcover   **$12.95**

Prices subject to change without notice.